DISCIPLINING THE

C000024144

For Matthew Godfrey

Ó orias de nem Whopper

Disciplining the Divine
Toward an (Im)political Theology

PAUL FLETCHER
Lancaster University, UK

Routledge
Taylor & Francis Group

LONDON AND NEW YORK

First published 2009 by Ashgate Publishing

Published 2016 by Routledge
2 Park Square, Milton Park, Abingdon, Oxon OX14 4RN
711 Third Avenue, New York, NY 10017, USA

Routledge is an imprint of the Taylor & Francis Group, an informa business

Copyright © Paul Fletcher 2009

Paul Fletcher has asserted his right under the Copyright, Designs and Patents Act, 1988, to be identified as the author of this work.

All rights reserved. No part of this book may be reprinted or reproduced or utilised in any form or by any electronic, mechanical, or other means, now known or hereafter invented, including photocopying and recording, or in any information storage or retrieval system, without permission in writing from the publishers.

Notice:
Product or corporate names may be trademarks or registered trademarks, and are used only for identification and explanation without intent to infringe.

British Library Cataloguing in Publication Data
Fletcher, Paul
  Disciplining the divine : toward an (Im)political theology
  1. Trinity
  I. Title
  231'.044

Library of Congress Cataloging-in-Publication Data
Fletcher, Paul.
  Disciplining the divine : Toward an (Im)political Theology / Paul Fletcher.
    p. cm.
  Includes bibliographical references.
  ISBN 978-0-7546-6716-2 (hardcover : alk. paper)—ISBN 978-0-7546-6722-3
(pbk. : alk. paper) 1. Trinity. 2. Theology. 3. Philosophical theology. 4. Church.
I. Title.
  BT111.3.F54 2008
  231'.044—dc22

2008037177

ISBN 13: 978-0-7546-6722-3 (pbk)
ISBN 13: 978-0-7546-6716-2 (hbk)

Contents

Foreword

The following book is the first – and, tragically, now also the last – work by the theologian and philosopher Paul Fletcher. He died suddenly, and very prematurely, in July 2008, when the manuscript for *Disciplining the Divine: Toward an (Im)political Theology* was in press. As with all posthumous publications, it is tempting to assign this book a symbolic importance that Paul himself would never have intended it to have: *Disciplining the Divine* was always meant as the beginning, not the end, of a line of enquiry. Yet, what follows is, nonetheless, the record of a life of reading, thinking and writing – for this was also a work long in preparation and the remarkable depth and passion of its scholarship can be seen on every page. In the best sense of the word, *Disciplining the Divine* can even be read as a kind of intellectual *autobiography* that charts its author's own very distinctive philosophical and theological itinerary over more than ten years. Where, then, did that journey begin?

It is entirely typical of its author that he should describe *Disciplining the Divine* as arising out of a failed love affair (p. xi) – not with a person, in this case, but with a theological doctrine: the social model of the Trinity. As a philosopher and theologian, Paul genuinely lived his ideas: he spent seven years of his life, from 1984 to 1991, as a Christian Brother living and working in London, Plymouth, Liverpool and at a leprosarium in Liberia. One of the dominant notes of the book you will read is, thus, a marked impatience with a certain kind of philosophical idealism that seems to assume that war, poverty and injustice can be abolished on the level of thought alone. To start with, as the preface to this book makes clear, Paul was attracted to the social model of the Trinity precisely because it seemed to offer the possibility for a politically and materially engaged Christianity that spoke directly to the world in which he lived and worked. If the desire for a genuine Christian political theology was what originally drew him to the work of Jürgen Moltmann and the other social modelists, though, it was this same desire that left him disappointed by it: Paul was increasingly disillusioned by the restrictions placed upon the social work of the Brothers in inner-city Liverpool and left the order shortly before taking his final vows. In one sense, *Disciplining the Divine* is the story of this disappointment – and of what came to fill its place.

To Paul's eyes, the greatest strength of the social model of the Trinity – its desire to be relevant to the world, to modernity, to the here and now – is perhaps also its fatal weakness. It begs the question with which *Disciplining the Divine* opens: what exactly is this thing called 'world' that all are compelled to address, live in, engage with? As the Introduction to the book makes powerfully clear, post-Copernican theology is haunted by the fear that it is not merely anachronistic but *anatopistic* – it does not just belong to the wrong time, but to the wrong place, even the wrong world. Not only did the Copernican revolution of the sixteenth century realign the earth in relation to the sun but, as Jacob Taubes has argued, it also dislocated the entire cosmological framework, of creation, of hierarchy, of grace, of providence and redemption, in which human existence hitherto found its meaning. What rushed to fill the void left by the collapse of the transcendental world of Christian cosmology is a new world that we have learnt to call 'the immanent', which is peopled by a new, apparently sovereign, self-authorising and self-legislating, species we have learnt to call 'the human'. Yet, it would be quite wrong to see Christianity as merely the passive victim of this process of secularisation, because it was complicit in it, responded to it – even drove it, at every stage. For Christian theology as a whole – both Catholic and Protestant – the loss of the God of cosmology means that He must be located elsewhere and increasingly that place is *anthropology* – what Paul calls the deification of the subject. If Christianity succeeds in finding a new *topos*, though, it is only secured through a kind of theological scorched earth policy that succeeds by laying waste to what was once its natural territory. On the one hand, theology abandons the study of nature, the world and truth to science. On the other, theology retreats to the interior, privatised faith of the liberal, autonomous individual. In this sense, Christianity re-makes itself entirely in the image of a secular, liberal modernity that remains fundamentally alien to its history, doctrine and cosmology.

For Paul Fletcher, it is precisely this world, this modernity, this here and now, that the social model of the Trinity seeks to address, and here we come to the crux of his critique: what begins as a well-intentioned attempt to fashion a theology that is relevant to modernity surrenders too much ground to that modernity and eviscerates its proper site of authority. Such is the charge that *Disciplining the Divine* levels at the social modelists: an entirely laudable attempt to critique the social and political order of liberal modernity ends up legitimising that order. To Paul's way of thinking, the fundamental modernity of the social model can be traced all the way back to its inaugural gestures. From its uncritical embrace of the Cappadocian concept of the Trinity to its – frankly inaccurate – dismissal of Augustinian trinitarianism, the social model is shown to depend not simply on a scholastic modernism but on a barely concealed political agenda driven by contemporary concerns. However, if its popular appeal depends less on its theological authenticity than on its allegedly unique ability to respond to contemporary social, political and theological problems, even this claim to 'relevance' is questionable. Whilst the social model's concept of God as a community of persons-in-relation is depicted as a means of challenging the sovereignty of the individual in liberal modernity, Paul once again shows that the theological doctrine remains complicit with the very order it seeks to overcome: its much-vaunted concept of 'personhood', in particular, is little more than an abstract, prescriptive ideal of the human that bears little resemblance to the actual relations between human beings. Perhaps the most ambitious claim of Moltmann and the other social modelists, though, is that the Trinitarian concept of God also represents a political challenge to the a-Trinitarian, monarchical God of monotheism and His secular surrogates: the king, the sovereign and now the dictator. If the idea of God-as-trinity does *theoretically* seem to offer a less authoritarian paradigm of theologico-political power than its monarchical equivalent, it will come as no surprise by now to learn that *Disciplining the Divine* remains sceptical of its *practical* efficacy: we need only call to mind the numerous military juntas of the last 50 years to recognise that dictators do not always come in ones. In Paul's account, what we seem to dealing with here is once again a well-meaning but ultimately naive theological idealism which holds that, if only we could secure the right *idea* of God, everything else will fall seamlessly into place.

In the final analysis, though, what destroys the social model of the Trinity is not just that it reproduces the modern liberal order it seeks to call into question but that it fatally *misunderstands* the nature of that order. It is at this point that *Disciplining the Divine* moves from a powerful critique of theological doctrine to a far-reaching and intellectually formidable diagnosis of the meaning of modernity itself. To be sure, liberal modernity expels Christian theology to the margins of the *polis* but what we must recognise – and what the social modelists do not recognise – is that the current order is *itself*, at root, a species of political theology: modern politics is predicated not on the separation of the sacred and the secular but upon the sacralisation *of* the secular. From a Christian eschatology that subjects all worldly or temporal power to a divine judgement delivered at the end of time, we move to a modern political order that, by a remarkable sleight-of-hand, both secularises eschatology and sacralises historical power. On the one hand, the time of the end is naturalised into little more than a historical process of completion or fulfilment. On the other, specific manifestations of temporal power acquire divine sanction as the agent or *telos* of that historical process. Quite simply, the *saeculum* or age itself – whether it be Constantine's empire or neo-liberal, post-ideological modernity – becomes deified: it is the time of the end realised *within* time, here, now. Just as the social model of the Trinity reproduces modernity, so it also reproduces its distinctive theologico-political order: what starts out as an attempt to offer a theological corrective to an essentially secular order unwittingly participates in the theologising of the secular itself. Such is the banal tragedy of Trinitarian politics: Moltmann's well-meaning attempt to triangulate the relation between socialism and capitalism in the 1960s ironically ends up sacralising the post-ideological, 'third way' technocracies of Bill Clinton and Tony Blair in the 1990s. Perhaps the defining form of this new political theology, though, is what Michel Foucault and latterly Giorgio Agamben call biopolitics – the politics of 'life' itself, of bare or naked life, of *zoē*. If there is no other time than now, if there is no other order than this order, then there can be no other life than this life and so the only theologico-political project becomes the essentialising, capitalising and securing of this precarious life. This is the time of the end in which we all now live but Paul Fletcher succeeds in showing that even in its utter immanence this life remains essentially religious. For Paul, in other words, liberal modernity stands revealed as nothing other than the radically de-eschatologised political theology of life itself – what we might call *biopolitical* theology.

What – if anything – can Christian theology do to renew its *topos* in the face of a modernity that both starkly refuses and ruthlessly assimilates its historic terrain? It is with this urgent question that Paul Fletcher concludes *Disciplining the Divine* and begins to open up a new field of enquiry. After very careful consideration, we have taken the decision to change the subtitle of the book from Paul's own original choice of *Beyond the Social Model of the Trinity* to *Towards an (Im)political Theology* in order to give the reader a better indication of the direction in which his work was going. For Paul, it is this concept of an *im-political theology* – and here he draws upon and extends the work of Taubes, Agamben and the Italian political philosopher Roberto Esposito – that best enables us to question the *biopolitical theology* that is modernity. Neither an attempt to retrieve its original *topos* – which is lost forever – nor an attempt to imagine another world – which is impossibly utopian – what Paul calls im-political theology is the affirmation of a form of life that remains irreducible to the modern politicisation of theology and theologisation of the political. Faced with the demand to be relevant to a modern time that is utterly alien to it, Christianity must instead embrace its *irrelevance*, its ana-chrony or untimeliness, or, better still, its adherence to a different, non-teleological model of time – what Paul calls (after St Paul) the time *between* time and the end of time, the time that it takes for time to end, the time that remains. Such a time is neither the messianic future heralded by neo-liberal capitalism nor the insipid millenarianism offered by the social model of the Trinity, but the promise of a new form of life, a new race and a new community: it makes possible a radically transformed form of being-with that cannot be represented by – and thus radically de-legitimises – any juridical, economic, theological or political form of sovereignty. Perhaps it is here, more than anywhere else, that we can see the importance of Paul's work, not simply for Christian theology, but for contemporary political thought as a whole: what the possibility of the *im*-political – of a form of life that is indescribable according to the categories of the political – makes visible is quite simply the political *itself* in all its power, violence and contingency. If Paul had lived, one of his future projects would have been to offer a new genealogy of the theologico-political machine – unfolding from Machiavelli, through Hobbes and Kant, all the way up to the contemporary age of security – that we call liberal modernity. This future will, sadly, now never happen. In *Disciplining the Divine: Toward an (Im)political Theology*, however, we catch a glimpse of what it would have been like, and so it is with love, gratitude and admiration that we present the work of Paul Fletcher to the reader.

Michael Dillon and Arthur Bradley

Preface

As we head towards the end of the first decade of this new millennium, we languish in the wake of a deluge of endings. After the end of art, or at least its spiritual vocation (Hegel), the end of philosophy (Heidegger), the end of history (Kojève), the end of the nation state (Guéhenno) and the end of ideology (Bell), what of theology? Excepting the views of its practitioners, the majority of whom wish to remain in employment, theology is regarded as marginal to the contemporary concerns of western culture, politics and social affairs. Occasionally a learned theologian or bishop will be offered a place amongst the new priesthood of techno-scientific societies – the ethical advisory committees. Such token and peripheral appointments confirm rather than undermine the fact that theology is still widely understood as being constituted by those *bêtes noires* of an enlightened modern world: dogmatism, superstition and heteronomy. If there is any place that remains for the theologian in this context it is merely as the curator of a museum of heritage. She tends to the relics of western 'civilisation', giving special attention to those artefacts that represent the basis of our moral frameworks.

Such a bleak opening – acceding to the end from the very beginning – is no pessimistic exercise in fatalism or cynicism. On the contrary, it is an honest appraisal of the contemporary state and status of theology in so-called western advanced societies. Such an assessment should hold little in the way of a surprise. In a 'postmodern' context, theology is experiencing something of a revival but it still has to attend to the wounds it received at the hands of modern 'Man' in his quest for autonomy, certainty and sovereignty. This book will consider the effect of, and one significant response to, these wounds. In doing so it charts the way in which Christian thought and practice attempted to make itself acceptable within a new epoch that was born out of the creation of the dominant philosophical, scientific and cultural discourses of modernity. Thus the nature of the central concerns of this book: the major attempt in the twentieth century to revivify Christian doctrine through the championing of the social model of the Trinity and the concomitant rise of political theologies engendered by this doctrinal phenomenon.

Nevertheless, I ought to confess that, like all love affairs that end in grief, this book is the product of a disappointment. After being introduced to the social model of the Trinity in the 1980s by Daniel W. Hardy, I became an enthusiastic adherent of the model, its socio-political relevance and its ability to usher theology into pastures new. It was when I returned to inner-city Liverpool from Durham that I began to see the problems with many recent political theologies and this utilisation of doctrine in particular. (There was also the case of the girlfriend who said that she had 'serious reservations' about courting someone who was so passionate about the social model of the Trinity!) Yet this study remains faithful to the spirit in which the affair began: a desire to reflect on the political ramifications of Christian thought and practice, and a serious belief in the importance of such a project.

In many respects the Introduction traverses old territory: the modern demise of theological concepts and discourses. The manner in which a cartography of the present is sketched, however, relies more on the status of metaphysics in relation to physics than questions of particular philosophical or social transformations, themes that tend to dominate expositions of the late-medieval and modern decay of theological authority. The purpose is to disclose the importance of the displacement of a cosmological context in which discourses concerning supernature depended in large part on the status of created nature. The subsequent modern implosion of theological space, its relegation to what Karl Barth called the 'apologetic corner', provides the backdrop for a whole range of attempts to relocate and revivify theological discourse. One factor that bridges all these attempts is the relegation of doctrinal and dogmatic formulations to the margins of theological enquiry. However, a recent and influential example of such a relocation is the ecumenical appropriation of the social model of the Trinity and it begins and ends with a confident incorporation of doctrine and a conviction concerning its application in theological, anthropological and political reflections. For this reason alone, and many more besides, the social model of the Trinity commands serious and thoughtful attention.

The first part of the book, 'Modelling' (Chapters One and Two) outlines the central concerns and proposals of what I call the 'social modelists'. Here I explore the rise of this particular conceptualisation of God and the manner in which it draws on specific patristic and biblical sources in order to make the case for its relevance to modern life beyond, as well as within, the Church. This narrative also accounts for the general suspicion – if not loathing – of the Latin tradition of trinitarian theology. Augustine is seen as the theoretical origin and most important proponent of a school of thought in which God's unity is more important than his intrinsic relationality. Yet my intention is to be more than expository. Chapter Two will consider in some detail a number of claims that legitimate the supposed *theological* supremacy of the social model. Drawing on the work of a series of significant scholarly studies in which patristic specialists have revisited and reassessed the relationship between Latin and Greek attempts to develop orthodox trinitarianism, and by returning to the some of the important sources themselves, I will begin to question the historical, hermeneutical and theological assumptions that the proponents of the social model take for granted. The point of these chapters is not to establish a authoritative and definitive role for the patristic doctrine of God in contemporary theology, in a manner that would mirror the methodology of the social modelists, but to understand something of the opportunities and limitations that reflection on the trinitarian nature of God bestows on the modern theological endeavour.

The second part of the study, 'Identifying', (Chapters Three and Four) explores and interrogates the reasons for, and the dangers of, the popular consensus that surrounds the social model and its perceived superiority in responding to *cultural* issues and concerns. Here I attend to the important utilisation of the model in the face of modern shifts in the notion of subjectivity and the manner in which the unfolding of trinitarian relations provides a Christian model for intersubjectivity and community. My hope is to illustrate that this programme of cultural analysis and doctrinal relevance is well intentioned but fatally flawed.

In the third part of the book, 'Living', an examination is undertaken of the *political* and *societal* implications that a range of social modelists believe can be drawn from a rightly understood trinitarian theology. These chapters sympathetically engage with the attempt to make theology relevant within a public space, but charge theologians with a cardinal sin: they simply do not understand the principles of formation which underpin contemporary western politics or appreciate the manner in which these principles affect selves and communities in the context of global liberal governance and its attendant practices of sovereignty.

On the basis of these critical interventions, I offer, in the fourth and final part of the book, 'End Matters', an analysis of the manner in which the failure of this particular relocation of doctrine arises out of a number of fundamental accommodations which theologians are only too happy to make but because of which they remain tied to the demands of modern relevance. Christian theology continues, therefore, to be anatopistic, out of place, and the final chapter marks an effort to interrogate and reconfigure the topology of Christian political thought in the midst of this dislocation. In short, this constructive essay develops a theological politics, but does so in negative terms through a political interpretation of the Christian eschatological imperative as the 'time between'.

*   *   *

The motivation for this study has been generated and sustained by my friends and colleagues over a number of years. The Department of Religious Studies at Lancaster University has provided many opportunities for discussion and reflection. I am particularly grateful to Gavin Hyman, Chakravarthi Ram-Prasad, Patrick Sherry and David Waines and for their support and friendly disagreement. In the wider community at Lancaster I have a number of interlocutors who have provided a rich intellectual forum and some lively discussion. In particular I wish to thank my colleagues from 'The Political and the Religious' reading group that met for a number of years under the auspices of the Institute for Cultural Research: especially Michael Dillon, Kirsten McAllister and Paolo Palladino. I also have long-standing debts to Ann Loades and Colin Crowder at the University of Durham, to Fergus Kerr who encouraged me to write this book and to Gerard Loughlin and Mark Vernon for the many stimulating and sensible questions they put my way. Finally I must thank Sarah Lloyd, my editor at Ashgate, who has exhibited both patience and perseverance as this text moved towards its present state.

Introduction
The Dislocation of Theology

At the very beginning of what is probably his most famous work, *The Crucified God*, Jürgen Moltmann outlines the fundamental challenge which confronts Christian theology and practice in the modern world. Moltmann characterises this challenge as historically specific, a predicament that is best described as a 'double crisis: the *crisis of relevance* and the *crisis of identity*' (Moltmann, 1974, p. 7). These interrelated dilemmas are easily identifiable, intelligible and, one could argue, empirically as well as anecdotally noteworthy. If, on the one hand, the church seeks to be relevant to its historical context then it must risk the security of its identity, the protection of its boundaries. Yet, on the other hand, if the church seeks to retain some large measure of its identity it must risk irrelevance and marginalisation.

Moltmann's dictum was written in the aftermath of 1968, the apotheosis of European social activism. Appropriately enough, his attempt to overcome the 'double crisis' of Christianity's character and significance in the world is marked by a desire to bring the church into a dialectical relationship with a godless world through the cross of Christ. There is no doubt that at least an echo of the logic of Moltmann's challenge can be detected in a variety of situations – academic, journalistic or populist – where the church is often implored to undergo institutional and devotional 'makeovers' in order to align itself with those values and practices that are generally regarded as normative or, at the very least, those that resonate with the consensual realism of modern liberal societies.

Nonetheless, while that may be true, there is a sense in which both the need for relevance and the necessary retention of some kind of ecclesial identity arise from a single, though largely unacknowledged and unexamined, presupposition. Moltmann's laudable concern is to place the church of the crucified Christ in the midst of the sighs and struggles of socio-political reality as a liberatory force and presence. In doing so, however, he is accepting that the constraint of historical immanence is the condition of possibility of both identity and relevance for the church *qua* church. Christian identity and a relevant social solidarity are both discerned and clarified 'in between' the dialectical poles of (historical) event and (eschatological) future through the dynamism of history itself. *Now* is the time of relevant identity in the light of a hope that is historically uncovered. Yet there is something questionable in what is unarguably a sophisticated justification of the priority of the immanent. As a theological strategy it is nothing other than the tacit approval of the expropriation of any elements of Christian experience that remain anachronistic, such as analogy, cosmology and particular species of metaphysics, the subsequent conversion of this expropriation into a reason for survival and the acceptance of the transient or the contingent as the normal condition of Christian existence.

Moltmann's strategy, however flawed it seems, is symptomatic of the problems that face any theologian who attempts to respond to modern principles of relevance that are now ubiquitous. For, if the challenges faced by theologians in the latter half of the twentieth century were considerable, they have only intensified with the dawn of the third millennium. In the contemporary western world, immanence is the necessary condition of *any* claim to value and authenticity. Immanence underpins the seemingly endless passion of the seasoned TV reporter – 'how did it feel?', 'what are your emotions at this precise moment?' It underscores the compulsive injunctions of contemporary capitalism – 'Because you're worth it' or 'Just Do It!' Every form of affective and reflexive life that seeks to bear authority must be immediate, forcible and, most crucially, must hold to the illusion of singularity. In many respects, however, this modern dream of the unique importance of what is self-produced reflects the fundamental banality of consumer-inspired living and the emptiness of cultural forms that promise excitement, self-actualisation and the perpetual fulfilment of our desires. It is a more than bizarre fact that, despite the intensity of these intrusions, hopes and prescriptions, we find ourselves sitting in armchairs watching people sitting in armchairs in the latest incarnation of 'reality TV', while the vast majority of reports that are disseminated on our 'real-time' networks are old news or well-managed revelations that inform us about tomorrow's news. Despite these modish and urbane deceptions, the exaltation of the immediate is not restricted to the vagaries of popular and consumer cultures or to those aspects of our lives that eschew reflection on the substantive and the meaningful. In 1896, for example, Maurice Blondel identified immanence 'as the very condition of philosophizing' (Blondel, 1964, pp. 151–152). The crucial place of *immanence* as the fundamental element of thought, according to Blondel's analysis, suggests that only those phenomena which are engendered by the *individual* are worthy of the name 'truth' because 'there is nothing in the nature of historical or traditional teaching or obligation imposed from without which counts …, no truth and no precept which is acceptable, unless it is in some way autonomous and autochthonous' (p. 152). Blondel's statement is as true as ever and we might add that, along with Moltmann and many other modern theologians, immanence has also become the very condition of theologisng. Yet Blondel's account offers little more than a rather belated diagnosis of the modern propensity to reject any bonds sustained by pre-ordained hierarchies or a pre-critical blend of faith and reason that are understood, in a modern context, as little more than dogmatism, heteronomy and superstition. And a major reason for this rejection is repeatedly ignored.

The Passing of Place

It is a fundamental, but seldom acknowledged, fact that many of the basic categories of theological reflection are meaningless in the modern world. The principle of the relation between heaven and earth, of the integral orders of the celestial and ecclesiastical hierarchies, is fundamentally antiquated in the wake of those revolutions – Copernican and Kantian – that inaugurated the natures and cultures of modern immanence. When Augustine portrayed the church as a pilgrim body with a definite, if dependent, relation to the city of God, his terminology was employed for more than an illustrative purpose. 'For the City of the saints is up above, although it produces citizens here below, and in their persons the City is on pilgrimage until the time of its kingdom comes' (Augustine, 1972, p. 596).[1] Outlined here is a spatial as well as spiritual categorisation of the *civitas terrana* and the *civitas dei*. Such a delineation of space is also the marker of divergent ends, within the context of which the insinuation of a vertical axis made sense, the kind of sense that is all too hard to grasp in a post-Copernican universe. The subsequent crisis of the meaning of theological space and identity, generated by the loss of place and perspective, is formulated by Nietzsche in a way that is relevant here: 'Since Copernicus man has been rolling from the centre toward X' (Nietzsche, 1967, p. 8). Theology no longer retains a warrant, whether provisional or ultimate, to provide meaning and specification to the status of the world. The cosmos no longer provides a supra-individualistic framework upon which social and ethical structures might be coordinated and assessed. What Nietzsche alerts us to is the fact that we are lost without compass or direction in a world that is no longer a providential home and which is little more than a fateful territory of loss. 'Since Copernicus,' he cries, 'man seems to have been on a downward path, – now he seems to be rolling faster and faster away from the centre – where to? into nothingness? into the *piercing* sensation of his nothingness?' (Nietzsche, 1994, p. 122).[2]

In response to Nietzsche's lament, it would seem judicious to ask whether his evaluation of the status of modern life and living is rather unbalanced, if not melodramatic. When it is possible to align as sober a figure as Alexandre Koyré, the eminent historian of philosophy and science, with the unapologetic nihilist, however, there seems to be something substantial in Nietzsche's verdict, even if

---

[1]   It is important to note that, although Augustine employed a range of ancient cosmologies within his *corpus*, the vertical axis remains a constant. Whether the influence came from ancient physics (Empedocles), Plato or the image of a spherical sphere, the point of reference is constant. His cosmology or, as Leo Ferrari shows, his *cosmography*, stands as 'a branch of metaphysics that deals with the nature of the universe'. See Ferrari, 1996, p. 132.

[2]   It is also worth noting that the proclamation of the death of God in *The Gay Science* is presented by Nietzsche as an event that is intelligible in cosmological terms. 'What were we doing when we unchained this earth from its sun? ...' (Nietzsche, 1974, pp. 181–182).

it is grounded in a uniquely psycho-poetic appreciation of the human condition rather than a straightforwardly empirical interrogation of the vicissitudes of historical development. According to Koyré, the Copernican revolution can be characterised as a 'fundamental process' in which 'man … lost his place in the world, or, more correctly, lost the very world in which he was living and about which he was thinking, and had to transform and replace not only his fundamental concepts and attributes, but even the very framework of his thought' (Koyré, 1957, p. 2). The world in question here boasted an internal organisation that reflected divine providence and which portrayed a ladder, composed of both material and spiritual elements, rising from the terrestrial heart right up to the empyrean. With its passing, we have nothing less than 'a very radical spiritual revolution of which modern science is at the same time the root and the fruit' (p. 1). A dislocation that is both essential and existential is the consequence of what is more than a simple 'scientific' innovation, a feature of modernity that is recognised by both Koyré and Nietzsche. Copernicus initiated a revolution that impacted upon more than knowledge. Pre-modern cosmologies, especially in the Christian examples of an Aristotelian-Ptolemaic kind, had the rank of a spiritual exercise or art as well as that of scientific theory. Such aesthetic and spiritual concerns are at the heart of the ordering of the cosmos, a factor that is evident in Ptolemy's *Almagest* where physics and metaphysics are indivisible in practice as well as theory:

> In addition, as to the excellence (*kalokagathia*) that concerns practical actions and character, it is [astronomy], above all things, that could make men see clearly; from the constancy (*homoiotēs*), good order (*eutaxia*), symmetry (*summetria*) and calm (*atuphia*) which are associated with the contemplation of divine things, it makes its followers lovers of that divine beauty, accustoming them and reforming their natures (*phusiō*), as it were, to a similar spiritual state (Ptolemy, 1957, I: 7.17–24.).

Astronomy has a metaphysical as well as physical significance.[3] The theologico-material arrangement of Being and beings suggests that the realm of the divine, which touches upon the outermost heaven of Ptolemy's cosmos, has an eternally distant but existent connection with the world. Such a God might be 'far away from the objects we directly observe with our senses' (Toulmin & Goodfield, 1961, p. 143) but humanity and all of creation is located in its relation to the divine – 'up above' *means* up above. The material structure of the cosmos directly reflected a hierarchy of being and physically advanced beings in this cosmological picture were also metaphysically superior. In turn, lower beings and purposes could not be dismissed because they underpinned and enabled that which rested upon them

---

[3]   Cosmology and astronomy also share a doxological significance in that ritual, liturgical and agricultural calendars and the timings of monastic prayer were dependent upon a heavenly *computus* and an integral relationship between the earth and its cosmic surroundings. See McCluskey, 1998.

(see Spaemann, 1984, 91–92). Theologically, this spatial arrangement constitutes a meaningful correspondence between creation and Creator and offers a structure within which the earth reflects, and participates in, heavenly perfection: the one, the good and the beautiful. The world is nothing less than cosmographic, the place in which the Word, as it is also outlined in scripture, is intelligibly written and in which analogy seems fitting.

The point of this all-too-brief consideration of the demise of that which we now entitle, in a distinctly modern and objectifying terminology, a 'worldview', is not to clamour for a return to a golden age. One cannot retrieve a point before which the *universum*, namely Being, became an object placed before the subject. The purpose of this narrative of disappearance is, rather, to provide the appropriate backdrop for an honest appraisal of something of greater consequence that arises as a result of the cosmic transformations of modernity. That is to say, if the ontocosmological context in which Christian identity and truth develops is intimately related to the very significance and authority of truth itself, what becomes of truth – biblical, creedal, doctrinal and dogmatic – when that context disappears? It is this problem that haunts modern theology and which remains valid for us today.

The Triumph of Immanence

If anything conveys the seriousness of this question then it is Jacob Taubes's contention that the 'Catholic Church was right in attacking the Copernican theory' (Taubes, 1961, p. 72). The purpose of this assertion is not to reclaim, as would a creationist, what is scientifically anachronistic in order to prove that a Christian datum is more 'true' than post-Copernican cosmological theories. For Taubes the Jewish philosophical theologian, the reasons for the truth of the claim lie with the theological consequences of a celestial revolution in which the realm of material reality is definitively lost for religious reflection and experience.[4] As much a period of ontological revolution as a scientific revolution, the early-modern period witnessed the stripping away of concepts and connotations in which the theological and material coexisted through a fecund and providential schema that constituted the cosmos. The eventual outcome of this revolution was the abandonment of the world to the onslaught of mere disinterested fact. It is not simply that the destruction of the cosmos led to the 'loss, by man, of his unique and privileged position in the theo-cosmic drama of creation of which man was, until then, both the central figure and the stake' (Koyré, 1957, p. 43). This is undoubtedly true, as Koyré suggests, but of equal, if not greater, consequence was the attendant loss

---

[4]   Of course, this may be news to New Age devotees of various kinds but, as I hope my argument will demonstrate, the various loci of 'nature worship' and the terms in which religious experience of nature or nature mysticism are made meaningful simply disclose the pre-eminence of immanence and the loss of what we might call experience. For more on this point, see Fletcher, 2003.

of analogy and proportion, what we might call a geometric or qualitative relation of spatial integrity. In its place arises a very different attitude towards the natural and supernatural, expressed in the new cosmologies (Taubes, 1954a, p. 116) that emphasise an arithmetical, quantitative plane of relation and separation.[5]

Not only was the cosmos lost to human being, then, but the very framework in which being human had its place and its role in relation to providential grace, meaning and destiny was shattered. The world could no longer provide a home: 'Man at this time was a traveller who was no longer astray *in* the world, but rather a traveller led astray *by* the world' (Michel, 1962, p. 110).[6] The cosmological revolution of the sixteenth century – Copernicus's *De revolutionibus orbium cœlestium* was published in 1543 – did more than demand a relocation of the earth in relation to the sun and the planets. It required a radical dislocation of the setting in which truth might be secured, in which to be 'human' had meaning, because the world could no longer be read as the book of creation in which the words of the creator might be discerned as productive traces of grace. Human being had recourse to a very different set of indicators in the quest for a home, a world that could be built on sure foundations.

> Because he had lost the cosmos that had been the framework of his existence and the object of his knowledge, he was driven back to search for certainty and order *in himself*. Through all the cult of scepticism and stoicism, through all the criticism of tradition and institutionalism, there emerges always and everywhere this question of the subject, this question of an autonomy which is both a witness to and a creator of reason, this question of an individuality that is a 'world' by itself, and the truth about the world as *thought* (Certeau, 1966, p. 6).

The turn to the subject is one of the inevitable realignments which occurred in the wake of the loss of any absolute co-ordinates, when 'theistic religion stands without a cosmology and is therefore forced to retreat into the domain of man's inwardness' (Taubes, 1961, p. 73). When the ancient cosmology is discarded, God must be sought elsewhere and the Copernican universe provides the conditions for the transformation in the modern understanding of the divine through novel arrangements of spatiality: varieties of deism, in which God is historicised as the 'beginning' but then is pushed beyond the boundaries of correspondence, a notion that Samuel Clarke, in his first reply to Leibniz, suggested would open the way to the 'notion of materialism and fate' (Loemker, 1969, p. 677); an assortment of pantheisms which conflate 'above' and 'below', and which indicate that while the

---

[5]   For a sustained analysis of this calculative transformation of the world, see Patočka, 1996, pp. 53–77.

[6]   Contrast this moment of ontocosmological crisis with Rémi Brague's conviction that, within the medieval context, 'Neither of the two questions, "who am I?" and "where am I?" – or, if we wish, "what is man?" and "what is the world?" – could be answered without an answer to the other' (Brague, 2003, p. 88).

essence of the modern age is rupture and separation, its central thrust is towards unification in *thought* (Schlegel, 1991, pp. 31–32); and a condition which in many respects underlies the first two, the deification of the subject. Through this interpolation of the world and its creator in a single subject, modern Christianity is forced to relocate those elements that were cosmically related to the divine through analogy. The consequences of refusal are, to use Moltmann's terms, an increasing irrelevance and marginalisation.

An early example of this process of relocation is Johannes Kepler's attempt to situate God within the immanent universe, a process that serves to confirm the loss of a Christian theological cosmology. As Koyré puts it, in Kepler's heterodox schema, 'The sun represents, symbolises, and perhaps even embodies God the Father, the stellar vault, the Son, and the space in between, the Holy Ghost' (Koyré, 1957, p. 286). The step from an envelopment of the divine within the world to a retreat into the domain of anthropological inwardness is little more than a modest realignment of metaphorical propriety. In her post-Copernican rendering of 'The Interior Castles', Teresa of Avila presents such a relocation through her application of a spiritual symbolism that is cosmological in form and content (Certeau, 1966, p. 7). The model for her spiritual and conceptual configuration of the spiritual life is the structure of the universe as presented by Peter Apianus in the 1539 edition of his *Cosmographia* (Koyré, 1957, p. 7). This cosmic structure – characterised as 'a typical pre-Copernican diagram of the universe' by Koyré – placed the earth against the celestial sphere, proceeding from the moon via the other six planets to the highest heaven occupied by God and the saints: *Coelum emporium habitaculum Dei et omnium electorum*. What is remarkable about Teresa's application of this cosmology is that she inverts its schematic significance. Michel de Certeau's study of the problems of spiritual experience and its cultural manifestations makes this point all the clearer. 'Saint Teresa's symbolical theme is no longer concerned with the structure of a cosmic *object*, but with a cosmic *subject*: it transposes the old cosmology into the form of anthropology' (Certeau, 1966, p. 7). In the act of rearranging the specific cosmological positions of subject and object, Teresa offers a thoroughgoing expression of the eradication of a cosmic experience. The cosmos is related to the spiritual individual in the form of a concept of the human as *microcosm* but, unlike the patristic use of this concept (if not the actual term),[7] the early-modern mystical rendition of the 'human' relates to the interior life of individuals as an alternative site of the cosmos rather than any analogical correspondence between 'human nature' and the structure of the world or, as part of this (super)natural order of things, the divine (see Dupré, 1993, p. 97). It is certainly no accident, then, that while Teresa makes use of the concentric circles of the pre-Copernican cosmology, they now mark 'the interior development of the soul which is due to the "sun" within the human heart, and no longer an ascent through a series of heavens' (Certeau, 1966, p. 7). Teresa's 'interior castles' offers a

---

[7]   The classical source for the notion is Plato's *Timaeus*, a text that was extant, at least in part, in Latin translation during the Middle Ages. See Plato, 1977, 30B, p. 43.

spiritualised rendition of an already dominant narrative that espouses the departure of a world in which analogy has substance and which, in its wake, sketches the birth of a universe in which the subject is alienated from all natures but one – the immanent nature of anthropology. Despite the success and importance of Teresa's innovative reconfiguration of the cosmos as a spiritual metaphor, the interiorisation of the world signified that the Christian conception of space and place had been assigned to antiquity, a process that finds its climax in Newtonian physics and the Enlightenment creation of the 'dark Middle Ages'.

> Ptolemy's system could already appear to the Enlightenment writers of the seventeenth and eighteenth centuries as an almost perverse aberration representing a kind of autism of the human race. They failed to realise that this reproach itself merely displayed a new form – this time a historical rather than a cosmological form – of egocentrism. One saw oneself as having arrived at the pinnacle of possible development and of self-liberation precisely in that one was able to bear reason's stern decree that one could no longer see oneself as being in the centre of the universe. In return for that, one could charge the dark Middle Ages with geocentrism as the expression, in the form of a system, of a superficial self-deception – as though the Middle Ages had invented it expressly to meet their own needs (Blumenberg, 1987, p. 230).

Atheistics and Astronomy

From the perspective which interests us here, this modification of the place and status of anthropology in relation to the *world* – an anthropocentric universe displacing a geocentric cosmos –is a hugely significant factor in the well-established and familiar contention that the subject of modernity is a disengaged, sovereign self for whom any and all phenomena are merely objects of sensual intuition and rational interrogation. In his oft-quoted poetic celebration of practical reason, Immanuel Kant proposes an analogy between the law-determined astronomy of Newton and the moral law within (Kant, 1956, p. 166).[8] What is noteworthy in this 'analogy' is the paucity of its metaphorical correspondence due to the fact that the world in between the law-determined starry heavens and the moral Kantian subject is essentially a dramatic stage upon which duty must overcome the sovereignty

---

[8]   It should also be remembered that Kant presents the relationship to nature in strikingly Baconian terms in the preface to the second edition of the first *Critique*: 'Reason ... must approach nature in order to be taught by it. It must not, however, do so in the character of a pupil who listens to everything that the teacher chooses to say, but of an appointed judge who compels the witnesses to answer questions which he has himself formulated' (Kant, 1929, p. 20, B xiii).

of evil (Kant, 1960, p. 85).[9] Nevertheless, the deification of the subject finds its climax neither in idealism, and its divinisation of the concept, nor in Romanticism, and its quest for the omniscient self.[10]

It is with the post-idealism of Ludwig Feuerbach that we witness the full maturity of the Copernican system and the nature of the anthropocentrism it engenders:

> If one may say that Feuerbach takes the Copernican schema as his guide, one must reckon with the fact – which already holds for Copernicus himself, and is found again and again – that the surrender of cosmic anthropocentrism presupposes or compels people to adopt conceptions that are centred on man in a different respect (Blumenberg, 1987, p. 87).

Peculiar to Feuerbach is the manner in which the deification of the subject is developed, and here the link with Copernicus is an essential factor. It is certainly true that he understood himself to be an 'overthrower' in the Copernican or Kantian mould, one who liberates humanity from the illusion and false security of superstition (Feuerbach, 1964, p. 10). It is also true that Feuerbach intensifies Kant's metaphorical correlation of the starry heavens and anthropological categories through 'the rational axiom of a homogeneity of nature' (Blumenberg, 1987, p. 88).[11] Besides these affinities with radicalism and juristic naturalism, Feuerbach develops his criticism of religious and idealist personalism, especially in the legal and political spheres (Breckman, 1992), through the figure of a cosmic character. In his celebrated Hegel critique of 1839, Feuerbach unveils this unparalleled and near-absolute creature. 'The being of man is no longer a particular and subjective, but a universal being, for man has the whole universe as the object of his drive for knowledge. And only a cosmopolitan being can have the cosmos as its object' (Feuerbach, 1972, p. 93).

The immediate result of the constitution of a 'cosmopolitan being' is a theoretical congruence between the figure of humanity, now reconfigured in unqualified and unlimited terms, and the deposition of God as an astronomical necessity.

---

[9] It may also be important that Kant's love of the two poles of beauty – deep within and far above – are intrinsically linked to his Pietist upbringing. See, on this point, Loades, 1985, p. 106.

[10] Although Romanticism comes close: witness Friedrich Schlegel's quest for omniscience (Schlegel, 1991, p. 70) and Ludwig Tieck's rendition, in his novella of 1839, *Des Lebens Überfluß* (The Superfluity of Life), of two lovers who seek to renounce the world and 'old experience' (p. 900), or more correctly its status as the 'philosophy of poverty', in order to embrace a 'pure knowledge' (p. 942) that rejects any worldly mediation (Tieck, 1965, pp. 893–943).

[11] Indeed, Feuerbach claims, in a notably Kantian idiom, that 'It is true that the stars are not objects of an immediate intuition, but we know the main thing – that they obey the same laws as we do'. Quoted in Blumenberg, 1987, p. 88.

Just as astronomy distinguishes the subjective, apparent world from the objective real one, so 'atheistics' – in reality, theonomy, which is distinguished from theology in the same way that astronomy is distinguished from astrology – has the task of distinguishing between the divinity, which theology regards as an objective reality, and the subjective reality. Theonomy is psychological astronomy' (Feuerbach, 1964, p. 332–333).

The transformation stimulated by the specific character of the foci of Feuerbach's conceptual ellipse, the theonomic and the astronomic, is usually and correctly interpreted as resulting in an essentially reductionist critique of religious sources and concepts. In his work of the 1840s and 1850s, after his renowned break with Hegel and Hegelianism, Feuerbach does indeed subordinate theology to anthropological categories. Even more significant, however, is the effective transposition of human being. 'While bringing down theology to the level of anthropology,' argues Jacob Taubes, 'Feuerbach exalts anthropology to the level of theology' (Taubes, 1961, p. 70). The inversion of respective ranks of mundane and spiritual entities reveals that the deification of the subject presupposes the death of God, a point that Nietzsche was to repeat so forcefully some forty years after the publication of *The Essence of Christianity*. In this respect, Feuerbach accomplished a comprehensive 'Copernican' revolution as he forged a novel image of the world and of the status of the human. As an object of these various revolutions, God is either seconded as part of the material universe (as with Kepler) or is explained in functional terms (as with Newton and Leibniz).[12] It is for this reason that God's death is set in motion by the astronomic revolution and effectively concluded with a fundamental commitment to its theonomic, that is to say, anthropological counterpart. On this basis it seems more than a little odd that Karl Barth is able to claim that this noteworthy, even outstanding, adversary of all things Christian 'belonged, as legitimately as anyone, to the profession of modern Protestant theology'? (Barth, 1957, p. xi).

It is worth dwelling on the puzzling assertion which Barth sets before us. If we are looking to resolve the paradox presented by him, how the self-confessed 'overthrower' of Christianity can be claimed as a genuine Protestant theologian, an important clue can be uncovered in Feuerbach's own analysis of Protestantism and its productive, revelatory significance in relation to Catholicism. 'The distinction between Protestantism and Catholicism – the old Catholicism, which only exists in books, not in actuality – consists only in this, that the latter is Theology, the former Christology, i.e., (religious) Anthropology. Catholicism has a supernaturalistic, abstract God, a God who is other than human, a not human, a superhuman being'

---

[12] Amos Funkenstein offers a neat summary of the significance of these critical moves in the development of modern natural and material philosophies: 'As a scientific hypothesis, [God] was later shown to be superfluous; as a being, he was shown to be a mere hypostatization of rational, social, or psychological ideals and images' (Funkenstein, 1986, p. 116).

(Feuerbach, 1957, p. 336). In the same section of the appendix to his *magnum opus*, entitled *Man is the God of Christianity, Anthropology the Mystery of Christian Theology*, Feuerbach emphasises the unquestionable differentiation between God and humanity in the now forsaken Catholic theology of old. 'Catholicism has, both in theory and practice, a God who, in spite of the predicate of love, exists for himself, renouncing his existence for self' (p. 337). While the otherness of God is certainly guaranteed in the supernaturalism of important strands of pre-Reformation ideas of the divine, the truth of theology's content, according to this master of suspicion, is only revealed in Protestantism. God, in a Protestant guise has, 'at least practically, virtually, ... not an existence for himself, but exists only for man, for the welfare of man' (ibid.). In summing up his view of these contending perceptions of God, Feuerbach makes it clear that 'in Catholicism, man exists for God; in Protestantism, God exists for man' (ibid.) and boldly suggests, in a footnote, that 'It is true in Catholicism also – in Christianity generally, God exists for man; but it was Protestantism which first drew from this relativity of God its true result – the absoluteness of man' (ibid.).

Notwithstanding his preference for the historically fresh representation of God existing for man, Feuerbach goes on to identify a problem which remains at the heart of the Protestant endeavour. The latter exhibits a positive tendency to understand the purpose of God in immanent, 'natural' or human terms but clothes this revolution in extrahuman, supernatural discourse: 'it has emancipated the flesh, but not the reason' (p. 338). The rationale which both informs and provides the end point of *The Essence of Christianity* is to resolve this contradiction (see Taubes, 1961, p. 71). Barth's assessment of Feuerbach as a legitimate member of the fraternity of Protestant theologians makes perfect sense from the perspective of this problem. Feurbach has disclosed the essential problem for Christian theology in the wake of its ontocosmological character: how is it that God can be thought in immanent terms? But this is not the only issue we must probe.

Because of the importance of Feuerbach's critical analyses of religion in general and Christianity in particular, and in view of the fact that his materialism was to prove so influential in propagating a hermeneutics of suspicion as the primary methodological tool of modern western thought, it is tempting to understand 'Protestantism' (in Feuerbach's terms) as only a theological attempt to find an appropriate response to the conditions of relevance that were established in the wake of the scientific revolution. Yet, as our examination of the passing of the Ptolemaic world demonstrates, and which the concomitant creation of a fundamental split between the natural and supernatural worlds confirms, Protestantism is as much a cause as it is an effect of the transformation at issue.

From Cosmos to Culture

Nothing highlights the character and extent of the change that has taken place with the arrival of these revolutions – those that were at least initiated by Copernicus and in some ways concluded by Feuerbach – than the manner in which the tension identified by Feuerbach is played out in early-modern Christianity. The significance of this tension, and the magnitude of pressure that is placed upon traditional theological categories, can be clarified when we consider those kinds of data that make sense and carry weight in the theological context of a nascent modernity that has succeeded in discarding the cosmos. Unsurprisingly, much of this data is related to the inner, moralistic and voluntaristic character of what Feuerbach recognises to be a specifically Protestant practice. What is more, these characteristics are sharply distinguished from external authorities, bar scripture, that claim the natural spheres of human life and exteriorised truth for their own. Thus, scripture itself, as the book of God, is differentiated from that other book of God – the world, its structures, its time and its very profanity – in a manner that abandons any notions of intertextuality and integrity. The predicament that arises from this estrangement is that the Bible almost becomes a world of its own, a world that renounces the world.

In a study by Peter Harrison (1998) which interrogates the relationship between early-modern biblical hermeneutics and scientific developments, we can clearly discern the manner in which Protestantism discarded the post-Ptolemaic world, and all that this entails for Christian theology and its socio-cultural identity. According to Harrison, it was the tendency towards a literal interpretation of the Bible and the rejection of the *quadriga*, the four senses of scripture, which largely contributed to the development of 'a new conception of the order of nature' (p. 4). The overriding emphasis on a 'different way' of reading the Bible (for 'different' here read 'literal' and dependent upon the pre-eminence of authorial intention) provided the suitable conditions for a jettisoning of 'traditional conceptions of the world' (ibid.). In other words, it was not simply that science was responsible for the reconfiguration of theological idioms and practices; theology itself abandoned the world to the vagaries of science. Scientific conceptions and theories, according to Harrison, shaped and, to a certain extent at least, determined hermeneutical practices that underpinned Biblical interpretation. This relationship to science also ensured that 'the text of scripture was for the first time exposed to the assaults of history and science' (p. 268). What resulted from this diremption of the study of nature and the contemplation of the Bible, and the resultant objectification of both entities, is summarised by Harrison in the broadest terms: 'the transformations which brought on the birth of modernity moved western culture from the era of "the two books" to that of the "two cultures" ' (p. 267).

If this is true, and Harrison's reflections are to be taken seriously (as I believe they are), we can conclude that the Christianity which is bequeathed to a post-Reformation world is established on those truths which can be 'scientifically' garnered from the text and the author's intention or that which is relevant to the practical, individual life of Christians within a strictly demarcated cultural sphere. The destruction of the integral relationship between the book of creation and the book of the Bible removes the natural context of grace and divine efficacy, for the most part, and resituates it in the hidden recesses of the heart which remains outwith the critical parameters determined by scientific enquiry. The fact of dislocation now becomes the pretext for the relocation of truth in the favoured spaces of faith, trust and voluntaristic decision. At the same time, the Bible itself is re-read through a 'scientific' or evidentialist monocle and anything and everything that is, from the perspective of this new cultural domain, extra-biblical is treated with an apposite dose of suspicion. The formation of two cultures not only creates the need for a theology in an immanent key; theology itself is beholden to the methods and means of the immanent.

Sent to the Apologetic Corner

It ought to be said in passing that it would be both erroneous and absurd to conclude that the transformation of theology and its attendant conceptual bearings is a wholly Protestant affair, at least in terms of denominational affiliations and identities. Many 'Catholic' theologians were *also* unwitting agents of the creation and marginalisation of a distinctively Christian culture that itself was eventually determined on the basis of the pre-eminence of scientific methods and metaphysics (see, for example, Buckley, 1987, pp. 42–67). Furthermore, Catholic polemics against the Reformation inclination towards the exclusive authority of scripture were increasingly couched in terms of the *sensus litteralis* at the expense of allegory (see, for example, Howell, 2002, pp. 25–28).One could also argue that the growing tendency within modern Roman Catholicism to standardise liturgy and to concentrate authority on the person of the Roman pontiff introduced immanent and positivistic criteria of truth that were also 'Protestant' in character. Finally, and most crucially, Roman Catholic 'supernaturalism', largely associated with neo-scholasticism, is the mirror image of the Protestant tendency towards immanence. Humanity may be left to its own political and social devices in the former but the method of distinction is the same: the fundamental division of nature and grace. The point that I wish to make, if we might consider the issue in general terms, is that the refusal or radical diminution of the status of the world as integrally related to the knowledge of the incomprehensible God is a 'Protestant' experience. From the perspective of the wide variety of theological, philosophical, scientific, social and economic transformations of the modern period, 'Protestant' is a synecdoche, a denomination *pars pro toto*. In Feuerbach's use of the term, which at the very least resonates with orthodox Lutheranism, this is due to the fact that a *theologia gloria* is unseated and supplanted by a scientific metaphysics and the categories of anthropological immanence. Subjective predicates are at the heart of theological utterances; theological utterances are weighed in relation to immanent categories.

Barth himself summarises the issue at hand in his interrogation of 'whether and in what measure religion, revelation and the relation to God can be interpreted as a predicate of man' (Barth, 1957, p. xx). Barth's response commences with a helpful contextualisation of theology's Feuerbachian predicament in which he questions the role of Christianity, theology and theologians in addition to his rather damning judgment on the over-excessive pretensions of modern 'Man':

> This formulation of the problem was brought about by the embarrassing situation – the 'apologetic corner' – into which modern theology, with decreasing power of resistance, has allowed itself to be pushed, through the rise of a conceited and self-sufficient humanity, a tendency to be observed from Pietism through the Enlightenment to Romanticism (ibid.).

Theological space is atrophied as the criteria of truth are found elsewhere. As Christianity reconstitutes itself either by abandoning itself to the truth of the new science or to the characteristics of the new *anthropos*, theological space is progressively and ineluctably squeezed and compacted. Sent, then, to the 'apologetic corner', the very status of Christian truth is related to fewer of those mediatory artefacts via which the faith was developed and transmitted in its natural, theological, doxological and teleological configurations. These elements are outdated in the midst of these new times of meaning and outlandish in these new territories of truth. The principal casualty of this attenuation of space that constitutes the 'apologetic corner' is undoubtedly those extra-biblical elements that are intrinsically tied to a metaphysics that is antiquated by the rise of modernity: creeds, dogmas and doctrines. These articles of faith cannot survive methods of enquiry and analysis which demand a clarity of meaning and significance that is comparable with those that are garnered in a scientific context. Moreover, they do not have the luxury of an authoritative status that comes with 'revelation' and all that it entails.

The examples of the marginalisation of extra-biblical data in the modern period are legion, not least because the anthropological criteria of truth and meaning seem to exclude the truth claims embodied in so many doctrinal statements and upon which their authority rested. In 1675, for example, in a letter to Henry Oldenburg, the Secretary of the Royal Society, Benedict de Spinoza expressed his complete and utter bafflement with the doctrine of the Trinity. Spinoza was driven to distraction when the Christian churches advocated and defended the doctrine because 'they seem to me to speak no less absurdly than one who might tell me that a circle has taken on the nature of a square' (Spinoza 1995, p. 333). Spinoza highlights the theological dilemma of modernity. It is not only that Christian thought must face the challenge of how one might articulate the supernatural in natural terms but that, once doctrine is subject to immanent critique, its very meaning is in crisis. Doctrine, from an immanent perspective, simply fails to add up.

Once again, it is the theologians who are as culpable as the sceptical or materialist opponents of 'superstition'. There are manifold examples of the manner in which early-modern Christian thinkers responded to intellectual, political and cultural forces and predicaments in a manner which served to bring about the subordination of doctrine *within* a theological setting. For our purposes, it is worth isolating three important developments in modern Christian thought which arise as a corollary of the loss of a place and space within which theological discourse is fitting and fruitful. These new formulations for a transformed locale include a commitment to *sola scriptura* at the expense of any extra-biblical co-ordinates for Christian life and practice, a subjective rather than ontocosmological tendency evident in early-modern Christianity which definitively abandons the world to the exigencies of a natural science that posits a *mathesis universalis* as a world-formula, and the inclination within the afterlives of Reformation and counter-Reformation theology towards an understanding of doctrine as essentially oppressive. It is to these three principles of modern Christianity that we must now turn.

Scriptural Precedence

It is a well-known tenet of the Reformation that the church was to be neither the sole key-holder to the truth of revelation nor a hermeneutical authority which held the scriptures and the people of God at a safe distance from each other. Quite the contrary was the case for Luther and Melanchthon. In the view of the Reformers and their followers, according to Ernst Käsemann's concise summary, 'the relationship of the community and the Word of God is not reversible; there is no dialectical process by which the community created by the Word becomes at the same time for all practical purposes an authority set over the Word to interpret it, to administer it, to possess it' (Käsemann, 1969, p. 261). The scriptures were understood as actively critical and questioning of the church, its articles of faith, its conduct, structures, and its people. The result, to once again borrow Käsemann's description, was that 'in the evangelical conception, the community is the flock under the Word as it listens to the Word. All its other identifying marks must be subordinate to this ultimate and decisive criterion' (ibid.). Yet the emphasis upon scripture as the sole benchmark of truth and authenticity was, at the same time, a surrender of the long-established interrelation of faith and reason, a relation that could survive neither the strictures of the new science nor the strictly policed limits of the apologetic corner. On the one hand, we have the development of a modern philosophy (which of course includes natural philosophy) that sought to develop an indubitable and sure route (that is, a *methodos*, a path) to knowledge; on the other hand, we see a biblical culture which demanded a similar level of unquestionable and indisputable certitude for its own preferred approach to truth: 'Anyone is mistaken who seeks to ascertain the nature of Christianity from any source except canonical Scripture' (Melanchthon, 1969, p. 19). The reason for Melanchthon's confidence and inflexibility is that 'truth' has no need of any other – relatively corrupt – mediation because of the fullness of what is revealed in the books of the Bible. 'For since the Godhead has portrayed its most complete image in them, it cannot be known from any source with more certainty or accuracy' (ibid.). It was faith and trust in Christ rather than understanding of the attributes and predicates of Christ which, after Luther and Melanchthon, secured Biblical sanction and deserved theological attention (Powell, 2001, p. 12).

It ought to be emphasised that Luther, Melanchthon and their followers were doctrinally orthodox in that they acknowledged, for instance, the authoritative standing of the doctrine of the Trinity.[13] Their reasons for doing so, however, constituted the very principles of weakness and vulnerability from which the doctrine was to relentlessly suffer in the modern period. Scripture was marginalised on the basis of a theological desire for an untouchable authoritative area, a space that was destined to become a ghetto. So secure were the boundaries that delimited a scriptural culture that any other symbols and writings of the faith were, according to the *Formula of Concord*, 'merely witnesses and expositions of the faith' (Tappert, 1959, p. 465). This process of demarcation ensured that 'the distinction between the Holy Scripture of the Old and New Testaments and all other writings is maintained, and Holy Scripture remains the only judge, rule and norm according to which, as the only touchstone, all doctrines should and must be understood and judged as good or evil, right and wrong' (ibid.). Moreover, the removal of the tenets of Christian practice and reflection from their productive location within a multifaceted 'world' engendered a homogeneous understanding of the faith. Indeed, despite the obvious tendency within the medieval church to provide a 'detailed clarification and systematization of doctrine necessary for forming and ensuring uniformity of faith in western Christendom' (Southern, 1995, p. 238), on the eve of the Reformation doctrinal pluralism is the norm (see Pelikan, 1984, pp. 10–68; Rupp, 1978, 287–304).

It is with the coming of the modern period that we witness the definitive subordination of doctrine to scripture, the curtailment of the former's pluralism and the destabilisation and deterioration of its authority. The status of a particular creedal statement was dependent on its attestation by scripture and its purpose was largely defensive. Thus doctrine develops as a set of secondary proof texts which secure the true territory of the faith and put to the test the truthfulness and reliability of its proponents. The inherent problem with this total differentiation of a scriptural culture from the culture of the rational, aesthetic and cosmological is that scripture itself is soon subjected to the standards and measures preferred within the dominant culture of immanent critique. The space within which Christian truth is meaningful is progressively marginalised.

The principles of this marginalising tendency that were constituted within a theological context remain undiminished in the modern period. In a famous systematic exposition of the twentieth century that is notable because of its amplification of the central tenets of Protestant theology, Emil Brunner discloses the conceptual limitations and theological boundaries that are a concomitant feature of this modern alteration of the meaning and significance of the theological tradition. In relation to the priority of revelation, Brunner sketches a hermeneutical

---

[13]   Although Pierre Caroli did accuse Calvin of Arianism on the basis of the latter's treatment of the doctrine of the Trinity in the first edition of the *Institutes*. As Bernard Reardon shows, Calvin clarified his orthodox trinitarianism in subsequent editions. See Reardon, 1981, pp. 203–204.

circle through which the interpretation and validity of doctrine is established. 'All sound doctrine', he suggests, 'claims to be based on Truth.' Furthermore, the breadth and significance of this claim is predicated on the fact that,

> its foundation does not lie in human knowledge, but in divine revelation. But this basis is at the same time a condition; Christian doctrine can only legitimately make this unconditional claim to Truth in so far as it is based on revelation. Thus its *basis* becomes its *criterion* and its *norm* (Brunner, 1949, p. 43).

Here Brunner exhibits both the centrality of the anti-speculative strand within Protestant thought and the subsidiary nature of doctrine in relation to scripture. Indeed, these elements receive a summary treatment in Brunner's assessment of the doctrine of the Trinity where he proposes that the 'starting-point of the doctrine of the Trinity is, naturally, not a speculative one, but the simple testimony of the New Testament' (ibid., p. 206). (It is difficult not to question Brunner's confidence here. How, one might ask, can the doctrine be garnered from the data of biblical revelation, 'naturally' as it were? Arius, as much as Athanasius, was convinced of his position on the basis of revelation!)

With regard to the defensive function of doctrine, Brunner brings together the precedence of Biblical testimony over speculation and an emphasis upon the essentially apologetic nature of doctrine in his examination of the doctrine of the Trinity:

> The ecclesiastical doctrine of the Trinity, established by the dogma of the ancient Church, is not a Biblical *kerygma*, therefore it is not the *kerygma* of the Church, but it is a theological doctrine which defends the central faith of the Bible and of the Church. Hence it does not belong to the sphere of the Church's message, but it belongs to the sphere of theology; in this sphere it is the work of the Church to test and examine its message, in the light of the Word given to the Church. Certainly in this process of theological reflection the doctrine of the Trinity is central (ibid.).

Doctrine is here presented as a consequence of revelation and of the pressing need to defend the content and identity of the truth of revelation before those who would question its veracity or distort its truth.[14] Brunner here is echoing the theological method of Luther and Melanchthon who, as Samuel Powell demonstrates, came to see in the case of the Trinity that 'the doctrine in its technical formulation is absent from the Bible; the most that could be accomplished would be to show that it is implied by scripture' (Powell, 2001, p. 4). These two giants of the Reformation

---

14   It should also be pointed out that Brunner actually thinks that the classical doctrine is erroneous in some ways. In short, he perceives the manner in which the three persons are placed 'side by side' to be the creation of 'a speculative truth, which is really an illusion' (Brunner, 1949, p. 225).

inadvertently, though definitively, introduced a conceptual partition 'that would in future generations make the doctrine of the Trinity a matter of suspicion. Luther and Melanchthon had unwittingly driven a wedge between creeds and Bible by insisting that the creeds are subject to inspection and criticism according to their agreement with the Bible' (ibid., p. 22). As the poor cousin of scripture, doctrine was now subject to the burden of 'proof' on the basis of revelation and stripped of any cognitive or traditional authority of its own. In contrast, one of Luther's primary intellectual enemies saw the possibility of overcoming the limitations of reason to 'convert probability into certainty' by using the authority of the ecumenical councils and the consensus of the people of God 'as criteria of truth' (Rummel, 2000, p. 57). The adversary was Erasmus of Rotterdam who, on the basis of his scepticism, incited the famous rejoinder from Luther that 'The Holy Spirit is no Skeptic' (Luther, 1972, p. 24).[15] The very possibility of considering a range of foundations alongside revelation that underpinned authoritative theological utterances was outside the scope of Luther's radical twin principles of theological elucidation: *sola scriptura* and *sola fide*. The ultimate consequence of the dependence upon these 'revolutionary' coordinates, to borrow Ritschl's term, was that creedal statements became 'worthless for the faith which consists in trust' (Ritschl, 1902, p. 395).

In line with this subordination of doctrine is the tendency to underscore the activity of God within salvation history. Harmless though such a stress might well have been within the theology of the Reformation, its effect can be discerned in an increasing emphasis upon the economy of God and the refusal to speculate on the nature of the divine because 'revelation does not disclose to us God's nature in its eternal essence' (Powell, 2001, p. 4). So it is that the parameters of the analysis of divine things are established on the limits of revelation and the concomitant lack of any ecclesial or material mediation of authority. The Biblical culture shaped by early-modern theological responses to the new cosmologies had already laid the foundations for its self-attenuation within the very principles of its constitution. Brunner's exposition of the doctrine of the Trinity illuminates this fact, especially in his rejection of any speculative move which tempts us to 'step out of the Biblical line of "saving history" and place the Father, the Son and the Holy Spirit "side by side" ' (Brunner, 1949, p. 227). Reason, within the culture of Christianity, must be renounced.

Despite what we might term the 'anthropocentric reserve' of Brunner and Reformed theology more generally, the terms and boundaries within which theology must take place accord with the principles of anthropological immanence. This is why what is given is sufficient, what is mysterious is out of bounds, what is unknown must remain unacknowledged. The theology of modernity is expressly or tacitly based on this foundation (and for this reason it is theology itself, and

---

[15]   The full sentence reads: 'The Holy Spirit is no Skeptic, and it is not doubts or mere opinions that he has written on our hearts, but assertions more sure and certain than life itself and all experience.'

not simply a seemingly self-sufficient 'secular' culture, that is responsible for the passing of theology).

The Irrelevance of Doctrine

If the Christian complicity in the constitution of two cultures is to some extent comprehensible, it is essentially because the site that comes to be inhabited by our early-modern forebears is a secure and discrete territory in which the meaning and authority of revelation is sheltered from inappropriate speculation and inadmissible enquiry. Nevertheless, the evolution of an anti-speculative tendency within modern theology spawned a twofold division that both determined the constraints of what comprises true Christianity and left a hiatus into which the scepticism and speculative abandon of 'secular' discourse was to rush. The two cultures of Bible and world are eventually transposed into a more radical division of world and interior redemption. Saving faith is efficacious; speculative prying into divine matters is illusory. In many respects, it is the Pietistic developments of the seventeenth and eighteenth centuries which provide an exemplary case of the amplification of Reformation tendencies in the face of the evolution of critical and sceptical questioning of the Bible's veracity and the tradition's significance. There is, however, another important reason why an understanding of the Pietist movement is essential for any honest evaluation of the dislocation of doctrine in the modern world.

In Pietism, we are forever being informed, inwardness is the principal characteristic of a true and authentic Christian life. Thus, Bernard Reardon, who demonstrates that in Pietism 'the cardinal Lutheran doctrine of justification *sola fide* signified above all the individual's inner re-birth' while its formal definition was 'something wholly subordinate' (Reardon, 1988, p. 7). Of course, this assertion is absolutely correct. Indeed, the 'founder' of Pietism, Johann Arndt,[16] strove to recapture and redeem the lost impetus of the Lutheran Reformation by eradicating the impediments of ritual, dogma and scholasticism, which he deemed to have undermined and obfuscated the individual and interior relationship to God. However, to appreciate the full force and contribution of Pietism within eighteenth century Christianity and society, we must adjoin rather than append what for Reardon is a mere supplement to his criticism of the near-solipsistic tendency of the movement. He continues: 'What emerges as its most positive features were its ethical and philanthropic concern, and its belief that the real value of Christian doctrine is to be assessed in moral terms' (ibid.). Pietism is nothing less than an attempt to retrieve the world, a world that is lost to Christian faith and practice,

---

[16]   This is by no means a universal opinion but in what remains the pre-eminent analysis of Pietism in English, F. Ernest Stoeffler's *The Rise of Evangelical Pietism* (1965), the author makes a convincing case for his claim that the 'father of Lutheran Pietism is not [Philipp Jakob] Spener but John Arndt' (p. 202).

through the medium of morality and good works as a proper and necessary complement of conversion and the relationship to the person of Jesus Christ. As a thoroughly anti-intellectual phenomenon, Pietism also endeavours to transform the scholasticism and theologism of the Reformation churches through the practical exposition and grounding of the truths of the faith that are to be garnered via revelation. These two poles – of the world of moral transformation without and the world of faith within – enable the constant and fluid renewal of the ecclesial space in between. The central Pietist co-ordinates of belief and action are thus:

> The need for, and the possibility of, an authentic and vitally significant experience of God on the part of individual Christians; the religious life as a life of love for God and man, which is marked by social sensitivity and ethical concern; utter confidence, with respect to the issues of both life and death, in the experientially verifiable authenticity of God's revelation in Christ, as found in the biblical witness; the church as a community of God's people, which must ever be renewed through the transformation of individuals, and which necessarily transcends all organizationally required boundaries; the need for the implementation of the Reformation understanding of the priesthood of all believers through responsible lay participation in the varied concerns of the Christian enterprise; a ministry which is sensitized, trained, and oriented to respond to the needs and problems of a given age; and finally, the continual adaptation of ecclesiastical structures, practices, and verbal definitions to the mission of the church' (Stoeffler, 1973, p. ix).

Pietism exudes a sense of simplicity. In the last of these Pietistic characteristics we witness the manner in which the external elements of Christian life and practice are perceived as ancillary to the immanent and experiential. Experience of God within one's own individual heart was the foundational principle of the Pietist reform. The overarching emphasis on this experience of faith, which even in its undisclosed form (that which Zinzendorf called *fiducia implicita*) was superior to a faith that was made manifest to others (Zinzendorf, 1983, pp. 304–305), ran parallel to a basic distrust of dogmatic or doctrinal statements and to the labour of the mind more generally. It was the role of the Word of God, and it alone, to fertilise and to fructify the spiritual life of the individual (Spener, 1983, p. 32), but even the Word had to be verified as authentic by a litmus test that exalted the experiential above all.

The leaning towards an elimination of a sense of the significance and importance of doctrine is not at all surprising in a movement that raises the *ordo salutis* (order of salvation) of the individual believer above every other concern (see Schmidt, 1876, pp. 488–499). That is not to say that the content of dogmatic theology, for example, is different from mysticism. It is the *form* of prayerful experience which enables the transcendence of the limitations of the processes of thought and analysis. The latter, in contrast, only utilise a small part of mind and spirit. God is revealed to the believer directly through experience, an experience that is elevated above the doubtful speculation of scholasticism, the corrupted analyses of faith that are polluted by the worldly methods of the philosophers and experience is raised beyond, and even verifies the authenticity of, the biblical witness itself. It is from this perspective that we must understand the Pietist search for the purest explication of the faith. Count Nicholas von Zinzendorf even went so far as to bypass traditional dogmatic and exegetical methods in order to focus on the experience of Jesus Christ and interior redemption. This experiential method precedes any academic theology and, in consequence, the testimony of the Triune God was to be gathered, first and foremost, from the hearts of the faithful (see Powell, 2001, pp. 33–35). Even the revelatory texts themselves, having been sidelined with the rise of natural religion, were now inferior to the most slippery of anthropological categories and were principally quarried for apologetic material.

As we have seen, a vital complement to this unparalleled emphasis on internal revelation and salvation was the principle that one must be moral and embody an ethic that accorded with the life of the Spirit. The Christian life is now first and foremost bounded by individual experience and moral duty, characteristics that transcend any ecclesial commitment or identity and which render immanent the boundaries and purposes of the religious life. It is for this reason that Robert Norton can apply the dictum of the seventeenth-century divines to the Pietistic movement: *theologia habitus practicus est* (theology is a practical discipline) (Norton, 1995, p. 59). A new human being was born of the Spirit; a morally transformed world was the product of a spiritual renewal. In fact, Zinzendorf and the Moravian Brotherhood established a whole range of communities in which members lived a life of practical piety for the conversion of the erring and the comfort of the weak. Edification of their fallen brothers and sisters went hand in hand with the centrality of conversion and the renewal of ethical requirements for individuals and societies (see Stoeffler 1973).

If Pietism is distinguished by its diremption of the world into an interior space in which dwells revealed truth and an exteriority that is to be laid claim to through the practice of morality, a feature that is all the more amplified with the overassertive moral defence of religion in 'neo-pietism' (Stoeffler, 1973, p. 242), it is but a small step to the anthropological moralism of a Kantian variety.[17] To be sure the salvific economy of experience is soberly expunged in the exploration of the postulates of practical reason and the colonisation of the interior world by the moral law. The anti-metaphysical gestures – especially concerning the doctrinal expressions of the Divine nature – are nevertheless repeated with interest in critical philosophy's division of the noumenal and the phenomenal worlds. The difference between Pietism and critical philosophy is that where the former noted two worlds constituted by faith and ethics respectively, the latter attempts a reunion of worlds

---

[17]   A point developed in Georges Gusdorf's analysis of the Enlightenment: 'Pietism is an intermediate phase in the process of a human consciousness on its way towards emancipation. The God of Pietism is the God who hides in the secret of the heart' (Gusdorf, 1972, p. 80).

through the pre-eminence of the moral law within and its application without. With the artfulness of philosophical sublimation, those very categories of moral action which are derivative in Pietism turn out to be paramount for a 'conversion' away from radical evil that is the very precondition for religion.

In Kantianism, as with Pietism, revelation is subordinated. Although Kant makes this point clearly enough (Kant, 1960, p. 123), it is presented with unparalleled lucidity in a book that was the very first 'Kantian' analysis of religion to be written and in which the ramifications of the subordination of revelation (begun most definitively within late-Pietism) are made apparent. In his *Attempt at a Critique of All Revelation*, published in 1792, a full year before Kant's own *Religion* book, J.G. Fichte outlined the fate of religion, revelation and doctrine when subjected to the demands of practical reason: '*only that revelation can be from God which establishes a principle of morality that agrees with the principle of practical reason and only such moral maxims as can be derived therefrom*' (Fichte, 1978, p. 134). As with Kant, religion is cultivated on the fertile land of the ethical, which in turn develops from reason. Religion finds itself answerable to the moral law and, in consequence, at the bar of reason.

> If certain dogmatic assertions contradict the final purpose of the moral law, they contradict the concept of God and the concept of all religion; *and a revelation that contains assertions of this kind cannot be from God*. Not only can God not justify assertions of this kind, but he cannot even allow them in connection with a purpose that is his own, because they contradict his purpose (ibid., p. 135).

The logical end of the creation of two post-Copernican cultures is complete in this assertion; a unified culture is founded on the immanent necessity of the juridical schema of practical reason. If, in a Reformation context, doctrine was dependent on the Word alone for its (already diminished) authority, Fichte has completed a transformation in which revelation is also subject to an external criterion of truth. While for Pietism this criterion was experience, for Kantianism it is practical reason. God, in this light, has no real relationship to the world *as such* but only to the extent that he is the ideal of the concept of duty (Kant, 1993, p. 204). Scripture, correctly understood, simply points our 'attention to the motives for obedience' (Fichte, 1978, p.111), motives that can, independently of revelation or the tradition of the Church, be demonstrated through reason. If doctrine is to be at all useful it must serve the ethical commonwealth, but with the caveat that such a service is only pertinent if it transmits pure religious faith (Kant, 1960, p. 101).

Any posthumous existence of a pre-Copernican metaphysics in which doctrine had a significant place evaporates in Kantian hands into *utility*; in this process, the tension which Feuerbach would later isolate has already been taken to the point where any theological content is of peripheral importance. Transcendent discourse is uncovered and laid bare by the immanent gaze of the critical method so that theology is wholly refigured as essentially anthropological. This development is inescapable as any assessment of Kant's treatment of the doctrine of the Trinity demonstrates. As an integral part of his assessment of the manner in which God is related to the human race in essentially moral terms, Kant limits his discussion of the divine to 'what He is for us as moral beings' (Kant, 1960, 130). There cannot, of course, be any discussion of God's nature in a Kantian schema, a point succinctly reiterated by Barth when he suggests the following:

> It is difficult and even impossible to relate the patristic doctrine of the Trinity to the improvement of life that is to be brought about by man himself in the heart or in the moral attitude of man. That doctrine clearly draws attention, rather, to a being and action of God in himself. For that reason it is contestable (Barth, 1972, p. 106).

It is by taking the doctrine well beyond the parameters of contestability, beyond any boundaries that were in any way meaningful for the Church Fathers, that Kant can endorse a (now) legitimate description of God in one of only very few passages in which he even alludes to the doctrine of the Trinity:

> Now the universal true religious belief conformable to this requirement of practical reason is belief in God (1) as the omnipotent Creator of heaven and earth, *i.e.*, morally as *holy* Legislator, (2) as Preserver of the human race, its *benevolent* Ruler and moral Guardian, (3) as Administrator of His own holy laws, *i.e.*, as *righteous* Judge (ibid., p. 131).

This is nothing more than the definition of the identity of the divine on the basis of the 'universal' human experience of the threefold quality of a morally desirable government – legislative, executive, and judicial – 'as combined in one and the same Being' (ibid.). Kant is refiguring the Trinity as the model form of government for the ethical commonwealth, a Trinity that is dependent not on revelation, certainly not on doctrine, but on Montesquieu's delineation of the most suitable form of constitutional, that is to say, *political*, arrangement (Montesquieu, 1989, pp. 156–157). Feuerbach's assertion that Protestant theology understands God in immanent terms but conceals this truth with a supernatural disguise is confirmed in this passage. Moreover, Kant is legitimating modern liberal political settlements, in which the balance of powers is essential, by means of an authoritative association with a divinely sanctioned order that is proximate. Kant has fashioned the definitive liberal political theology that refuses a hierarchy of Being and, in its place, posits a world in which 'balance' is essential (in this case a triune God who personifies the modern political settlement which is symbolised by the balance of powers). With the replacement of hierarchy by the notion of balance, we see that the 'guiding principle remains within the limits of immanence and yet drives the different antagonist forces … to a synthesis with the help of a purely immanent balance of conflict and mediation' (Taubes, 1996, p. 265). The Kantian God is the distillation of an illusory dream in which difference and conflictual particularity are enlisted into a single system of liberal equilibrium and rational peace without any need or desire for divinely constituted or revealed co-ordinates.

Nevertheless, Kant not only enacts a version of what for Feuerbach is a universal Protestant phenomenon. In a later reflection on the place and purpose of the Trinitarian doctrine, he refuses even this safe recourse to immanent utility:

> The doctrine of the trinity, taken literally has no practical relevance at all, even if we think we understand it; and it is even more clearly irrelevant if we realise that it transcends all our concepts. Whether we are to worship three or ten persons in the Divinity makes no difference: the pupil will implicitly accept one as readily as the other because he has no concept at all of a number of persons in one God (hypostases), and still more so because this distinction can make no difference in his rules of conduct (Kant, 1979, pp. 65 & 67).

Such an exemplary rejection of doctrine on the grounds of its conceptual incongruity and its practical irrelevance is, in many respects, contrary to the earlier example we find in *Religion within the Limits of Reason Alone*. However, on closer inspection we see that Kant shrewdly inserts a hermeneutical caveat which ensures the continued relevance of doctrine (as long as it is a *theoretical* teaching of scripture). We must 'read a moral meaning into this article of faith' so that 'it would no longer contain an inconsequential belief but an intelligible one that refers to our moral vocation' (ibid., p. 67). If doctrine is to have any kind of life and relevance it must be understood symbolically because, as with scripture, its representations are inadequate to its object. Doctrine (as with scripture) is neither useful nor true unless it is tamed and refigured, exposed and explained according to the true doctrine of practical reason. In this light, we can see that doctrine and scripture are *indistinguishable* from an immanent perspective; the 'apologetic corner' has contracted to almost nothing.

Doctrinal Fetters

The employment of theological discourse by Kant underpins, historically and contingently, the attempt to provide a theoretical substructure that engenders a universal applicability of moral maxims. All legitimate moral action must be understood as arising from the free and autonomous operation of the individual's moral forces. The moral agent cannot act feely if he or she is compelled to act from without, even if the compulsion emanates from some higher force 'with respect to whose working man could only behave passively' (ibid., p. 73, trans. modified). As Hannah Arendt has shown, this obsessive rejection of heteronomy results in a familiar modern theme: the privatisation of freedom (Arendt, 1977, p. 147).

The modern period is one which presents us with a universe in which, contrary to the purpose and prescriptions of a closed world, we are offered infinite productive possibilities and for which 'the idea of open-ended self-determination'

(Dupré, 1993, p. 126) is consistent with the anthropocentrism and egocentrism of post-Copernican philosophy. Selfhood is a project that is only possible if government of the self is attained by the self through the refusal of external authorities of any kind. The transformation of the good into an exclusive and voluntaristic end also undermines and antiquates the notion that natural, ecclesial and communal life participates in the divine image. Social and ecclesial forms are the result of 'inter-individual' and 'contractual' constructions that are formed rather than essentially formative (see ibid., p. 131). Moreover, doctrinal authority – an ecclesiastical device that had already been marginalised within the Christian church – is perceived in this new context as oppressive and dangerous for human beings, as well as useless for understanding the nature of a faith that is largely unintelligible to human reason. A good example of this estimation of doctrine, and why doctrine must consequently be rejected, is provided by the Roman Catholic theologian Gerald O'Collins.

The supremacy of a narrative of individual freedom within the theological context of our times is offered by O'Collins in a reflection that is entitled 'The Case Against Dogma'. His rejection of the significance and benefits of any pre-critical baggage that continues to be carried by the church is concisely presented via a fourfold denunciation that constitutes a manifesto of theological and ecclesiastical freedom. The first and recurring principle of O'Collins' passionately argued polemic is that dogma 'readily suggests a denial of liberty' (O'Collins, 1975, p. 9). On the grounds of this generalised conception of the illiberal status of the doctrinal and dogmatic traditions of theology, a more focussed denunciation is proffered in which the crisis of authority in the face of its questionability is conspicuous. 'Dogma connotes a lack of openness and an adherence to rigid systems. It denies the dignity of an enlightened man to submit only to what he has critically examined and accepted on appropriate grounds' (p. 13). The third principle through which O'Collins demonstrates his dissatisfaction with dogma is predicated on the fact that the church has annexed and, therefore, arrested the significance of the divine–human relationship. 'By venturing to "define" some revealed doctrine, councils and popes seemingly commit themselves to set out in precise words, and fix linguistic barriers for, some aspect of God's mysterious dealings with mankind' (p. 18). Finally and most damning is O'Collins' return to the fundamental problem with the role and status of dogma. In order to disclose the urgency of this contemporary theological predicament, he poses a rhetorical question to which the answer has already been secured by his critical stance. 'Is dogma no more than a mask for such political and religious tyranny, a tool used to block human freedom and happiness?' (p. 22). In the face of an inescapably negative assessment of the basis and authority of doctrine, there is only one way to overcome the difficulties inherent in its very purpose and the tyranny of its utilisation. If the church is to embrace and foster an ethic of flexibility, openness and freedom then the necessary conclusion is that for the future, according to O'Collins, 'one can only hope that the Church as a whole will agree to dispense with doctrine' (p. 99).

There is little doubt that this illustration of a distaste for all things dogmatic is an inevitable modern response to the unyielding and inflexible position of the Roman Catholic church with regard to dogmatic assertions (and the creation of a distinction between the latter and doctrine) that is inaugurated by the Council of Trent. The experience of opening out to the world that began with the Second Vatican Council engendered a number of critical assessments of a church that had, until then, been defined by parameters that were constructed in line with a redoubtable and ingrained siege mentality. Hence the desire to envision a future that is radically different to the past is both comprehensible and justifiable. In presenting this future in such stark and uncompromising terms, it is certainly the case that O'Collins' proposal marks a rupture that is historically particular for the Roman Catholic church but which, as we have seen, is a conceptual and concrete fissure that is practically and ontologically universal in the wake of Copernicus and Kant. Freedom and autonomy, *self*-regulation and *self*-determination, are the great themes of the age and they require the repudiation of dogma and doctrine as authoritative texts and contexts.

We must conclude from O'Collins' denunciation of the rigidity and absolutism of doctrinal assertions that any commitment to hierarchy, analogy or particular species of metaphysics is fundamentally unsuitable and unethical in the context of modernity. This point is clarified when, despite the lack of a sustained and nuanced discussion of the rise, development and purpose of dogma in his polemic, O'Collins implicitly creates a historical model of the irrelevance of doctrine that presupposes the primacy of human nature, that is, human rationality, in determining the shape of the church to come. Tradition gives rise to a staid and stagnant church; human deliberation engenders dignity and dynamism. This model is certainly not novel within the wider theological arena, but O'Collins pushes the boundaries of its significance. If we consider Ernst Troeltsch's earlier formulation of such a model for an assessment of the doctrine of the Trinity, a formulation that directly resonates with the ontocosmological demise that is charted in our narrative, we can see the manner in which explicitly doctrinal categories were transformed on the basis of the prevailing anthropological principles: 'Now that ancient cosmology has been eliminated from theology, and with the accompanying emergence of a human-historical view of Jesus, the Christian concept of God has grown independent of this basically Neoplatonic formula' (Troeltsch, 1991, p. 105). The 'humanisation' of doctrine is in every respect disclosed in this passage as well as the demands of a 'new time' in which the rigidity of metaphysics is renounced and, in its place, the authoritative categories of human potential and experience are embraced and celebrated. However, while Troeltsch is satisfied with an immanent 'human-historical' reconfiguration of divine identity and meaning, O'Collins appeals for the total subjection of doctrinal propriety to the needs and desires of the free individual. To be situated within the demands of scripture and tradition while one stands in the midst of the modern world is to be subject to an alien power. To be free, self-authenticating and self-determining is to stand outside the difficult demands of doctrine that have no 'reasonable grounds' for the 'enlightened man'.

In short, to be free means to stand outside the church *as such* and to construct a space of critical engagement in which the self has sovereign authority over the determination of the divine, over what 'boundaries' might be 'fixed' or, indeed, unfastened in the individual's dealings with God.

It is at this point that the 'apologetic corner' has imploded into naught. With the apotheosis of the subject, those 'other' factors that traditionally inform Christian thought and practice – including God himself – are to be decided on by the self for the self by means of the attributes of the self. Doctrine is an unnecessary and dangerous hindrance and any recourse to its authority is tantamount to a sanctioning of oppression and division through the artificial and contingent construction of boundaries. But this refusal of any truth external to the subject is an inevitable negative corollary of the loss of an integral cosmos. While it is a foundational norm of the metaphysical tradition of the west that the theoretical sciences precede the moral and political interrogation of the norms of human being and action because man is not the highest being of the universe (Aristotle, 1976, 1141a, p. 212), the creation and subsequent destruction of the apologetic corner is made possible by the end of this ontological-anthropological arrangement. The overthrow of metaphysics and the primacy of the immanent within the very task of theology are not simply historical dynamics through which the ascendancy and superiority of the attributes of the human reach a climax. A decisive factor in the midst of these modern upheavals is that the freedom which is implied and enacted is a purely negative action: to be unhampered, to be unfettered, to be unhindered in one's movements and aspirations (see Virilio, 2000, p. 7).

Any genuine theological engagement with the historico-theological conditions of the present must not forget this essentially negative identity of the quest for freedom from doctrine and its demands. The legacy of this pursuit of freedom is the subsequent institution of opposition as a first principle of moral and social being. But just as our story is one in which the 'spatial' relationship between supernature and nature is rendered opaque and obscure to the point of a radical disassociation in strictly theological terms, so too is it a 'secular' story of the acquisition and appropriation of supernature. There is a structural analogy between the diremption of nature and grace as a modern fact and the requisition of transcendence as an anthropological necessity. The constitution of the apologetic corner is made possible by the partition of the transcendent and the immanent; the acquisition of the transcendent and its authority *by* the immanent is predicated on its annihilation. Negation masks ontological larceny. Only in this light do the well-worn mythologemes which authorise and determine the modern status of politics, nature and history acquire their true sense.

That is why the force and consequence of such a negation engenders much more than the relegation of doctrine to the status of mere (erroneous) opinion or privately held conviction. The divinisation of anthropology as a central theme of modernity's overcoming of theology is simultaneously the enactment of an occupation of material space in which, and upon the basis of which, grace is disavowed. It is from this perspective that the modern division of sacred and profane powers – cosmologically, juridically and socially – can be seen as not simply a new arrangement of authority but the political and anthropological transformation of theology and doctrine. The significance of this rearrangement of meaning and value was powerfully underlined by Erik Peterson in a searing polemic written in the 1930s:

> The liberalism that asserts that theology and politics have nothing to do with one another, was the same liberalism that separated State and Church in politics and for which in theology the membership in the body of Christ was only a matter of personal opinion and Christian dogma was only a mere subjective expression of opinion. It is clear that a privatisation of faith, such as that carried out by liberalism, had to have a detrimental effect on every aspect of dogmatics. There God was stripped as far as possible of his transcendent character so that he could be absorbed into a private religious relation. There the God become Man became a liberal bourgeois who in fact worked no miracles but made up for it by preaching humanity, whose blood was in fact not a mystery but who died for his conviction, who in fact did not rise from the dead but lived on in the memory of those close to him, who in fact did not proclaim the end of the world and his Second Coming but taught us to see the beauty of the lilies in the countryside. There the Holy Spirit also was no longer honoured as the third person of the Trinity but only related psychologically to the so-called religious experiences of one's own soul. The assertion that politics and theology have nothing to do with one another could therefore be implemented by liberalism only in such a way that the Christian faith was heretically distorted (Peterson, 2004, p. 239).

Is it a surprise that theology has, in a modern context, withered as it is steadily eviscerated? Inevitably distorted by the claims and demands of an immanent agenda, theology, according to Franz Overbeck, 'is now of even less significance than a handmaid (*ancilla*), in the sense that it could possibly fulfil an ancillary role, but its services are just not required' (Overbeck, 2001, p. 63).

A New Beginning?

It is in the context of this type of theological distortion, where doctrine is reconfigured according to anthropological criteria, that Karl Barth's reintroduction of a doctrinal sensibility finds its peculiar and important place. From a position, outlined in the second edition of *The Epistle to the Romans*, where Barth presents the Resurrection as an elementary 'disturbance' of a humanistic equilibrium (Barth, 1933, p. 462), to his shattering of an anthropo-ontological foundation of theology in *Church Dogmatics* (1975, p. 245), it is almost as if the 'heresy' of liberalism actually serves to reveal the fundamental task of theology. The force and attraction of Barth's work lies, to a certain extent, in the manner in which he utilises the critical situation of a theology that is conceptually and culturally overwhelmed. It is as if he begins from a principle by which it is only when the artefact is irreparably damaged that its fault lines become surprisingly obvious, the disclosure of which enables theology, at the end point of its demise, to establish its essential purpose. With regard to *Romans*, the 'dangerous memory' of the resurrection surges forth at the instant of crisis; by the time of *Church Dogmatics*, a theology of the event gives way to an architectural endeavour that remodels the foundations upon which the purpose and scope of theology can rest.

We must not forget, however, that Barth is very much a modern theologian. His refutation of traditional ontology and natural theology, along with his rejection of *analogia entis* as 'the invention of Antichrist' (Barth, 1975, p. xiii), indicate that there can be no return to (or restoration of) an ontocosmological theology.[18] But from his work on *Romans* to the *Church Dogmatics*, Barth challenges the hegemony of immanence: initially, through his anti-Hegelian separation of history and eschatology; eventually, through the construction of a dogmatics based on a *theologia crucis* as an act of obedience (ibid., p. 14) rather than subjective presumption (p. 23).

To fully appreciate what Barth has enacted, let us recall my criticism of Jürgen Moltmann with which I commenced this introductory chapter. There I charged Moltmann with championing a mode of theologising in which reason's expropriation acts as the condition of theology's very survival. In contradistinction, Barth delineates a form of theology that, on the basis of revelation, has an expropriative force, a force which strips the rational presuppositions of liberal humanism of their unwavering ground and opens onto the possibility of a vulnerable discourse about God (and its criticism and correction) 'according to the criterion of the Church's own principle' (ibid., p. 6). There are no anthropo-ontological standards by which dogmatics is measured (p. 12) and the task of dogmatics is an act of faith (p. 17) that finds its criterion, as with the church, in the Word (p. 47). This renewal of the theological enterprise is also the renewal of the formulation and status of doctrine. Since the point of departure for the 'doctrinal task' is the truth of God that is realised in revelation, only from this point, and only for this reason, can theology recover from the onslaught produced by the dominant and dictatorial presuppositions of modern epistemology (see Barth, 1928, pp. 218–271).

The novelty of Barth's refiguration of the doctrinal task arises from the interconnection of an emphasis upon *ecclesia* which places the subjectivism and anthropocentrism of modernity under the banner of questionability – thus *church* dogmatics – and the exposition of God's self-revelation as the datum which confirms humanity as the predicate of the divine – thus the *Word* is the criterion of the task of dogmatics. It is precisely this correlation, which begins with the revelation of the Word that 'creates the fact that we hear the Word' (Barth, 1956, p. 247), that, in turn, breaks apart the immanent ground of modern anthropocentrism and creates the fissures from which a theological aperture is constructed, an opening through

---

[18] I will return to this thorny problem in Chapter Seven.

which we can understand and practise the doctrinal task anew. And for Barth, this aperture leads directly to the doctrine of the Trinity:

> The doctrine of the Trinity is what basically distinguishes the Christian doctrine of God as Christian, and therefore what already distinguishes the Christian concept of revelation as Christian, in contrast to all other possible doctrines of God or concepts of revelation (Barth, 1975, p. 301).

While many of the critics of Barth's trinitarian theology have levelled quite devastating charges at his feet (see, for instance, Moltmann, 1981, 139–144; Williams, 1979, p. 188), the fact remains that this privileging of the doctrine of the Trinity has enabled a revolutionary transformation in the fortune of trinitarian theology. As more and more theologians took notice of, and heart from, Barth's uncompromising stance, the latter half of the twentieth century was characterised by a return of the doctrine to a central position within the task of theological enquiry. Yet it was not simply Barth's *assertion* of trinitarianism that prompted this important change of emphasis. Barth also reconceived theological anthropology in line with the doctrine of God, an innovation that enabled theologians to confront the subjectivism and egotism of modern humanistic thought.

In this respect, Barth was undoubtedly influenced by Dietrich Bonhoeffer. In an essay entitled 'Creation and Fall', first published in 1937, Bonhoeffer reflects upon the theological significance of human freedom. Human freedom, like creatureliness itself, argues Bonhoeffer, is certainly not a quality, 'something that exists, something that is' (Bonhoeffer, 1966, p. 37). The identity of the creature arises from being against, with and dependent upon the other. 'The "image ... after our likeness" is consequently not an *analogia entis* in which man, in his being *per se* and *a se* (*an und für sich*), is in the likeness of the being of God' (ibid.). Rather than conceiving God in ontotheological terms, Bonhoeffer asks us to think of him 'inasmuch as he is the God who in Christ bears witness to his "being for man." The likeness, the analogy of man to God, is not *analogia entis* but *analogia relationis*' (p. 38).

In his examination and explication of the doctrine of creation, Barth distils the force and substance of Bonhoeffer's analysis by placing the divine–human relation before a more explicitly trinitarian backdrop. Barth acknowledges that there is a correspondence between the prior relationship of Father to the Son (and the Son to the Father) and the relationship between God and humanity. Nonetheless, Barth is very careful about the nature of this 'correspondence':

> This is not a correspondence and similarity of being, an *analogia entis*. The being of God cannot be compared with that of man. But it is not a question of this twofold being. It is a question of the relationship within the being of God on the one side and between the being of God and that of man on the other. Between these two relationships as such – and it is in this sense that the second is the

image of the first – there is correspondence and similarity. There is an *analogia relationis*' (Barth, 1960a, p. 220).

The utilisation of *analogia relationis* enables a renewal of trinitarian theology in tandem with a reconception of theological anthropology. These rearrangements endeavour to escape the shattering criticisms levelled at natural theology in the modern period while simultaneously underscoring the absolute dependency of the 'human' on the divine. This two-pronged revitalisation of theology was also a twofold attack on the pretensions of liberalism, and it inspired a vast array of theologians to turn to the explication and construction of Christian doctrine by means of a relational theology of God and humanity. In this way, the social model of the Trinity was made possible as a modern response to the challenges of modernity. It is to this important attempt at the *relocation* of doctrine that we must now turn.

PART I
MODELLING

Chapter One
Trinitarian Formulae

In the context of modern Christian theology, Karl Barth's advocacy of trinitarian theology as *the* pivotal element of the dogmatic task prompted an undoubted fascination with the doctrine of the Trinity. By the last quarter of the twentieth century, doctrine *per se* had been revitalised in the wake of this return to the 'trinitarian homeland' (Forte, 1989, p. 5). While trinitarian theology had by no means disappeared prior to Barth's intervention, it had certainly found itself positioned at the periphery of influential systematic and dogmatic theologies. As Claude Welch had argued in the 1950s, in 'the dominant systems of theology in the nineteenth and early twentieth centuries, the Trinitarian conception was either ignored or relegated to a relatively unimportant place in the theological structure. There were exceptions to this trend ... but these were subordinate to the prevailing directions of thought' (Welch, 1953, p. vii). Consigned to the theological margins, trinitarian theology was suffering from a 'general malaise' (LaCugna & McDonnell, 1988, p. 191), a critical condition that could only be overcome by way of a fundamental shock to the theological system. It was Barth who imparted this timely jolt. The rehabilitation of the doctrine of the Trinity began from a variety of earnest analyses of Barth's unapologetic grounding of theology on a revelatory epistemology that questioned the pre-eminence of the sovereign subject of modernity and, running parallel to this critique, on the basis of his insistence upon an understanding of God that was necessarily situated within an ecclesial context. Barth brought together the trinitarian relations, revelation and human participation in the very mystery of God in a manner that was primarily dependent on God's free self-disclosure:

> We are not speaking only of an event which takes place on high, in the mystery of the divine Trinity. We are indeed speaking of this event, and the force of anything that is said about the knowledge of God consists in the fact that we speak also and first of this event. But we are now speaking of the revelation of this event on high and therefore of our participation in it. We are speaking of the human knowledge of God and the basis of this revelation and therefore of an event which formally and technically cannot be distinguished from what we call knowledge in other connexions, from human cognition (Barth, 1992, p. 181).

There is a fundamental challenge here to the modern rejection of speculative reflection on the doctrine of God on the grounds of its essential unknowability. Barth rehabilitates theology in a manner that is itself knowingly critical of the limitations placed upon the very task of theologising by the advocates of the critical philosophy and their theological disciples. In doing so, he brings the task of understanding and illustrating the specific nature of the immanent Trinity within the bounds of an unambiguous process; that of the discernment of the character of a God who reveals his very nature through his action within history, or in terms of the economic Trinity (a strategy most closely associated with Karl Rahner). Yet despite Barth's importance in the process of the renewal of Christian reflection on the doctrine of the Trinity, his contribution still fell short of the expectations of even the most sympathetic of commentators. In short, he was lauded for inducing a renewal but he was criticised for not advancing far enough along the very path that he had cleared, a path which enabled an expedition into the modern frontier territory of doctrinal renewal.

According to Colin Gunton, an advocate and expositor of Barth's work, the reasons for an apparent 'malaise' in trinitarian theology can be traced to the constant tendency, within post-Augustinian reflections upon the nature of God in himself, usually termed the immanent Trinity, towards abstract speculation (Gunton, 1989, p. 47). The entire history of western theology is implicated in a process of intellectual abstraction that serves to divorce our understanding of God from the history of salvation. Barth's challenge to this fundamental failing is presented by Gunton as a twofold process in which Barth effectively restores 'the link between history and the Trinity' and inserts 'into the Augustinian tradition … elements from the Cappadocian Fathers' (ibid.). The two foci of this sentence can act as useful keys to the recent success of trinitarian theology and to the context in which the doctrine of God has become the starting point or fulcrum of any truly authentic theological enquiry. As far as Gunton is concerned, however, this 'restoration' on its own is insufficient to deflect an enduring dissatisfaction with Barth's reconstruction of trinitarian doctrine. The motivation behind Gunton's sustained criticism of Barth is fuelled by a contention that while the latter formulated a theology of the Trinity that was superior to the well-worn ahistorical abstractions that dominate the western tradition, he regrettably failed to take his insights to their natural conclusions.

If Barth's most important contribution to our understanding of the triune God, at least in Gunton's view, is to be found in the shift towards 'a more truly relational conception of the Trinity' (p. 60), the Achilles' heel of his thought is to be found in exactly the same spot. Barth curtails and limits the significance of the relational God through his adoption of, and emphasis upon, 'modes of being' as a more adequate term for the divine persons. Because the modes of the Trinitarian persons are predicated on a prior substance or unity that engenders and enables any subsequent distinction, Barth's model of God gives an ineluctable primacy to the oneness of God. In consequence, the 'weakness of Barth's theology of the Trinity is that God's unity is seen as the *ground* of his threeness, rather than the *result*' (ibid.).

Gunton's criticisms of Barth echo those of Jürgen Moltmann whose problems with the author of the *Church Dogmatics* are also directed at the frailty of any notion of relationality in Barth's theology of God. The core of Moltmann's unease also rests with Barth's concept of 'modes of being', as a substitute for divine 'persons'. Moltmann, however, widens the scope of the context within which Barth's famous term fits. Modern, post-Idealist theology has seen the notion of divine substance transformed into a concept of divine subjectivity as it responded to the reification and divinisation of the self-sovereign subject. In the wake of this theoretical and cultural shift, the divine subject and the human subject have a relationship that is one of correspondence and, in the context of this historical change, 'it is quite understandable that the early church's trinitarian formula: *una substantia – tres personae* should now be replaced by the formula: one divine subject in three different modes of being' (Moltmann, 1981, p. 139). And this formula sums up the essential features of Karl Barth's 'trinitarian monarchianism', a conceptual principle that depends on a 'non-trinitarian concept of the unity of the one God' (p. 144). Barth's trinitarianism is of derivative or secondary concern and his theology constitutes the individual persons of the Godhead as little more than shadows of the essential unity of the divine.

Both Gunton and Moltmann call attention to an aberration within Barth's theology, yet while Moltmann believes that the fault lies with the influence of German Idealism, Gunton points to Barth's 'appropriation of the tradition' as a stumbling block to a more thoroughgoing recasting of the doctrine of the Trinity' (Gunton, 1989, p. 60). Notwithstanding subtle differences in their readings of Barth's failures, these two critics both accept that the larger part of the western theological canon (of which Barth is part) has offered a restricted and inadequate trinitarian theology because of this emphasis – even obsession – with the unity of God. 'Since God's lordship can only be fulfilled by a single subject, identical with itself, it follows that the unity of God himself is to be found in the unified lordship of God' (Moltmann, 1981, p. 63). In contrast, eastern theology has approached the question of the doctrine of God from a different and more suitable perspective, and this distinctive standpoint is neatly summarised by Ramiero Cantalamessa:

> In considering the Trinity, Greeks and Latins approached it from different aspects. The Greeks started with the divine persons (i.e., plurality), and thence arrived at the divine nature and unity. The Latins, on the other hand started from the divine nature or unity, and thence arrived at the persons (Cantalamessa, 1977, p. 61).

There is no doubt that this characterisation of the distinctive trinitarian traditions of east and west is something of an oversimplification. However, it effectively discloses the grounds upon which the critics of Barth establish their celebration *and* censure of his work. Barth's theology of the Trinity is deficient because it replays, albeit with modifications and minor improvements, the story of a western Christian theology that places unity before trinity. As far as the critics are concerned, the Christian God is not to be confused with monarchical monotheisms or unified sovereign subjects but is a triune God of Father, Son and Spirit. The question then arises: how might a more adequately relational Trinity be delineated? We shall return to this question in more detail presently, but first we must consider the biblical and extra-biblical foundations of any rekindling of a trinitarian theology. It is only in the light of these important sources of theological reflection that it is possible to understand the substance and attraction of the trinitarian theology that attempts to move beyond the Barthian legacy.

A Practical Revelation

Many of the more recent reflections on the doctrine of the Trinity have stretched and developed Barth's conception of revelation and have reconstituted the groundwork for a relationship between the immanent and economic Trinities by giving specific prominence to the historical relationship of Jesus to the Father (see Moltmann, 1981, pp. 16–20; Moltmann, 1985, p. 54). As Wolfhart Pannenberg argues, 'the doctrine of the Trinity is indeed the explicit articulation of what was implicit already in Jesus' relationship to the Father and His behaving as Son of this Father in the history of His earthly mission' (Pannenberg, 1991, p. 31). Salvation history, and especially its climax with the coming of the 'Son of Man' (Evans, 1999), or, in a different idiom, the Messiah and the gift of the Holy Spirit (Cunningham, 1998, p. 22), is the very source from which the dynamic task of formulating trinitarian doctrine springs. The practice of reflection and the search for meaning is seen to have commenced with the early Church but remains the ineluctable obligation of every generation of Christians. That is why, according to Robert Jenson, there is a profound correlation between the revealed Word and later authoritative formulations of God's own trinitarian nature and internal activity:

> To rehearse classic doctrine: there are in God two incommensurable 'processions,' of the Son and the Spirit, from the Father; therefore there is a unique relation of each of Father, Son and Spirit to the other two; and finally there are truly three in God. But these 'processions' are simply the biblical account in drastic summary, construed as an account of God's own reality (Jenson, 1995, p. 36).

What Jenson is enacting (along with a whole range of like-minded commentators) is a theological move in which the intra-trinitarian life of God – a life of interpersonal love – and the history of God's action within the world – a history of God's infinite love – are intrinsically related, a move that offers a hermeneutical key for trinitarian doctrine. Commencing from God's action in the world, the theologian may utilise the revelation of the Trinity in history as the narrative basis for an exposition of the very nature of God. The biblically sanctioned assumption that underlies a trinitarian theology which attempts to be adequate to the present can be summarised thus: that the acts of God '*in history* (and not ontology) were the original subject matter of trinitarian theology' (LaCugna, 1986, p. 173). It is this historico-revelatory origin that enables the theologians of the present to undertake the 'Trinity's recall from exile' in the present (Forte, 1989, p. 7).

Subjected to a revelatory criterion – that the doctrine of the Trinity is expounded on the basis of 'the New Testament's testimony to Jesus Christ, the Son of God' (Moltmann, 1981, p. 16) – trinitarian thought is given a dynamic backdrop on the stage which constitutes Christian theology and practice. The loving interaction of the Father, Son and Spirit functions as a point of departure for the wholesale reconfiguration of trinitarian thought and a radical reconception of its purpose within Christian practice. This second point is vital. In addition to an acceptance of the centrality of the biblical data of salvation history, resolutely promoted by Barth, a wide range of theologians have recently emphasised the manner in which the 'doctrine of the Trinity is ultimately a practical doctrine' (LaCugna, 1991, p. 1). Any reflection concerning the identity and status of the Trinity must relate to ecclesial practice and human experience or, more accurately, the ecclesial reflection on the nature of God, properly understood, actually allows us to faithfully interpret and understand human experience from the perspective of the nature of the divine (Moltmann, 1981, p. 153). In line with this concern, David Cunningham has claimed that the 'doctrine of the Trinity becomes meaningful *only* in the context of theological practices' (Cunningham, 1998, p. 3; my emphasis). Trinitarian theology as a practical concern proffers for the Church 'a wisdom, a discernment, a guide for seeing the "two hands of God" (Irenaeus) at work in our salvation' (LaCugna, 1991, p. 379).

A veritable flood of theologies, in which the doctrine of the Trinity acts as a methodological and doxological focus, find their theological authenticity and historical relevance in these two basic principles: that only a social and relational understanding of God is a faithful expression of Christian revelation and that such a conception of God points to a more truly Christian understanding and transformation of human existence. But what is so remarkable for the onlooker is the manner in which theologians from across the spectrum of denominational and theoretical boundaries commence their theologies from these two tenets. Indeed, we have nothing less than a 'Rainbow Coalition' of Roman Catholic (LaCugna, Forte, Bracken, Margerie), Lutheran (Pannenberg, Jenson), Reformed (Moltmann, Grenz, Gunton), Anglican (Brown, Hardy, Kevern), Methodist (Rudman), Orthodox (Osthathios, Timiadis, Zizioulas), liberation (Boff, Segundo) and feminist (Grey, Soskice) theologians whose critical and constructive assessments of the doctrine of God originate from this theological territory. Each and every theological subdivision includes a significant number of scholars who extol the virtues of a rightly understood 'relational' model of the Trinity as it is revealed by God's self-disclosure. Moreover, the members of this loose coalition champion a doctrine of the triune God which powerfully impacts upon our understanding of anthropology and practice.

It is certainly not a coincidence that theology and praxis coincide in the work and reflections of those who are part of this trinitarian consensus, the 'Rainbow Coalition'. Recent trinitarian theology has stressed this correspondence between the biblical witness of divine action within the world and the practical ramifications of the revelation of the very character of the God who acts. The narrative of encounter and providential grace offers more than a basic insight into particular or contingent historical relations between God and creation and, more importantly, operates as a measure against which to judge the authenticity and relevance of our doctrinal traditions and the manner in which they affect ecclesial life and practice. That is why, along with the critical distaste for an overarching emphasis upon the unity of God that is regarded as an unfortunate bequest of the occidental tradition, so many Christian theologians have tended to question the dominant tropes of western trinitarianism and have identified an alternative, more suitable, source for the doctrine within the reflective deposits of eastern Christianity. In this sense, Ramiero Cantalamessa's somewhat condensed outline of the variation within Latin and Greek approaches to the doctrine of the Trinity can act as more than a descriptive illustration. This trinitarian demarcation has been adopted with something approaching a normative force. The distinct characteristics of eastern and western trinitarianism offer a prescriptive benchmark from which theology might begin its composition of an authentic doctrinal enterprise. The constitution of a trinitarian theology that is attuned to the demands of the revelatory witness of the Word and the exigencies of the Christian life is to be found in the recovery of the theological endeavours of late-antique eastern Christianity, a task of thematic and doctrinal excavation which follows in the wake of a critical assessment of the western conception of God. Indeed, according to Christoph Schwöbel, it is the interlacing of these two features of the task at hand – the questioning of the western Patristic heritage and the retrieval of the eastern legacy – which 'must certainly be identified as one of the factors leading to a new interest in trinitarian theology' (Schwöbel, 1995, p. 5).

In line with this 'historico-geographical' delineation of a critically constructive trinitarian theology, all the theologians we have mentioned, and many more besides, perceive their task as relatively simple. First, it is the theologian's responsibility to offer a depiction of the divine that coincides with the possibilities and limits of the disclosure of God within salvation history. Revelation provides the essential material for the constitution of a faithful doctrinal formulation. Second, and concomitant, the theologian must resist an all-too-common temptation to impose familiar philosophical presuppositions and concepts onto the assorted and distinct elements of this revelatory data. Such a procedure would only obscure the nature and identity of the God of Jesus Christ. Third, the theologian must work to ensure that the very doctrine which establishes Christianity *as* Christianity – the Trinity – is placed at the centre of enquiry, reflection and practice. A process of this kind constitutes a vigorous theological response to the implacable modern challenges to western theology which, as we have seen, have led to the demise of doctrine in general, and of the doctrine of the Trinity in particular. Let us not forget that it was these central elements of the tradition that were deemed extraneous to the Christian life. Karl Rahner neatly summarised the effect of this marginalisation in his diminutive but influential study of 1967. 'Christians,' he argued, 'are, in their practical life, almost mere "monotheists." We must be willing to admit that, should the doctrine of the Trinity have to be dropped as false, the major part of religious literature could well remain unchanged' (Rahner, 1970, pp. 10–11). It is clear to Rahner that a fundamental problem of Christian thought and piety is the persistence of a hiatus that exists between Trinitarian profession and its meaningful endorsement in practice. But that is only half the story. The traditional inclination within the western tradition to hold the One God as prior to, and as the precise condition of, the Triune God has created a situation where the role of the Trinity as a 'living focus of life and thought' has been seriously undermined (Gunton, 1991, p. 3). We still live with the ramifications of the antique western failure to discern satisfactorily the significance of revelation, not least because 'as the history of Western theology and piety worked out, the doctrine of the Trinity did in fact become dysfunctional both in piety and theology' (Jenson, 1997, p. 113).

The Augustinian Psychological Model

The protagonist responsible for this woeful state of affairs is Augustine of Hippo who (along with his formidable heir Thomas Aquinas) dictated the terms by which the prevailing western conceptions of God were formulated. Augustine's prominence in western theology is simultaneously the key to his notoriety. That is why Christoph Schwöbel can claim that it 'would not be a gross exaggeration to see the mainstream of the history of Western trinitarianism as a series of footnotes on Augustine's conception of the Trinity in *De Trinitate*' (Schwöbel, 1995, pp. 4–5). There is little doubt that Augustine casts a long and persistent shadow across the history of theological reflection in the west and the terms, principles and tendencies he inherited and fashioned were constructed into a majestic but flawed *corpus*. In the eyes of many recent interrogators of his work, Augustine's primary failure arose because of his myopic delineation of the nature of the Trinity. The conflict with Arianism bequeathed to Augustine and the western church such a stress on 'the *homoousios* that the one nature or substance of God became the basis on which the entire doctrine of the Trinity was explained' (Kasper, 1983, p. 262). The fact that the initial (and continual) stress in *De Trinitate* was to be placed on a delineation of a unified substance meant that for Augustine the significance of triunity was of secondary and derivative concern. Hence, according to Kasper, western trinitarian reflection is predicated on the primacy of substantial unity within the Godhead: 'the distinction of the three persons was made within one nature' (ibid.). Augustine himself prioritised just such a conception of unified substance in his explication and explanation of God's nature, a fact that is evident in a unambiguous passage in the first book of *De Trinitate* (I. 7):

> Father and Son and Holy Spirit in the inseparable equality of one substance present a divine unity; and therefore there are not three gods but one God; although indeed the Father has begotten the Son, and therefore he who is the Father is not the Son; and the Son is begotten by the Father, and therefore he who is Son is not the Father; and the Holy Spirit is neither the Father nor the Son, but

only the Spirit of the Father and of the Son, himself coequal to the Father and the Son, and belonging to the threefold unity (Augustine, 1991, p. 69).

It is apparent from this passage that any consideration of the divine persons is preceded and succeeded, or, better, framed, by an insistence on substantial unity as the very principle of formation of our understanding of the Trinity. The problem with this structural supposition, according to Colin Gunton, is that *the* question of theology – which ought to be 'What kind of being is this, that God is to be found in the relations of Father, Son and Spirit?' (Gunton, 1991, p. 40) – is posed in terms that are alien to the witness and tone of revelation – 'What kind of sense can be made of the apparent logical oddity of the threeness of the one God in terms of Aristotelian subject-predicate logic?' (ibid.). Because of the strict limitations of his philosophical presuppositions, Augustine was unable to consider the divine persons in their particularity and retreated to a position where they were to be examined only in their relations (and here relation is a *logical* rather than an *ontological* category). In this way, Augustine secures the unity of God. But what of the God of salvation history and what of the significance of the biblical revelation of the very identity (or identities) of the triune God? For Gunton, this is the crux of the failure of western theology's most influential figure: 'Because the one God is the real God, and known in a different way from the God who is three, God as he is in himself would appear to be, or at least conceivably is, other than the God made known in salvation history. The outcome is either a modalistic conception of God, or two competing sources of knowledge which tend to discredit each other' (ibid., p. 33).

It is on the basis of such analyses that Augustine's doctrine of God is deemed to be a questionable and contestable contribution to western theology. The antique African bishop tends towards a heretical monotheism, or unitarianism, and seems blind to the exigencies of scripture. In addition, his theology of God takes as its methodological point of departure the (pre-Christian) Aristotelian interrogation of logical relations rather than divine revelation. There is, however, another element of Augustine's trinitarian thought that has led to censure and distrust of this brilliant thinker. Catherine Mowry LaCugna offers us a significant clue in her examination of 'Augustine's emphasis on the unity of the divine substance as prior to the plurality of persons':

> If divine substance rather than the person of the Father is made the highest ontological principle – the substratum of divinity and the ultimate source of all that exists – then God and everything else is, finally, *im*personal' (LaCugna, 1991, p. 101).

As far as LaCugna is concerned, the significance of a formal and impersonal exploration of the Trinity impacts upon more than any doctrinal or regulatory sensibilities within a theological context. As we shall see in subsequent chapters, Augustine's dominant role in the formation of trinitarian theology in the west triggered and sustained a whole range of important ramifications for 'politics, anthropology, and society as well' (ibid.). The fundamental route to the understanding of God's *oikonomia*, in the theology of Augustine, is provided within the individual soul, 'whose interior structure discloses the reality of the Trinity' (ibid.). This is the root and cause of an impersonal and anti-relational theology that has infected, say our critics, the majority of western interrogations of the nature of God.

The creation of a psychological analogy between the human soul and the divine Trinity is pursued in books IX and X of *De Trinitate*. The point of reference for this psychological analogy, or what Edmund Hill calls Augustine's 'mental model' (Hill, 1985, p. 124), is the immanent Trinity (God in God's self as opposed to God as known in his manifestation in salvation history). That is why the internalised and psychological activity of the mind loving in-itself is apt: just as the immanent Trinity concerns God apart from any external actions, so the psychological model considers the analogous relations within the individual human being aside from any intersubjective or external activities. Here the mind acts as a substantial unity (as does 'God' in Augustine's conception of the Trinity) while the three mental acts – remembering, understanding and willing – constitute relational terms (as do Father, Son and Spirit). This model provides Augustine with a powerful representation of that 'supreme and most high being of which the human mind is the unequal image, but the image nonetheless' (Augustine, 1991, p. 299).

The fundamental weakness in Augustine's doctrinal construction arises from this solipsistic formation of the *vestigia trinitatis* within the human soul. However, the problem here does not only lie in the fact that the psychological model shapes a conception of both God and humanity that is based on 'individualism' and 'intellectualism' (Gunton, 1991, p. 43). Just as crucially, Augustine's diremption of *theologia* and *oikonomia* tends to contradict revelation in its blurring of 'any real distinctions among the divine persons' (LaCugna, 1991, p. 97). God's very being, that is to say, *who God is*, is a question and a challenge that is resolved by a method in which Augustine fundamentally divides God's nature from the self-disclosure of divine identity in the economy of creation and redemption. That is why recent theology has repeated the charge that Augustine is fettered by a neoplatonic philosophy which provides the first principles of trinitarian thought, the result of which is the priority 'of an unknown substance *supporting* the three persons rather than a *being constituted* by their relatedness' (Gunton, 1991, p. 43). Even a thoroughly sympathetic critic such as Bertrand de Margerie who wishes to dispel a number of myths concerning *De Trinitate*, accepts that Augustine's theology of the Trinity has bequeathed to the western tradition a model that is too *intrasubjective* and, in consequence, strictly confines our understanding of the Trinity (Margerie, 1975, pp. 418–419). In this light, de Margerie augments Augustine's principal model with a number of analogies that he draws primarily from the New Testament. And in doing so, he infers that, while trinitarian models that are taken from scripture and art – for example, 'Roublev's admirable icon' (p. 419) – flirt with tritheism, they impact more upon the imagination and understanding of human beings than the abstract and individualistic psychological analogy.

The tragedy of Augustinian hegemony in western theological reflection, according to a number of influential commentators, is that a unitarian conception of God and the human has dominated the formulation of doctrine and, in consequence, the true basis and significance of God as *Trinity* is consigned to the realm of irrelevance. Indeed, as Stanley Grenz argues, Augustine established a 'long process' that has dominated western theology, even if we take into account the important supplementation and modification of Augustine's theology by Thomas Aquinas (Grenz, 2001, p. 39). In relation to Aquinas, it is argued that he falls more completely into Augustine's trap because of his invariable accentuation of the transcendental nature of the One and his distrust of the world and its plurality. But Thomas does not simply construct a theology in which the 'one God precedes and forms the foundation for the triune God: the divinity of the Absolute comes first and encompasses the personal relativity' (Forte, 1989, p. 5). He advances even further than Augustine: Thomas builds this substantial primacy into the architechtonic of the *Summa* where the consideration of the one God – *De Deo Uno* – precedes any analysis of the triune nature of the divine – *De Deo Trino*. The outcome of this hierarchical pre-eminence of the One is that 'knowledge of the existence and unity of God precedes revealed knowledge of the triune God and stands as the universal frame of understanding for the particular picture of the Trinity within the history of salvation' (Moltmann, 1984, p. 158). In both narrative and pedagogical terms the 'revelation' of God's nature is offered in the *Summa* from the prior and pre-eminent perspective of unity. In line with Moltmann's condemnation of Augustine's heir, it is also Colin Gunton's belief that Thomas's theology fails on this point: it is ultimately Parmenidean and Platonic and its refusal of plurality as a transcendental is a rejection of God's revealed nature (Gunton, 1993, p. 139). It is this elimination of a characteristic that is intrinsic to both divine and created natures that has led to the irrelevance of theology and 'the cultural fragmentation of Western life' (p. 140). In short, Aquinas prolongs a sad history of theological myopia inaugurated by Augustine and, in doing so, intensifies the crisis of western theology through the institutionalisation of a structural diremption of the One and the Three. The most damning conclusion of the social modelists is that this lamentable condition persists to this day.

The Cappadocian Relational Model

If the psychological model is replete with profound and far-reaching flaws, a suitably relevant and theologically superior model is required. This is no trivial matter because, as indicated by Robert Jenson, the dominance of the psychological model has threatened even the faithfulness and validity of the church *as* church:

> Reversal of Augustine's misstep is vital, for a religious fellowship in which the
> differentiating relations between Father, Son, and Spirit had ceased to shape ritual
> and theology would no longer be the church, no matter how otherwise dedicated
> to one or another Christian value or slogan (Jenson, 1997, pp. 113–114).

The stakes, according to Jenson, are undeniably huge because of Augustine's
blindness to the original biblical confession of faith that stands as a contradiction
to the unitarian tendencies of the Christian Platonists. In this context, the 'historical
deformations' (Moltmann, 1985, p. 55) of Latin scholasticism must be refused.
And, in its place, theologians must install a trinitarian theology that is adequate
to the truth of divine revelation in which it is disclosed that 'communion is the
first and last word about the mystery of the Trinity' (Boff, 1988, p. 16). Only on
this basis might the church truly be a genuine and valid ecclesial community, a
gathering that focuses its worship and reflection on the trinitarian God.

If Augustine (closely followed by Aquinas) is the *bête noire* of a wide range of
Christian theological critics, then their *bête blanche* – the tradition that constitutes
the underlying inspiration and historical counterpoint to the pre-eminent position
of the psychological model within western theology – is the theology of the
Cappadocian Fathers. These most eminent of Greek theologians, Gregory of
Nyssa, Basil of Caesarea and Gregory of Nazianzus, are championed by our
'Rainbow Coalition' because of the emphasis they place upon divine sociality via
the utilisation and elucidation of the analogy of the three persons (see Moltmann,
1981, p. 199). The manner in which sociality is stressed can be seen in the distinctly
gentle critique of Augustine undertaken by Bertrand de Margerie. We have already
seen de Margerie's attempt to complement the intrasubjective trinitarian analogy
with analogies that reflect more entirely (and faithfully) the social nature of
God. With this perspective in mind, we can more properly understand why he
chooses to introduce his extensive study of the history of trinitarian thought with
an unqualified statement of a normative image of God that guides theological
reflection.

> The regulative idea underlying our trinitarian analysis and synthesis is this:
> the total, though not adequate nor still less exhaustive, image of the trinitarian
> mystery in the created world is man, personal and familial, in the being of the
> mystery of the Church (Margerie, 1975, p. 13).

Margerie does not formally repudiate the 'personal' focus of trinitarian language
and identity, but augments the Augustinian strand of the tradition with a familial
model that acts as the climax to his study. This familial analogy is also utilised by
Jürgen Moltmann because of its intersubjective significance (1981, p. 199). Both
of these critics of the psychological model refer to Oration XXXI of Gregory of
Nazianzus, a powerful polemic in which the orthodox theologian responds to an
Arian's scepticism regarding the consubstantiality of Father and Son (Gregory of
Nazianzus, 1894, p. 321). The appropriate analogy for the Trinity, the means by

which we might contemplate 'intelligible realities in a sensible image' (Margerie, 1975, pp. 368–369), is, according to Gregory, the trinity Adam-Eve-Seth. The primordial biblical family offers us a vision of consubstantial persons, or three individuals of one human nature, an analogy that creates an aperture through which we can begin to penetrate the mystery of the social and relational dimension of divine being.

The force of this figurative and heuristic use of an inter-relational analogy is pursued within the theology of the Cappadocians at the level of ontology. In contrast to the logical definition of relations which dominates antique Latin reflection on the nature of the divine, the Greek understanding of relation is placed at the core of the being of God. Moreover, while it is significant for the critics of the occidental tradition that this is the very point at which Augustine differs from the Cappadocians, it is also the feature of Greek theology that incites Augustine himself to express a theological and philological bewilderment with the trinitarian speculation of the eastern Church. After outlining his contention that God is one and that 'whatever God is called with reference to self is both said three times over about each of the persons, Father, Son and Holy Spirit, and at the same time is said in the singular and not the plural about the trinity', Augustine confirms that his understanding of divine being is equivalent to the Greek *ousia* which he translates as 'substance' (Augustine, 1991, p. 197–198). He then suggests that,

> The Greeks also have another word, *hypostasis*, but they make a distinction that is rather obscure to me between *ousia* and *hypostasis*, so that most of our people who treat of these matters in Greek are accustomed to say *mia ousia, treis hypostaseis*, which in Latin is literally one being, three substances (ibid., p. 196).

It is here that Augustine betrays a complete ignorance of the significance and importance of what John Zizioulas calls the 'Cappadocian revolution' in trinitarian theology (Zizioulas, 1995, p. 47). The dynamism of this revolutionary trajection is a profound theological adjustment that Augustine fails to understand because in his mind, and in common usage prior to the Cappadocian departure from that linguistic norm, 'the term *hypostasis* was fully identified with that of *ousia* or substance'. The innovation that the Cappadocians introduced into trinitarian discourse was the identification of 'the idea of person with that of *hypostasis*' (ibid.). The effect of this consummate innovation, according to the proponents of the relational model of the Trinity, is that the 'Cappadocian Fathers gave to the world the most precious concept it possesses: *the concept of person, as an ontological concept in the ultimate sense*' (ibid, p. 56).

The importance of this witness to the inter- and intra-subjective life of the Godhead can be calibrated in a manner which exceeds the significance of the term 'person' for human self-understanding (a theme which, in any case, we shall examine in Chapter Three). The development of a new and productive linguistic and theological idiom enables the cultivation of a theological space in which triunity, that is to say, the very nature of God, might be adequately articulated. And this idiom accords with the claim of the social modelists that the formulation of a 'trinitarian dogma begins with the experience of three distinct subjects – Jesus, God, and the Spirit – and not with the abstract conception of "deity" and/or "unity" ' (Hopko, 1992, p. 146). The act of revelation of Father, Son and Spirit is central, from this perspective, in the constitution of a reliable trinitarian theology and, as a corollary, in the foregrounding of the Cappadocian analysis of the divine nature. Thus the distinction and interrelation of the two foundational terms in eastern trinitariansim offers an understanding of God's nature and activity that parallels the self-disclosure of the Christian God in scripture and salvation history. The emphasis upon *hypostases* is warranted, then, because, rather than being opposed to a sense of divine unity or the being of God as a general feature of revelation, it enables 'the concrete individual embodiments of this common being' (Kasper, 1984, p. 259). The common experience of the church, of the interaction with the world of a threefold God in history, is reflected in the prominence given within Greek patristic thought to this conception of divine persons, persons who are not mere addenda to the essential identity of God but who constitute the very being of God: 'Hypostases come into being as complexes of "idiomata," i.e., individualizing characteristics. These "idiomata" are here understood not as accidents but as constitutive elements of the concrete existent' (ibid.).

The Cappadocian revolution provides a theological conduit through which God's activity in history as *trinitas* is realigned with the eternal threefoldness of God in Godself. The consequence of this linguistic and theological revolution is not only that we might understand the peculiar and paradoxical nature of the Christian God in a more adequate manner but, just as crucially, that humanity and the church configure the divine life and character in a fashion that is analogous to the way in which God approaches and engages with the world. It is a trinitarian theology that is infused with revelatory significance and anthropological consequence. We can glean from a rightly framed doctrine of the Trinity both who the trinitarian persons are and what they are. And, in doing so, we are better able to assess how the church is called to be an *imago trinitatis*. Consequently, the Cappadocian distinction between *hypostasis* and *ousia* – the distinction that Augustine was unable to fathom – is crucial to the formulation of a faithful doctrinal framework, a framework within which response to divine donation and disclosure is made truly possible. Priority here is given to the notion of *hypostasis* because it differentiates the Cappadocian theology from that of the Augustine and his followers:

> The word *hypostasis* came to designate personal uniqueness. It articulated the experience that *who* God the Father is is not *who* God's Son and Word is, who is not *who* the Holy Spirit is. The word *hypostasis* affirmed that the Father, Son, and Holy Spirit are three distinctly existing and acting subjects (*hypokeimena*) of divine being, action, and life, each subsisting in his own right, uncompromisingly existing as *three* in who they are and how they act in their identical divinity (Hopko, 1992, p. 147).

The depiction of the three hypostases as acting subjects of self-communication and interrelation engenders a more profound and concrete understanding of the characterisation of God as love (see Moltmann, 1981, p. 153). The action of God in God and in relation to the world is nothing other than the action of Father, Son and Spirit as 'a mutually involved personal dynamic' (Gunton, 1993, p. 163). Such a theology of God demands that contemplation of the Trinity begins with the threefold identity of the divine persons and only then might it progress to a consideration of God's unity. 'What then emerges,' suggests Jürgen Moltmann, 'is a concept of the divine unity as the unity of triunity' (Moltmann, 1981, p. 19). In the light of this insight, Thomas Hopko's insistence that divine unity or *ousia* must be 'enhypostasized' finds its theological context.

> The word *ousia*, or essence (being, substance, or nature), came to designate *what* a person (or even a thing) is, not in the specificity of its particular existence but in the generality of its being. In this view, no essence exists except as 'enhypostasized' concretely as a uniquely distinct 'mode of existence' (*tropos hyparxeos*). This metaphysical insight, born from the need to articulate the theological experience of the Holy Trinity, came to be formulated with linguistic, logical, and theological precision by the Cappadocian Fathers following the doctrinal witness of St Athanasius (Hopke, 1992, p. 147).

The concrete identification of *ousia* with the prior conception of hypostatic distinctiveness promotes a doctrine of the Trinity that is opposed to the monolithic and static monotheisms of the western tradition. That is why, in an attempt to ensure the unity of God, even if this unity is derived ontologically from the dynamic relations of the hypostases, so many of the proponents of the relational model of the Trinity utilise the concept of *perichoresis*, a mutual incoherence or inter-penetration of the divine persons. But, as Colin Gunton reminds us, the 'three do not merely coinhere'. In a more radical sense, the Father, Son and Spirit 'dynamically constitute one another's being' (Gunton, 1993, 164). It is the fellowship of the three persons and not a prior substantial unity which enables Christians to say that God is One. 'Because of their eternal love, the divine persons exist so intimately with each other, for each other, and in each other that they themselves constitute a unique, incomparable, and complete unity' (Moltmann, 1984, p. 166). God is an ontology of communion which means, in contradistinction to the dominant western paradigm, that the 'substance of God, "God," has no ontological content, no true being, apart from communion' (Zizioulas, 1985, p. 17). This theology of dynamic interaction impinges upon our conceptions of church, fellowship and person to the extent that it undermines the impersonal and fundamentally patrician God of the Augustinian tradition and, so its advocates claim, offers a truly authentic and relevant doctrine of God. God 'in relation' is a loving, dynamic and excessive being, and the description of this relational God contrasts starkly with the discrete, static and self-contained model of the dominant occidental tradition.

A Relevant Theology

It is undoubtedly the case that the social or relational model of the Trinity has become so vastly popular that it is now the principal, even canonical, standpoint in recent accounts of the doctrine of God. Beginning from Karl Barth's insistence on a revelatory starting point for the exposition of a constructive outline of the nature of God, the proponents of the social model of the Trinity have left behind a western notion of trinitarian persons that is 'defined by their relationship to their common nature' (Moltmann, 1981, p. 171). In its place, the social modelists have championed a doctrine of God that 'has far-reaching consequences for the hermeneutics of the history of salvation and human experiences of God' (Moltmann, 1991, p. xii). And the reasons for its attraction and esteem are uncomplicated. The call of the church to fellowship, love and self-donation seems awkwardly out of step with the conception of a God who is self-enclosed and static, a God who is presented and represented as distant and unmoving. Furthermore, in the context of a Christian desire to propagate a theological and ecclesial context that is relevant to the needs and aspirations of the modern world, where the notions and practices of relationality and community are admired and advanced, the retrieval of the Cappadocian theology of the Trinity makes perfect sense. This social model is both fitting and relevant.

In terms of a general renewal of doctrine, the social model has revitalised interest in the nature of God and his relationship with the world, both in terms of the quest for a faithful understanding of what it is to be human and how a dynamic and self-giving Trinity relates to nature itself. Moreover, the church is challenged to critically reassess its identity, purpose and vocation in the light of the communion of God which exceeds simplistic boundaries of substance or absolute subjectivity. It follows from this challenge that the church must also look beyond its own borders to the needs and pain of the social worlds of others and, most crucially, to the status and significance of the eschatological community. The possibility of an ecclesial self-examination which eschews disconnected certainties and detached concerns is engendered by a doctrine of divine identity that is rich in relationship and marked by an active invitation to participate in the life of those relations. Trinitarian fellowship is not to be predicated on enclosure and restriction. Instead, human beings are drawn into a redeeming and healing relation to a God who is God-in-relation as such.

It is the force and appeal of these trinitarian ramifications that has fuelled a renewal of interest in trinitarian doctrine itself. Because this specific doctrine of God 'speaks' to a modern western context within which theology is homeless, it has provoked an unusual sense of confidence among the practitioners of a marginalised academic discipline. An essential aspect of this injection of theoretical buoyancy is that theology can now surpass its boundaries and offer a critical perspective on the nature of human identity and purpose. The social model brings with it a point at which theological conversation overlaps with the human sciences more generally, a site from which theology can offer its own dynamic analysis of history, the self, relation and ends. But we have to ask whether this confidence is warranted. Is it possible that a correctly understood concept of God can radically alter the fortunes of Christian theology? The need to raise these questions arises from the implications of our assessment of the modern trajectory of theology. As it has languished in the 'apologetic corner', theology as a discipline has tended to grasp at any conceptual tools that might reverse its demise; think only of the experiential and moral foundations of liberal Protestantism or the concrete, dramatic tenets of existentialist philosophy. In each case the celebration of relevance and renewal was relatively short-lived and theology once again sought a handmaid with whom to escape its self-imposed, immanent incarceration. Is it possible that the social model of the Trinity is one such episode, built on an understandable illusion but destined to bring little in the way of fundamental and prolonged change in the fortunes of Christianity? It is to this question that we must now respond.

Chapter Two
Trinitarian Concessions

According to the proponents of the social or relational model of the Trinity, contemporary theology has been granted an urgent commission. It must re-envision itself by correcting its exposition and understanding of its primary source and goal. The very existence and relevance of theology in the modern world is dependent upon a rejection of the Augustinian, Latin tradition of trinitarian theology. The composition of a germane theological enterprise must begin from the demands of a biblical account which gives precise witness to the nature and action of the Christian God. Only on the basis of divine revelation – and from no other source, whether that be theological, philosophical or devotional in nature – is it possible to begin the task of assessing a doctrine of God that is adequate to the calling of the church, the practice of prayer and the exercise of self-donation. In this light, it is hardly surprising that many theologians accept the widely held view that the failings and perversions of the western doctrine of God must be expurgated from the modern theological enterprise and, as a consequence, that this very task clears the ground and provides the foundation for a vital and constructive re-imagining of the theological task. A true and faithful understanding of God is distorted, our critics argue, by the supremacy of a monistic and strictly circumscribed image of God in the west, a representation of God that is dependent upon an understanding of the nature of the individual soul: 'Augustine reduced the image of God to the human soul: the soul which dominates the body corresponds to the God who dominates the world' (Moltmann, 1991, p. 61). Along with the need to re-envisage the nature of the divine life from a perspective other than that of the deficient Latin tradition there is a need to search for a suitable, alternative theological resource. In the view of the social modelists, the principal resource for the reconstruction of the doctrine of God, a vital and relevant tradition that stands as a counterpoint to the distortions of the western version of the doctrine of the Trinity, is provided by the retrieval of the Cappadocian, Greek tradition of trinitarian theology.

The task of the present chapter is to assess these two claims. For while the critical and constructive tasks of much recent trinitarian theology have undoubtedly stimulated a revival of interest in the significance of the doctrine, and have served to restore the Trinity to the centre of theological enquiry, the principal claims of the social modelists have attracted an important range of criticisms. Here we shall assess the theological foundations of the social model of the Trinity from three interrelated angles. First, and most crucially for our purposes, we shall examine the relationship between Cappadocian theology, particularly as it has been re-evaluated in recent patristic scholarship from the perspective of its pro-Nicene milieu, and its relationship to that which is appropriated and celebrated as 'Cappadocian' by a whole range of contemporary theologians. Second, we will assess the charges laid at the feet of Augustine and Aquinas by looking again at the content and context of their principal trinitarian reflections. Then, in the light of these assessments, we shall interrogate the status of the division between western and eastern theologies of the Trinity, focussing on its historical and hermeneutical relevance. In the light of these analyses, I hope to offer an overall appraisal and evaluation of the theological significance of this important, and predominant, strand of trinitarian theology. In doing so, I will undertake – all too briefly – an assessment of the function and limits of the theological enterprise in terms of where the theologian stands and what this stance entails.

The Cappadocians and the Moderns

In the opening pages of his analysis of the place of power (*dynamis*) in Gregory of Nyssa's theology of the Trinity, Michel Barnes offers a rather revealing insight into the academic popularity of this important Cappadocian father. Of the thousands of recent articles and books in which Gregory's theology is a point of focus or reference, the majority have been written by systematic theologians or by those undertaking general surveys of trinitarian doctrine (Barnes, 2001, p. 2). This recognition of the circumstances in which Gregory is appropriated and promoted is essential for understanding the manner in which his thought in particular, and that of the Cappadocian fathers more broadly, has been received and used: the trinitarianism of these Greek fathers is exposed and analysed in the service of a modern theological endeavour. Gregory is less the object of patristic scholarship, where his reflections are assessed within the context of late-antique history, thought and controversy, than a means to rejuvenate or complement contemporary formulations and approaches.

One must not, of course, reject or censure such employments and re-readings of Cappadocian theology *per se* (although we must remember that there is, in fact, no unitary theology which might be termed 'Cappadocian'). Hermeneutically speaking, the texts of Basil and the two Gregories may well illuminate or even resolve theological difficulties or challenges of which they knew nothing. But what no theologian of the present must forget is that the variety of texts that are authored by the Cappadocian fathers do *not* constitute a systematic or comprehensive theological overview of those concepts and problems, from the doctrine of creation to the doctrine of the last things, by which modern theology has come to navigate its vast territory. In this light, the very fact that the majority of Cappadocian texts are polemical or responsive in nature – that they offer specific (if often sophisticated) rejoinders to particular problems for, or challenges to, orthodox doctrine – should lead us to read them with care and sensitivity as well as delight.

It is exactly this sense of caution and the attendant responsibility to proceed with respect for the tradition of the Church that so many of the social modelists discount or overlook. Exemplary in this regard is Jürgen Moltmann's claim that the social analogy of the Cappadocians enables us to overcome a monarchical conception of the divine. For any theologians who happen not to be patristics specialists, the appropriate response to Moltmann ought to begin from a position whereby they treat the minimalism of this assertion with a sensible degree of scepticism. For it is a truism that social analogies for the divine image 'point to the fact that the image of God must not merely be sought in human individuality; we must look for it with equal earnestness in human sociality' (Moltmann, 1981, p. 199). The Cappadocians are not interested in an 'earnest' equality of unitary and plural analogies when it comes to confessing 'the incomprehensible unity of the incomprehensible and yet irreducible divine persons' (Ayres, 2004, p. 344). They are not interested in a general malaise in trinitarian theology or the need to create an arsenal of natural or social models of theological discourse so that the doctrine of God is relevant to modern anthropological or political crises. They are interested in the pursuit of truth, along with the prayerful quest for knowledge and the desire for sanctification that are understood as integral and harmonious exercises.

The Cappadocian fathers offer a number of examples where points of emphasis or accent reveal the contextual nature of their reflections. And the variety of these points of emphasis leads us to conclude that there is no straightforward or simple manner in which the plurality of persons in the Trinity is the point of departure, always and everywhere, for a 'Cappadocian' model of the Trinity. Let us illustrate this point by considering a short and important passage in Basil of Caesarea's *On the Holy Spirit*:

> Worshipping as we do God of God, we both confess the distinction of the Persons, and at the same time abide by the Monarchy. We do not fritter away the theology in a divided plurality, because one Form, so to say, united in the invariableness of the Godhead, is beheld in God the Father, and in God the Only begotten (Basil, 1895, §45, p. 28).

The passage is uncompromising in its commitment to an ontological unity within God, from which and through which the distinction of Persons is situated. When we consider the context of Basil's explanation of the concrete nature of divine unity, the reason for its foregrounding is clear. *On the Holy Spirit* is a polemical text that is penned in order to attack the position of Eustathius, Bishop of Sabaste. Eustathius had located the Spirit in an intermediate position between Creator and creature. This pneumatological site, 'in-between' God and the world, is exposed by Basil as nothing but a false and illusory region (see Meredith, 1995, pp. 30–31). Is it any surprise, then, that rather than accentuating the distinctive nature of the divine Persons, Basil should be seen here underscoring the essential and underlying unity of God? The question of plurality is approached with a degree of prudence that is most certainly apposite given the circumstances in which Basil composed his thoughts.

A slightly different consideration of the divine monarchy is provided in the *Theological Orations* of Gregory of Nazianzus. This reflection on the nature of God, which is found in the third of Gregory's famous sermons, succeeds a thorough and uncompromising examination of the incomprehensibility of God in the preceding *Oration*:

> The opinions about deity which hold pride of place are three in number: anarchy, polyarchy, and monarchy. With the first two the children of Greece amused themselves, and may they continue to do so. Anarchy with its lack of a governing principle involves a disorder. Polyarchy, with a plurality of such principles, involves faction and hence the absence of a governing principle and this involves disorder again. Both lead to an identical result – lack of order, which, in turn leads to disintegration. For us, however, monarchy is the most valuable, but not a monarchy defined by a single person, for unity establishing plurality is self-discordant, but the single rule produced by equality of nature, harmony of will, identity of action and the convergence towards their source of what springs from unity – none of which is possible in the case of created nature. The result is that though there is numerical distinction, there is no division in the substance (Gregory of Nazianzus, 2002, 29.2, p. 70).

It is evident here that Gregory is rather more circumspect about the unequivocal application of a 'model' to describe the nature of the trinitarian God. No natural analogy, let alone model, adequately describes the Godhead, a fact that is made explicit when Gregory warns us that 'to tell of God is not possible … but to know him is even less possible' (28.4, p. 39). Monarchy may well be a valuable idea when it comes to offering a portrayal of God but it falls well short of any claim to similitude. All that Gregory is willing to state clearly is a pair of affirmations which offer different weights to the question of unity and plurality; one declaration that is the staple fare of the social modelists, and one account concerning the nature of the Trinity that is at least problematic for, if not antithetical to, the 'Cappadocian' theology by which the prior sociality of God is unequivocally established and guaranteed. In the first place we have a claim that unity establishing plurality is self-discordant, an argument from which we might surmise that unity cannot have a simple and straightforward priority over plurality. But the caveat is decisive here; no such image, arrangement or model can be found in the world. There are no social or political models that approach a modicum of adequacy. Secondly, however, we have a statement which presents a rather different degree of nuance: that the three differ in number but not in substance (*ousia*).

The purpose for which Gregory composed his *Orations* will offer us both an important clue as to exactly what it is that he wishes to confirm and question about the nature of God and what it is that he wishes to precisely delimit in his reflection on the character of the relationship between Father, Son and Spirit. According to R.P.C. Hanson, the 'apophatic, agnostic theology' of Gregory, a theological disposition that is habitually operative in this Greek father's analysis of the nature of God's essence, marks a direct response to the 'trenchant, rationalist arguments' of the neo-Arian Eunomius (Hanson, 1988, p. 708). The essential aspect of Eunomius's argument, a viewpoint that prompts Gregory's impassioned response, is the former's proposition of a divine nature of the Father from which the Son must be excluded on rational as well as biblical grounds. The Son may well be the 'most perfect agent for all the creative activity and decisions of the Father' (p. 632), but his nature and significance do not accord with the pro-Nicene's 'outrageous' exaggerations. The Son does not share the essence of the Father to any extent and is both subordinate and inferior to the one God. Against the rationalism of Eunomius, Gregory offers a profound and appropriate sense of reservation. All examples which attempt to capture the transcendent harmony of the Christian God will fail; all monarchic, polyarchic and anarchic 'models', those that are unitary, plural or even multifarious, will only establish a God in whom disorder and discord result. Against the subordinationism of Eunomious, Gregory underscores the unity of the divine essence, an emphasis that is by no means rare.

The element of what we might call the 'ambiguity' of these reflections on the divine nature actually finds its undivided, originary coherence in the very acknowledgment that God 'is one and yet not one' (Gregory of Nyssa, 1893, p. 102), a coherence ignored or eschewed by the social modelists' obsession with plurality as a definitive and authentic model for the identity of God. For, while it is true that the *oikonomia* is the essential point of departure for the theology of the Cappadocians, the purpose of assessing the character of the operations of the trinitarian Persons is to understand something of what Lewis Ayres calls the 'texture of God's ineffability' (Ayres, 2004, p. 360). Or, at the very least, this is what Gregory of Nyssa is establishing in 'On "Not Three Gods"'. Here, there is no attempt to 'begin with a particular understanding of differentiation or individuation in the Godhead' (ibid.). It is true that such an account is able to follow from these trinitarian 'first principles' but the 'texture' of God's ineffability is disclosed, however imperfectly, through an examination of the unity of trinitarian operations which then leads to the assurance of unity itself from which the activities of the Persons of the Trinity are initiated.

There is no doubt that the Cappadocian endeavour to formulate and defend a pro-Nicene doctrine of the Trinity does take seriously – absolutely seriously – the triunity of God. But within the polemical context of fourth-century doctrinal development there is no simple (or simplistic) starting point from which the details and minutiae of the interrelatedness of God is pursued. Even the trinitarian 'formula' which now operates as something of a slogan for the social modelists, 'one *ousia*, three *hypostaseis*', is, according to Joseph Lienhard, 'more a piece of modern academic shorthand than a quotation from the writings of the Cappadocians' (Lienhard, 1999, p. 100). What we have witnessed within the so-called 'renaissance' of trinitarian theology, a process predicated on the priority of the social character of God's inner life and external action, is an appropriation of the Cappadocian fathers that is hermeneutically violent and historically dubious. Even the rather straightforward historical observation that the pursuit of an orthodox doctrine of

God in the fourth century was 'in fact complicated and exasperated by semantic confusion', that those holding opposing opinions on the order of relations between Father, Son and Spirit were using identical terms to mean very different things (Hanson, 1988, p. 181), is ignored or forgotten by those who would have us think that the only acceptable form of trinitarianism can be easily and comprehensively procured from the writings of these important fathers of the church. And if such problems are evident in the social modelists' reading and interpretation of those they fête and lionise, it is essential that their claims regarding the 'disaster' of Augustine's trinitarian reflections are approached with caution, in addition to a fitting dose of scepticism.

Augustine's Trinity

The dismissal of Augustine's theology of the trinity begins and ends with the claim that it is barely trinitarian. In addition to the tendency towards a modalistic understanding of the trinitarian Persons, Augustine, unlike his Cappadocian counterparts, is said to construct a philosophical rather than a scriptural conception of God's identity (Gunton, 1991, p. 42–43). In doing so, Augustine secures the divine unity for later Latin theology but does so at great cost. Such charges are now legion but what they seem to uncritically assume is that Augustine was expounding and elaborating his doctrine of God in a cultural, theological and political vacuum – which is to say, that he had no knowledge of the tradition within which he was situated, or rejected scriptural precedence because the neo-Platonists were clearer thinkers than the evangelists. This tendency to bracket out the questions and challenges to which Augustine was responding mirrors almost exactly the trend to elide the complex lexical and idiomatic experiments that the Cappadocian fathers undertook so that they might clarify the vocabulary through which they could comprehend the incomprehensible God who is both One and Three. Would it be too crass to suggest that the model for this late-antique theologian is the modern Professor of Divinity who fashions a thoughtful doctrine of God during a well-earned sabbatical? While such an analogy might seem to trivialise the projects of the social modelists, its purpose is to show that, yet again, the most striking aspect of this trinitarian project is its tendency towards a de-contextualisation and dismemberment of those texts it exposes and analyses (see Barnes, 1999, p. 148).

One of the most striking aspects of the modern study of Augustine's theology in general, a problem that is particularly relevant to those texts which offer a detailed interrogation of Augustine's theology of the Trinity, is that there has been a shocking reluctance to present any substantial and broad contextual analysis. Within the critical assessments and denunciations of Augustine's theology we are not given any cause to think that his discussions of God's unity are varied and diverse, each instance or set of instances dependent upon 'a particular idiom which evolved as the result of participation in a variety of traditions' (Ayres, 2000, p. 43). While such a lack of care is an omission for which theologians concerned with modern questions and contemporary problems should at least feel uncomfortable, it might also prompt us to accept that for many systematic theologians such an undertaking would be well-nigh impossible. It would probably be unfair and unwise to expect a generalist or a systematic theologian to master all the historical and doctrinal contexts within which Augustine's thought evolved. But two points still require the modern theologian's attention. It is important to note that a great many 'systematic treatments' of Augustine's elucidation of the doctrine of the Trinity 'are characterised by an avoidance of texts in the genre of trinitarian polemic, and a failure to take the polemical context of such writing seriously' (Barnes, 1995a, p. 245). As Barnes demonstrates, a close analysis of even *De Trinitate* will disclose a range of notable and often decisive clues as to the text's polemical intent, with the anti-Arian or anti-Homoian arguments that run through Book 2 of particular importance in this regard (p. 247). The relation of similarity (*homoios*) between God and the Son that is promoted by the Homoians constitutes an affiliation which is devoid of any reference to substance (*ousia*). Such critics of the Nicene orthodoxy are presented by Augustine with arguments that demonstrate how both the divinity and consubstantiality of the Father, Son and Spirit are revealed in Scripture.

It is also incumbent upon any theologian willing to offer a definitive judgement on Augustine's theology to read beyond *De Trinitate*, to consider the various letters (such as Letters 11, 14 and 120) or sermons (such as Sermon 52) where the evolution of the fundamental lines of Augustine's argument is evident. One essential reason for a broader assessment of Augustine's oeuvre lies in the fact that such a simple and mundane enterprise reveals quite startling similarities between the Augustinian and the 'Cappadocian' doctrines of God. In Letter 11, for example, we see a pivotal element of Nicene theology explained by Augustine in a manner that is consonant with orthodox anti-Arian polemics, whether 'Greek' or 'Latin' in origin. The letter offers a response to a forthright question proffered by Augustine's friend Nebridius who in a series of letters sought the clarification of a number of key theological issues that were central to the pro-Nicene trinitarian doctrine. Nebridius asks Augustine to account for how it is 'that if the Trinity do all things together in unity, then why is the Son alone said to be incarnated and not the Father and the Holy Spirit as well?' (Barnes, 1999, p. 155). Augustine offers Nebridius a concise summary of the orthodox doctrine when he claims that,

> according to the Catholic faith, the Trinity is proposed to our belief and believed – and even understood by a few saints and holy persons – as so inseparable that whatever action is performed by it must be thought to be performed at the same time by the Father and by the Son and by the Holy Spirit. Consequently, the Father does not do anything which the Son and the Holy Spirit do not also do; the Son does not do anything which the Father and the Holy Spirit do not also do; nor does the Holy Spirit do anything which the Father and the Son do not also do. From this it seems to follow that the whole Trinity became man, for, if the Son took on human nature and the Father and the Holy Spirit did not,

they no longer act jointly. Why, then, in our mysteries and our sacred rites is the
Incarnation celebrated as if attributed to the Son? This is a very deep question,
and so difficult and of such great import that it cannot be solved in a sentence,
nor can its proof be wholly satisfying (Augustine, 1951, pp. 26–27).

The recognition of the difficulty of answering this most basic of trinitarian
questions is also an appreciation of the problem of understanding a trinitarian
theology which one wants to believe (see Barnes, 1999, p. 157). It is not as though
the Catholic or pro-Nicene explanation is the only one available to Nebridius,
Augustine or any Christian at the end of the fourth century. Augustine has to
pursue a course of elucidation in which the inseparability of the operations or
activities of the trinitarian Persons is secured because this is a vital theme within
orthodox doctrine that is shared across the so-called 'Greek–Latin divide'. Indeed,
in Gregory of Nyssa's discourse *On the Holy Trinity*, we see a similar assertion of
inseparable operation being deployed.

If ... we understand that the operation of the Father, the Son, and the Holy Spirit
is one, differing or varying in nothing, the oneness of their nature must needs be
inferred from the identity of their operation. The Father, the Son, and the Holy
Spirit alike give sanctification, and life, and light, and comfort, and all similar
graces (Gregory of Nyssa, 1893, p. 328).

Common to a whole range of pro-Nicene theologies, this affirmation offers a
basis for establishing the basic and undivided unity of the Persons: 'the identity
of operation in Father, Son, and Holy Spirit shows plainly the indistinguishable
character of their substance' (ibid., p. 329). It is true that there are idiomatic and
analogical variations to the manner in which Gregory and Augustine develop an
answer to how the distinctive characteristics of Father, Son and Spirit might be
related to inseparability of action, but the contexts within which these answers
are formulated are strikingly similar: that of the need to explicate and defend pro-
Nicene doctrine in the face of alternative images of God which claim to have their
basis in revelation.

Contextual engagements which draw on the theological and historical
environment of Augustine's trinitarianism (let alone its legacy), such as those
provided by patristic scholarship, are rare indeed within the many recent
systematic theological assessments of those who propose the superiority of the
social model (Barnes, 1995a, p. 248). Whether this reluctance to pursue a whole
range of Augustinian texts is the result of the linguistic deficiencies of many a
systematic theologian (because so many of these other 'trinitarian' works remain
untranslated), as Barnes hypothesises, or an unwillingness to move beyond the
seemingly ordered and self-contained text of *De Trinitate*, are questions that
remains to be answered. But what is clear is that the 'rhetorical voice' of the
narratives constructed by Augustine's critics 'is one of comprehensiveness, but
the "historical method" supporting the narrative is in fact reductive. Stories of

increasing scope are told on the basis of diminishing experience and evidence' (ibid., Epp. 248–249). Even a cursory glance at Letter 120, for example, would force the critic of Augustine to think again about the claim that unity is everything in his theology: it is here that Augustine clearly suggests that there is no divinity apart from the three persons (Augustine, 1953, p. 306).

If these problems were not serious enough, there is an important challenge which must be confronted when reading the very work that is the focal point for the social modelists' denunciation of Augustine: to approach this text with attentiveness and sensitivity. For to read *De Trinitate*, a text that by no means exhausts Augustine's trinitarian theology, is to read a prayer. As with Gregory of Nazianzus's emphasis on the intrinsic relation of the quests for knowledge and sanctification, so Augustine begins this work by relating the purpose of revelation to the process of purification. This process is crucial for understanding the intertextual basis upon which the question of *oikonomia* and the nature of the Christian God are in fact intertwined. For the Augustine of *De Trinitate*, as Sarah Heaner Lancaster demonstrates, the 'first step in his process is to show that scripture does indeed authorise the kind of faith about which he speaks' (Lancaster, 1996, p. 128). Revelation and the action of God in and for the world stand as the necessary backdrop to the Augustinian expression of God's mystery. And it is not as though Augustine can be accused of pursuing, in this most cited of texts, an agenda that reduces the search for the nature and action of the triune God to a process of 'intellectualism' (Gunton, 1991, p. 43). Such a complaint totally misses the narrative trajectory and theological intention of Books IX–XIV. Here we see Augustine modifying his approach to the question of how we might come to know and appreciate the divine *mystery*. This development of his earlier sketch in Book VIII of a God – a Trinity – of love is by no means predicated on a the primacy of a rational or disengaged apprehension of the divine life. It is a prayerful and reflective acceptance that although we cannot 'penetrate directly and immediately into the innermost being of God, we can perhaps get more thoroughly acquainted with the divine mystery by looking at it indirectly' (Hill, 1985, p. 79). The cultivation of such a familiarity demands an activity or series of activities. Modern theology has in many respects forgotten what constitutes a mystery; it is a phenomenon which, 'in the old sense of the word, is more of an action than a thing' (Lubac, 1949, p. 60). And it is this action that *De Trinitate* prompts us to follow and repeat, an action of contemplation that is most certainly *not* that of the solipsistic, disembodied narcissist who is portrayed as imagining an impersonal God. The action of contemplation requires, in the words of Letter 11, a way of life in which the Christian might be formed according to the truth (Augustine, 1951, p. 29).

It is no coincidence, then, that the point at which Augustine announces that we have reached the very limits of ordinary human language, at the end of Book VII, is also the point at which the call to purification is most austerely sought (Augustine, 1991, p. 230). The move to Book VIII is also a move towards an understanding of the need to love God if any knowledge of God, any sight of God, is possible (p.

255). This crucial requirement of the theological task challenges any claim that Augustine is strictly delimiting his understanding of the divine nature through the exclusive use of images and analogies that are individual, internal or impersonal in kind. The image of the self is an essential point of reference and reflection in *De Trinitate*, but, as Lancaster argues, 'it is not entirely accurate to say that Augustine has relocated the economy to the "interior" so that we know God by knowing ourselves. If we contemplate only ourselves, we never truly know God' (Lancaster, 1996, p. 137). Love of God and love of neighbour are essential paths by which knowledge of God, however inadequate, might be attained. It is this need to love and to exceed the limits of self-contemplation that provide the background and basis for the 'psychological' analogy of the nature of God in the subsequent two Books. Yet it is an essential part of Augustine's preparatory work to demonstrate that, while the image of God in the human person does constitute an analogy of the divine processions, this image has an historical dimension that must first be addressed. Scripture has illustrated how the created *imago dei* originated in beauty and suffered disfigurement under Adam, only to find its restoration and renewal through the grace of Christ. The bond between salvation and the doctrine of God, or *oikonomia* and *theologia*, is held fast in Augustine's thought.[1]

But while it is obvious that Augustine is innocent of the heinous theological crimes attributed to him, what of Aquinas the western theological metaphysician *par excellence*? As we saw in the last chapter, he is accused of propagating and maintaining two major distortions of trinitarian theology: first, that the One God (*de Deo Uno*) precedes the triune God (*de Deo Trino*) in both essence and importance in the *Summa* and, second, that his explicit privileging of substance as the fundamental principle of the divine identity is nothing short of a rejection of the revealed, triune nature of God.

That these charges are based on a series of misunderstandings of the structure, form and content of Aquinas' theology is now a well-established fact. According to Fergus Kerr, the allegation that Thomas divides his analysis of God so that everything of significance about God is already established within his treatment of the One arises from an essay written by Karl Rahner in 1960. There, Rahner criticised the ubiquitous division between the examination of *de Deo Uno* and *de Deo Trino* within the Roman Catholic educational establishments of his time (Kerr, 2002, p. 183). On the basis of the dissemination and popularity of this essay, the criticism is now nothing short of canonical. Yet any examination of Aquinas' writings, particularly the *Summa*, will demonstrate that these titles do not exist (see Rikhof, 2002, p. 218). They are a later development through which Aquinas is commonly evaluated and, rather strangely, even endorsed. It is true that in his treatment of God Thomas considers the unity of God earlier than the trinitarian Persons, but he does so for a very good reason. Rather than presenting

---

[1]   In fact, Augustine examines the missions of the divine Persons (Book II) prior to the processions. One could suggest, therefore that the economy establishes the theology, *contra* the social modelists.

an ontological or theological priority for the unity of God, Thomas sketches his interrogation of God's nature on the basis of the historical narrative of revelation. Kerr offers a succinct statement of the character of this formal analysis:

> His conception of God is phased, so to speak: God as creator of whose existence the wisdom-seekers of the ancient world have knowledge; God as the Lord whom the people of the Law were commended to worship; and God as Trinity, of whom knowledge has been communicated by Christ to the apostles (Kerr, 2002, p. 184).

Far from rejecting the narrative of God's self-disclosure in history or Scripture, Thomas accedes to its formal or narrative demands in depicting the divine engagement with the world. The *Summa* enacts, dramatically and thematically, the economy of God or the historical missions of the Persons of the Trinity in a manner that is consonant with the objectives of his most trenchant critics. And one significant misrepresentation of Aquinas clearly demonstrates this point. He is accused and arraigned of attempting to disconnect creation from the divine missions and the economy of salvation (La Cugna, 1991, p. 167). But in the *Summa* it is quite clear, as Herwi Rikhof argues, that 'there are not just two parts to *de Deo*, but three. The *processus creaturarum* also belongs to *de Deo*' (Rikhof, 2002, p. 221). The creative and salvific acts of God are folded into an account of God's nature and its threefold revelation and are seen as integral to divine self-communication.

One of the reasons for these common misunderstandings and misrepresentations of Thomas's theology of God may well be the uncritical acceptance and use of alien and anachronistic terminology. The only antidote to this problem is the hard labour of reading and reflecting on what Thomas actually wrote and the theological and philosophical context within which he endeavoured to understand the unfathomable God. One final example is illustrative of this point. As we have already seen, the issue of the character of, and commitment to, the category of divine substance in Thomas's theology is one that exercises a number of critics. But the Thomistic notion of theistic substance should not be understood as 'the unknowable static inert substratum' (Kerr, 2002, p. 48) that modern critics of classical and medieval metaphysics would want us to reject. Rather, substance in its classical and Thomistic usage has dynamic connotations that are now largely forgotten or suppressed. 'Thomas's "supreme being",,' argues Kerr,

> far from being the static deity of substantialist metaphysics, is the subsistent (i.e. underived) sheer Act of existence, identically Intelligence and Will. Far from being a self-enclosed isolated substance, this sheer Act is also the freely self-diffusing Good, in effect self-communicative love (p. 50).

This Aquinas – dare we call him the 're-contextualised' and 're-membered' Aquinas? – is a theologian whose own search for God offers openings or apertures that might well complement, supplement or even surpass the efforts of the social modelists, especially in the portrayal of a God of loving interaction with creation and creatures. For this theism, in contrast to many another 'model', is an extravagant theism.

East or West?

There is no way that we can continue to accept the historical or theological validity of the social modelists' simplistic appropriation of a Cappadocian trinitarianism and their naïve rejection of Augustine's theology of God. It would be irresponsible to assume that the Greek–Latin divide is any longer tenable. But on the basis of this ineluctable conclusion, a question arises that requires our consideration. Why is it that this theological division between east and west is accepted as reliable, and continues to be deployed and possesses such authority? If the premises upon which the theological diremption is founded are not only misleading but downright erroneous then there are no grounds whatsoever for its esteem and ubiquity.

The most compelling answer to this question is provided by Michel Barnes's exposition of what is now known as the 'de Régnon paradigm'. In two important essays, Barnes has demonstrated how a late-nineteenth-century examination of the Trinity has strongly influenced subsequent assessments of trinitarian doctrine. In the first volume of this work, his *Études de théologie positive sur la sainté Trinité*, published in 1892, Théodore de Régnon came to two important conclusions, both of which are familiar to any readers of recent assessments of the Trinity and which served to manufacture, as it were, the rigid dissimilaries between the Cappadocian and Augustinian doctrines of God that are so often taken as read. First, it was de Régnon's contention 'that the core of Cappadocian theology is that it argued the unity of nature from the unity of activities' (Barnes, 1995b, p. 51). We have already seen how this claim, while certainly true in the case of the Cappadocians, is by no means an exclusive preoccupation. Augustine is similarly committed to the inseparability of operations. Second, and crucial to the formation of the now-common 'paradigm' is the argument 'that patristic trinitarian theology, as represented by the Cappadocians, proceeds from the diversity of persons while scholastic trinitarian theology, as represented by Augustine, proceeds from the unity of nature' (ibid.).

De Régnon develops his paradigm on the basis of the epistemological claim that the Trinity cannot be known in itself. God as Trinity is only subject to knowledge through an acknowledgement of the 'reality of the manifold expressions of its existence'. Barnes helpfully summarises the doctrinal significance of this epistemological stance: it requires the recognition of the 'authority or authenticity of the different (orthodox) accounts or doctrines of the Trinity' (p. 52). The two distinct accounts of the Trinity that are identified by de Régnon and are operative within the *Études* are the 'patristic' and the 'scholastic': the former is relates to the theology of the first four centuries of the Church where the encounter with God is always mediated by the category of person; the latter category is characteristically Augustinian and emphasises the 'inner-trinitarian relations' (p. 54).

The importance of de Régnon's analysis of the history of doctrine is not to be found, however, in the *Études* themselves. As Barnes makes clear, it is later scholars who identified the patristic category with Cappadocian or Greek theology, an association that de Régnon neither can nor would want to establish (ibid.). Indeed, if we consider the context within which the *Études* were composed, it becomes clear that de Régnon established his trinitarian categories in order to reject the position that his 'paradigm' has come to determine. He sought to bring the trinitarian doctrine of these two dominant eras into a mutual conversation from the perspective of the enduring mystery of the divine nature. It was clear for de Régnon, as Kristin Hennessey has demonstrated, that any one model or system would fail to illuminate and articulate this mystery sufficiently (Hennessy, 2007, p. 181).

It is evident that the 'de Régnon paradigm' was neither produced nor promoted by de Régnon. Yet the history of the reception of the *Études* is one whereby the text itself is forgotten but a caricature of its arguments and categories persists, and this is especially true of English-language scholarship of the last century and this. A hermeneutical key for the proper understanding of God's nature is taken as wholly valid, despite the fact that it is the product of an erroneous reading of a late-nineteenth-century text. A theological 'Chinese whispers' has provided the social modelists with an authoritative pattern by which to honour Cappadocian theology and condemn Augustine. The social modelists have not returned to the patristic sources themselves in the search for a renewal of the tradition that finds its coordinates from within the tradition. Rather, they 'exhibit a scholastic modernism, since they … take as an obvious given a point of view that is coextensive with the 20th century' (Barnes, 1995a, p. 238). In terms of the creation of a more truly *faithful* doctrine of God, this anachronistic and myopic project is anything but.

Standpoint and Setting

A major contributing factor to the theological failure of the social modelists' historical division between Greek and Latin theologies has to be the comportment of the theologian to doctrinal and dogmatic sources. As I explained in the Introduction, modern theology is marked by a tendency towards a positivistic method, especially in the treatment of its doctrinal tradition. The proponents of the social model seem to wholly accept and utilise this attitude with regard to their critical and constructive approaches to the doctrine of God. An analogy that helps us appreciate the significance of this theological method is provided by Michael Hanby in his discussion of the common misreading of Augustine's trinitarian theology. Hanby offers a distinction between first- and third-person perspectives. Those theologians who regularly attack Augustine's thought approach his reflections on the divine nature and economy from a third-person perspective. That is to say, they expound the antique bishop's theology from the standpoint of observers. Augustine, in contrast, considers the question and status of the economy from the perspective of the participant. This latter positioning of the theologian with regard to the quest for God, demands of her, Hanby reminds us, something that is unnecessary or superfluous for the positivist. Doctrinal data is, for the observing subject, little more than an object of analysis. To the participant, however, 'an account of how one's very capacity to recognise the economy *as economy* exemplifies one's location within it' (Hanby, 2003, p. 16). If one is located outside the economy, as the one who inspects the relevant data from afar, the doctrine of God, its purpose, authority and ultimate point of reference, has a markedly detached importance.

A positivistic theological standpoint has produced an important strand of theological reflection that is dependent upon a series of theological, historical and hermeneutical claims that are at the very least problematic. A cursory analysis of the relevant patristic literature demonstrates that the Cappadocian approach to the Trinity is nothing like an authentic counterpoint to the disaster of the Augustinian schema. There is no basis for such an assertion. Indeed, the reading of the texts of the Cappadocian fathers and Augustine is both limited in scope and myopic in practice.

The appeal of the social model does not rest with its veracity, however. One of the fundamental reasons for its popularity is the way in which it enables the student of theology to engage with questions and challenges that are presented by contemporary social, political and cultural forces. One such modern question and challenge that persists today is that of the status and consequence of the human person, a person who is seen as enduring the various malaises of modernity: fragmentation, atomisation and melancholy. The social model of the Trinity offers an alternative theological anthropology which directly confronts the anthropological disquiet of the modern human being. It is this project of the social modelists that will be the subject of the next chapter.

PART II
IDENTIFYING

Chapter Three
Trinitarian Persons

At the beginning of his assessment of the social formation of the Church and the potential principles upon which it might be restructured, Daniel Hardy offers a diagnosis of modern life that is widely held. We in western liberal democracies tend to find ourselves existing in contexts where there is little social cohesion and where the grounds upon which the meaning and objectives of institutional life are no longer vital or have disappeared (see Hardy, 1989, p. 21). Hardy identifies this crisis of sociality as arising from the modern turn to the subject, and suggests that if we are to overcome this predicament a rather different set of underlying tenets requires our commitment. The principles which Hardy believes will enable a more truly Christian approach to sociality can be summarised as anthropological and theological in nature. On the anthropological plane, sociality is an inherent attribute of human being *per se* – it is, as it were, simply there. Consequently, the desire to share life with another 'is not in the first instance a cultural or social necessity' (p. 37). We cannot reduce the human imperative to live socially to any appetitive or constructed requirement that is functional or instinctual in character. From the other plane, the divine or transcendent level, we are able to discern that it is the 'divine ordering' that 'ultimately implants in the human condition the "being-with" which is natural to it' (p. 42).

While many of the proponents of the social model would confirm Hardy's diagnosis, the urgency with which theology must embark upon a thoroughgoing interrogation of self and society is only heightened in the context of postmodernity. Fragmentation, in the view of Stanley Grenz, has reached the point at which we can identify a 'spiritual chaos endemic to the postmodern condition'. But this crisis of identity and social and cultural form is also the point at which we presented with the opportunity for 'a new quest for some semblance of meaning' (Grenz, 2001, p. 137). It is the kind of divine ordering which Hardy outlines that bestows a set of parameters for the constitution of new forms of meaning that are unapologetically theological. The divine ordering of society is understood according to the logic of a social dynamic of persons in communion through which, and by which, the Church and wider society might become more faithfully themselves.

In Hardy's twofold examination of the nature of human and divine being, we find a model of the intersubjective social character of personhood. The 'tri-personal community of God' (Gunton, 1989, p. 77) is indicative of the nature of true humanity, that is to say, the way we are, along with the organising precepts of ecclesial and social relations, or what we are communally. This arrangement of transcendent and human relations offers a portrayal of the 'person' or self who is interdependent, a portrayal which, in its refutation of the disengaged, sovereign self of modernity and its disavowal of the 'end of Man' proclaimed by postmodernity, 'comes closest to the self of scripture' (Thiselton, 1995, p. 78). The God who is revealed in salvation history, who is witnessed to in the gospels, is a God of mutual relationality. And this God offers the community of the Church, and the world at large, an image of how we might come to authentic self-understanding and fashion the community of the living in the order of divine identity.

To expose the contours of the self who is an image of the divine persons is not, however, without its difficulties. The modern critique of trinitarian dogma and the Enlightenment reconfiguration of the self as an abstract and detached phenomenon require that theology responds to the most formidable of challenges. In Walter Kasper's view, this constitutes the most serious point of trinitarian reflection because, in 'the modern period, person is no longer understood in ontological terms but is defined as a self-conscious free centre of action and as individual personality' (Kasper, 1983, p. 285). The significance of this modern change of anthropological focus is that an essential commission is conferred upon any theologian concerned with the doctrine of God:

> Above all, the issue is how, in continuity with and yet also in opposition to the spirit of the modern age, the human person can be properly understood as the image of the trinitarian God (p. 286).

It is Greek trinitarian theology which, according to the social modelists, offers the most helpful route to an understanding of this God revealed by scripture as trinitarian in nature. The focus on 'the divine persons in their self-manifestation' (La Cugna, 1991, p. 248) constitutes a basic ontology in which the 'social, communal, towards-another character of personhood' is evident. The benefit of this threefold image of God is that it reintegrates an ontology of self into categories of personhood but does so in a way which overcomes the self whom modernity fabricated. We cannot restrict our anthropological categories to those provided by modern philosophy or social theory because the response to divine personhood demands a 'praxiological' supplementation, an openness to others and the world which begins and ends with a God who is reciprocal relation.

A useful definition of the identity of this relational God is provided by Cornelius Plantinga, who succinctly captures the related and foundational characteristics of the divine persons who are disclosed by Cappadocian theology and who offer a model by which human beings might reconceive their individualities and social attributes:

> (1) Father, Son, and Spirit are conceived as persons in the full sense of 'person', i.e., as distinct centres of love, will, knowledge, and purposeful action ... and
> (2) who are conceived as related to each other in some central ways analogous to, even if sublimely surpassing, relations among members of a society of three human persons (Plantinga, 1986, p. 325).

It is important to emphasise the way in which the trinitarian hypostases are persons in the 'full sense'; they are not simply like persons or quasi-persons. Father, Son and Spirit are individuals in a way that we can fully recognise, they exhibit characteristics that any 'person' must possess to be identified as such. In addition, what we can ascertain of the divine life through the economy and revelation is its communal or relational nature and the ramifications of this life for practical living. Because the three persons are situated within a 'communal ontology' where 'their personal identities emerge out of their reciprocal relations' (Grenz, 2001, p. 332), we are presented with an incomparable model from which the purpose and shape of human existence is truly revealed. But that is not all that is revealed to us: on the basis of the divine life, we can now affirm that 'personhood, not substance, comes first in the order of being' (Vanhoozer, 1997, p. 174).

The Invention of the Person

If we are to understand how it is that the doctrine of the Trinity can facilitate and sustain a productive theological anthropology, then we must begin by identifying what it is within the tradition that engenders and enables this process. It is in the *corpus* of the Cappadocian theologians, we are promised, that an ontology of personhood is formulated, an ontology that is relevant to both divine and human life. And it is within the work of John Zizioulas that this promise is most fully exposed. In two of his most cited texts, *Being in Communion* and 'Human Capacity and Human Incapacity', there is a sustained attempt to outline and apply the principles of trinitarian identity to the concerns of theology and the church. These innovative tasks 'have been so influential', writes Stanley Grenz, 'that his major thesis, which forms the book's title, has become almost a methodological axiom of the order of Rahner's rule' (Grenz, 2001, p. 51). What Zizioulas offers for the theological construction of an apposite anthropology, a concept of the person that is derived from scripture and the doctrine of the Trinity, is a portrayal of personhood which transcends and corrects the failings of any number of prominent theories of the self.

The constructive task that Zizioulas sets himself in exposing the foundation of human personhood begins from a historical and conceptual critique of the western fixation with the individual. Theologically, it is Augustine (along with Boethius) who is to blame for the dominant western approaches to the question of human being. This one-dimensional anthropology developed historically, philosophically and theologically out of a mixture of two fundamental components: '*rational individuality* on the one hand and *psychological experience and consciousness* on the other' (Zizioulas, 1975, pp. 405–406). From these combined elements of basic human identity, the western tradition advanced a conception of the human understood as 'an *individual* and/or a *personality*, i.e., a unit endowed with intellectual qualities centred on the axis of consciousness' (p. 406). The resultant concept of the person established, without reserve, the importance of the autonomy of the self as a conscious being. In doing so, it delivered to western culture and thought a substantial foundation by which the notion of the human person could be fully secured. It is this fixed and rather stagnant conception of self that is deficient anthropologically and theologically.

In the light of this critical analysis of the substantial individual, Zizioulas offers a constructive alternative. He argues that 'the person can not be conceived in itself as a static entity, but only as it *relates to*' (pp. 407–408). In outlining the character of relating to, Zizioulas offers a description of personhood in which the dynamic movement beyond the borders of individuality is always already implicitly a fact.

> Thus personhood implies the 'openness of being', and even more than that, the *ek-stasis* of being, i.e. a movement towards communion which leads to a transcendence of the boundaries of the 'self' and thus to *freedom*. At the same time, and in contrast to the partiality of the individual which is subject to addition and combination, the person in its ekstatic character reveals its being in a catholic, i.e. integral and undivided way, and thus in its being ekstatic it becomes hypostasis, i.e. the bearer of its nature in its totality. Ekstasis and hypostasis represent two basic aspects of Personhood, and it is not to be regarded as a mere accident that both of these words have been historically applied to the notion of Person (p. 408).

The importance of this ekstatic and hypostatic portrayal of personhood lies in the two consequences of its formation. First, and as ekstatic, the Person cannot be delimited and enclosed, and it cannot be divided. Second, and as hypostatic, the Person is inimitable and singular. According to Zizioulas, the interrelation of these two terms, along with their effective consequences, enables us to discern the true ontological basis of personhood: 'it is not a quality added, as it were, to beings, something that beings "have" or "have not" but it is constitutive of what can be ultimately called a "being"' (p. 409). The ontology of the person is not that of the static and secure substance that has dominated the western theological and philosophical traditions; it is, rather, to be found in a being that breaks out of the fetters of substance in a dynamic process of communion.

> That for which an ultimate ontological claim can be made, that which *is*, is only that which can be *itself*, which can have a hypostasis of its own. But since 'hypostasis' is identical with Personhood and not with substance, it is not in its 'self-existence' but in *communion* that this being is *itself* and thus *is at all*. Thus communion does not threaten personal particularity; it is constitutive of it (ibid.).

The ontology sketched here offers a profoundly dynamic conception of the person in which it is only in-relation – in communion, freedom and love – that a self can genuinely be itself. The model or exemplar of this type of personhood is, Zizioulas reminds us, the God whose 'particularity is established in full ontological freedom'

(p. 410). To be truly free in this sense is only possible if one is 'uncreated' and unbounded by necessity. And only theology can tell of this person, for only theology seeks and understands the complete and genuine 'Person'. For without him there simply *is* no such thing as a person: 'If such a person does not exist in reality, the concept of the person is a presumptious daydream. If God does not exist, the person does not exist' (Zizioulas, 1985, p. 43).

The theological basis of the concept of person is essential for any clear perception of the nature of human being. Only in the light of God's personhood can the being of human being find satisfaction, a process and ultimately a goal which demands that the human must become an *imago Dei* (Zizioulas, 1975, p. 411). But in what ways can we be clear about that of which we are an image and that towards which we must move? It is clear that the potential to become like God is dependent on the revelation of God's own nature, a form of disclosure that Zizioulas identifies with the 'historic cross-fertilisation of Greek and Biblical thought that took place in the fourth century' (pp. 410–411). This is where we find the peerless relevance of the Cappadocian fathers for the construction and elucidation of a theological anthropology. In the place of the deadening influence of an individualisation 'that accounts for the impossibility of real communion' (p. 442), the Cappadocian fathers delineate a communal notion of being which uncovers historically and ontologically the very possibility of attaining the status of personhood. The essential legacy of Basil and the two Gregorys is that they 'gave to the world the most precious concept it possesses: *the concept of the person, as an ontological concept in the ultimate sense*' (Zizioulas, 1995, p. 56). With this designation of the origin, or better, invention of personhood, Zizioulas is reminding us that it is only because of the Cappadocian modification of the trinitarian vocabulary that we can relate the nature of God to the content of the human being who yearns to be like Him. It is only with the 'Cappadocian revolution' that this possibility is truly revealed.

The revolutionary change inaugurated by the Cappadocians relates, of course, to the shift in the use and meaning of the term *hypostasis*. Prior to the 'Cappadocian contribution', the term 'was fully identified with that of *ousia* or substance'. The new application of the term identified 'the idea of person with that of *hypostasis*' (ibid., p. 47). We have already seen the way in which this lexical shift was in fact revolutionary; in the light of its new use, Augustine was left in a state of confusion.

> The Greeks also have another word, *hypostasis*, but they make a distinction that is rather obscure to me between *ousia* and *hypostasis*, so that most of our people who treat of these matters in Greek are accustomed to say *mia ousia, treis hypostaseis*, which in Latin is literally one being, three substances (Augustine, 1991, p. 196).

Augustine, as the paradigmatic theologian of the Latin convergence of self and Trinity in individualistic terms, is joined in the expression of confusion by a

Christian philosopher who also tends towards what Zizioulas calls the primacy of 'individuation'. Boethius misinterprets (as Zizioulas would see it) the meaning and purpose of hypostasis not because he is baffled, as with Augustine, but in that he cannot help but extend the significance of the term to the rational substance of the individual self. In a passage from the *Contra Eutychen* he suggests that,

> the Greeks far more clearly called the individual subsistence of a rational nature (*naturae rationabilis individua substantia*) by the name *hypostasis*, while we through want of appropriate words have kept the name handed down to us, calling that *persona* which they call *hypostasis*; but Greece with its richer vocabulary gives the name *hypostasis* to the individual subsistence (Boethius, 1973, pp. 86–87).

The *persona* in this regard is arithmetically distinct, one and only one on the basis of an ontology which, from the perspective of the Cappadocian revolution, has little or nothing to do with the proper meaning and significance of *hypostasis*. Boethius has violently squeezed the *hypostasis* into the metaphysics of individuation that it was meant to surpass. The sacred identification of person-in-communion is damaged or destroyed in this process.

In contradistinction to the western predisposition to individuality, the Cappadocian revolution offers to human existence and thought a prototype of being-with in which the uniqueness (rather than individuality) of the person is offered as a point of anthropological reference. It is a form of distinctiveness that cannot be enclosed or fettered by the demands of rationalism or arithmetic. Rather, the Cappadocian invention offers a concept of personhood which describes and accounts for the excessive and communal origin of the self. As a form of creative theology, Zizioulas's contribution has prompted a whole range of theologians to engage more fully with the relational nature of divine and human persons. In doing so, however, many of those who are indebted to the Cappadocian revolution have sought to supplement the notion of 'being as communion' with the spatial categories that fall under the term 'community' and with the performative concept of 'communication'.

The Communicative Person

A theology of the Trinity, in which the unprecedented and radical conception of person finds its true origin and meaning, not only 'opens the way for a truly theological anthropology' (Grenz, 2001, p. 57) but allows us to perceive the proper social setting for the development of authentic human personhood. An anthropology that begins from this God-given tenet may well use the resources of the human sciences but does not, indeed must not, abdicate the role of identifying the true nature of the human person to secular philosophy or social theory. It is the triune life of God which 'becomes the final touchstone for speaking about human personhood' (ibid.). We must conclude, then, that any 'borrowed' anthropological theories must be used only to the extent that they assist in the delineation of a concept of person that remains faithful to this 'final touchstone'.

The methods by which the proponents of the social model have attempted to 'flesh out' the divine concept of personhood are multiple. A common theoretical tool used within a number of assessments of this strand of theological anthropology is personalist philosophy. Identified most fully with Martin Buber and his construction of a self who is constituted only in relation to another, famously abbreviated as I-Thou, personalism enables the two basic components of identity (whether human or divine) to be maintained as harmonious correlation. While the modern concept of person has emphasised the importance of individuality to the point at which its understanding of self is enclosed and discrete, personalism holds together the two elements that it claims are constitutive of a true self rather than a caricature: personality and mutuality. 'The "I" can only be understood in the light of "Thou" – that is to say, it is a concept of relation. Without the social relation there can be no personality' (Moltmann, 1981, p. 145). The concept of personhood gains much from such a 'thick description'; it also moves closer to its true point of reference, the divine community. Indeed, as Hans Urs von Balthasar has persuasively argued, the vision and purpose of personalist philosophy can only really be realised from a theological perspective. 'The dialogical thinkers,' Balthasar suggests, 'are philosophers who need theology to carry out the project of their thought' (Balthasar, 1985, p. 45). Only on the basis of a trinitarian community of persons can we view the genuine form and performance of the interpersonal. In that community, 'personality only exists as interpersonality; subjectivity as intersubjectivity' (Kasper, 1983, p. 289). Indeed, the intersubjective reality of personhood that is revealed by the Trinity is such that it cannot be erased. It is present and operative even where there are relations of 'apparent inequality' (see La Cugna, 1991, p. 257).

One weakness of personalism, certainly within a theological context, is the lack of the kind of active and interactive dimension that would complement the ontological description of personality, a dynamic aspect of interpersonality that is essential for an authentic understanding of 'being in communion'. In the opinion of some social modelists, personalism as a philosophical system is in need of exactly this type of augmentation. Because the trinitarian God as God-in-relation determines the awareness and pattern of human identity, human beings must be able to observe the nature of the being of God as a substance-in-relation, an organic interpenetration, and understand themselves accordingly. Just as the divine community *is* God and is the very foundation upon which the substance of God is predicated, so the human being as related *becomes* something more than a self. From this perspective, the social modelist is able to observe, according to Joseph Bracken, an idea of community that is true to the *imago dei*. It is an idea that begins with,

> the social nature of man and suggests that just as the organic unity of a physical
> substance with respect to its immanent operations transcends the merely
> extrinsic unity of order present in a simple aggregate, so the unity of persons-
> in-community transcends the unity of individual substance. The community as
> such is an ontological totality which is greater than the sum of its members, just
> as the substance or organism is an ontological totality greater than the sum of its
> operations. (Bracken, 1973, p. 171).

It is clear how the arrangement of the divine Persons and the traditional language
of trinitarian description – especially substance and operations – inform this
organicist model. A metaphysics of connectedness provides a suitable ground upon
which the terms by which God is understood and worshipped might be relocated
onto anthropological territory.

Nonetheless, there is one term that is still missing from the personalist
and organicist models of divine and human interpersonality. If we are to take
seriously the perichoretic relation of Father, Son and Spirit, it is essential that this
interconnectedness is understood in communicative terms. As Verna Harrison has
shown, in the later vocabulary of Maximus the Confessor and John of Damascus,
the term *perichoresis* indicates a '*communicatio idiomatum*', a communication,
exchange or interchange of individualising characteristics (see Harrison, 1991,
p. 55). Without this insight into the self- or inter-communicative nature of God,
the vision of the trinitarian community is in danger of falling short of the lexical
precision of the Greek fathers. But with due attention to this most crucial of facets,
it is possible to sketch the concept of the human person by drawing faithfully
upon concepts and ideas that are reminiscent of those presented by this innovative
tradition of trinitarian theology. It is with a suitable level of consideration to the
meaning and status of communication that Alistair McFadyen has formulated a
concept of personhood for which the social model of the Trinity is the ultimate
point of reference. It is a mode of personhood in which and for which the three
persons who 'mutually inhere' within the Trinity (La Cugna, 1991, p. 270) are the
horizon of significance.

Early on in his analysis of the character of the self, McFadyen provides a clue
as to the theme that might constitute the heart of his theological anthropology.
He suggests that the personalism of Buber, Barth and Bonhoeffer assisted his
audacious attempt to refashion the Christian understanding of the person:

> The key insight which grew out of engagement with these attempts to formulate
> some middle way between individualism and collectivism was the fruitfulness
> of understanding personal being and identity in terms of communication
> (McFadyen, 1992, pp. 6–7).

The desire to find a way through the modern predicament of individualism versus
collectivism, right versus left, freedom versus responsibility is shared by a number
of the social modelists. Thus, Colin Gunton suggests that another way of being

human must be sketched theologically because 'the individualist teaches that we are in separation from our neighbour, the collectivist that we are so involved with others in society that we lose particularity' (Gunton, 1993, p. 169). The teaching of Christianity teaches something quite different from either of these (largely) secular options and this is where the importance of communication is revealed. Communication in the Christian narrative is not simply the essence or degree zero of subjectivity. Rather, it is the dynamic vehicle of an identity that is forged through time as human beings are constituted in relationship. As McFadyen sees it,

> We become the people we are as our identities are shaped through the patterns of communication and response in which we are engaged. We carry the effects of the communication we have received and the response we have made in the past forward with us into every new situation and relationship. This happens most obviously, but by no means primarily or exclusively, through memory, and is what I later term the 'sediment' which is laid down through our communication history. It is this which makes us the people we are (McFadyen, 1992, pp. 7–8).

Formed through and by their communicative interaction with those around them, human beings are temporal animals who become what they are in their passage through time and their contexts in space. The 'sediment' of which McFadyen talks is similar in function and consequence to a narrative that delivers diverse elements and experiences into a unified 'identity'. Thus the person is ultimately 'dialogical (formed through social interaction, through address and response)' but must also be seen as 'dialectical (never coming to rest in a final unity, if only because one is never removed from relation' (p. 9). There is always a provisionality present within the formation of identity because of the dependence of the latter on relationality: 'Persons are the manifestation of their relations, formed through though not simply reducible to them' (p. 40).

Thus far the theory of subjectivity that McFadyen is delineating depends chiefly on the social, historical and linguistic contexts in which individuals find themselves (in both senses of the term). Yet this de-centred, relational self is supplemented – if not supplanted – by another self. This subsequent theoretical move ensures the integrity of the individual self and is made in order to safeguard personal identity in response to the possibility of the fragmentation of the individual. Although he purports to 'describe individual identity in terms of a response' (p. 47), McFadyen's central concern is to provide an intelligible and palpable foundation to the self:

> The basis of the position I shall be taking on these issues is the understanding of persons as individuals whose consciousness, experience of and interaction with the world are internally centred. Conducting oneself from a personal centre of being and communication is what makes self-direction – that is, personal control of and intervention in oneself and one's interactions – possible. In other words, personal centering enables performance as a subject in communication,

being an I for and before others and for oneself (through self-reflection and consciousness) (p. 69).

The provisionality of identity in communicative relation is augmented, or to be more accurate anchored, by a reflexive, conscious 'I'. The possibility of a dialogical identity is predicated on an anterior, internal unity that centres the self and provides a fixed location from which to securely engage with the ebb and flow of communicative interaction. Yet, the formation of this centre, and the resultant self-consciousness, is mediated through communication itself. Such a circular strategy has its antecedent in Pannenberg's insistence that the 'consciousness of the ego's unity is mediated through experience of the world, insofar as this experience allows the ego to become aware of its own body as existing within the context of a world and to construct a social and spiritual self in connection with it. This is the self to which one refers when one says "I"' (Pannenberg, 1990, p. 53). There is a significant convergence between the two notions of a subjectivity grounded in consciousness. It is evident that, for both Pannenberg and McFadyen, the person is an internally centred reality. Moreover, this centering in consciousness is facilitated, indeed engendered, by the external world of experience. Thus with a strong foundation, there is the 'basis for the unfolding of individual particularity and individual awareness of identity' (ibid., p. 54).

There are, then, two distinct though interrelated movements in the production of subjectivity, the formation through communication and the solidity of centred being: 'personal identity is a structure of response sedimented from a significant history of communication. A person is centrally organised and, on that basis, may exercise a degree of autonomy as a subject of communication' (McFadyen, 1992, p. 113). Here we see the dialectical nature of subjectivity as a dynamic unfolding with a secure point of fixity, a personal, centred identity that is both formed in connection and communication with others and fundamentally 'owned' by the individual:

> My self-understanding is embedded in my communication, and your understanding and response to it will be embedded in yours. So I receive a reflection of myself in your response. Dialogue may be considered as a process of self-transcendence (movement towards the other) and return (receiving oneself back from the other). Through giving and receiving ourselves in this way we can come to a new understanding of ourselves (p. 125).

Understanding one's self is based on a 'genuine mutuality' that is fuelled by a dialectic of egression and return. As a process of coming-to-be, self-understanding is produced by an autonomous self reaching out. The other mediates and augments self-awareness.

The terms within which this mutuality is generated are very similar to, and largely dependent upon, Jürgen Habermas's formal context for genuine non-distorted communication. The Habermasian project takes as its point of departure the need to reconfigure the subject of modernity and, as a concomitant, the requirement to open up rationality as a multidimensional reality. Only through a radical reassessment and remodelling of reason can the failed project of modernity be brought to its proper and fruitful consummation. The means through which this might be attained is the diremption or at least sub-division of reason in relation to the exigencies and character of different contexts or lifeworlds in which human beings operate. Habermas claims that the subject can be reconstituted on the basis of the self being mediated through communication. The intersubjective self is constructed through a dialectic that brings into play a universal logic of rationalisation and the historical contingency of individual situations. This quasi-transcendental allows the creation of a public, communal sphere that is ideal, non-coercive and inclusive. The ideal speech situation and participants' communicative competency are the building blocks that Habermas contributes to the possible reconstruction of a framework within which authentic subjectivity can flourish. Participants are safeguarded from the domination and totalisation of a purposive rationality and, as a consequence, from the worst excesses of modern subjectivity. Just as crucially, Habermas also claims that his hypothesis is more socially and politically applicable than the 'presentism', relativism' and 'cryptonormativism' associated with the postmodern dissolution of the self (Habermas, 1987, p. 287).

In line with the Habermasian ethic of communication, McFadyen outlines two important characteristics of mutuality. First, he suggests that 'communication and understanding' are to be rational and, second, that 'communication will have to be free of constraints, coercion and all other forms of distortion' (McFadyen, 1992, p. 165). These formal injunctions are imposed so that a genuine form of communication can be secured. Reciprocity is perverted if subjects communicate outside a context in which misunderstanding is formally excluded:

> Unlimited, constraint-free explication, in which the autonomy and responsibility of each partner in and for communication is respected and intended as means are found to ensure formal reciprocity in the relation (i.e. non-privileged distribution of dialogue roles, or symmetrical binding by norms), exhibits a formal ideal for communication. It is this ideal to which all communication is or pretends to be orientated (it is therefore anticipated in its distortion), and which presents the codification proper to the ideal form of life in God's image (p. 187).

This ideal speech situation ensures both formal reciprocity and provides the grammar or mores that are proper to the way of life of Christians in relation to and with God. Indeed, McFadyen goes as far as to suggest that such an ideal or formal situation 'indicates the form of interpersonal life as intended by God at creation' (ibid.). A communicative, mutual concept of personhood represents a pre-lapsarian and post-redemptive ideal that mirrors the 'dialogical form of God's communication' as triune intersubjectivity (p. 207). This statement of commitment to the ideal speech situation points us to the model for McFadyen's theological anthropology. He suggests, early on in his study, that one of the two 'theological components' in his argument is the concept of 'human existence in the image of the trinitarian God' (p. 17).

The Communicative God

It is now possible to understand the significance of a concept of personhood that is shared by God and the human self. The narrative we have followed is one whereby God, like the human being, is characterised formally and ontologically as being in Communion, formed and realised in Community and oriented towards perichoretic Communication. It is the trinitarian God who, according to the social modelists, can redeem the totalising subject of modernity and the fragmented and broken identity of the self of late- or postmodernity. In line with McFadyen's 'communicative person', there are a great number of attempts to apply the terms and images of a perichoretic trinitarian personhood to these two anthropological predicaments of modern times.

In response to the violence and manipulation that defines and controls the decentred self of postmodernity, Anthony Thiselton posits a self who – via the application of the working hypothesis of a promise that he believes is present in the context of both Christology and a perichoretic Trinity – it is possible to reconstitute.

> [This promise] transforms the self because, like the experience of resurrection, it *'reconstitutes' self-identity* as no longer the passive victim of forces of the past which 'situated' it within a network of pre-given roles and performances, but opens out a new future in which new purpose brings a 'point' to life. The self perceives its call and its value as one-who-is-loved within the larger narrative plot of God's loving purposes for the world, for society, and for the self (Thiselton, 1995, p. 160).

This reconstitution is possible 'from ahead' as we are invited to a form of reconstituted identity in relation to the person of Jesus (see p. 163). Thiselton does not offer a programme or sketch of practices through which the self might be reconstituted in this relation but his claim is nonetheless bold. He presents an understanding of the interrelationality of the Trinity, like Moltmann, Boff and Gunton, that drives the radical nature of his alternative to many modern and contemporary anthropological discourses.

With the attempt by Colin Gunton to formulate a trinitarian anthropology we are presented with a rather less self-assured pattern of intersubjective existence. Highlighting the importance of the analogous character of statements that we make of God, Gunton charts a course between the perfect mutuality of the divine persons and the broken context of nature, human and otherwise. It is proposed, as a consequence, that we should not press models of God too far in their application to individual, social or communal life. Nevertheless, Gunton argues that the perichoretic model of the Trinity challenges our conceptions and description of subjectivity and persons in society. On the basis of the doctrine of the relational God we can conclude that 'a doctrine of human perichoresis affirms, after philosophies like that of John Macmurray, that persons mutually constitute each other, make each other what they are' (Gunton, 1993, p. 169). But the modern, isolated subject is not the only target of Gunton's notion of perichoretic personhood; following the lead of John Zizioulas, Gunton asserts that the contemporary fragmentation of culture is due to a more ancient concept of person, the unitary conception of God. Only through a more properly triune conception of the divine might we conceive of and perform an authentic plurality in unity (see ibid., p. 177).

The championing of a social, perichoretic understanding of the Trinity is due, to a large extent, to the crisis of subjectivity and of social form that is an evident part of modern life. If a social and communal model of God provides a significant challenge to, and an alternative way of being within, this context then it offers hope of a more truly 'human' social setting. Thus, if human beings are able to embrace their vocation as the *imago Trinitatis*, then 'since God's nature is triune, a society of mutual relationships, life in human nature and the Church is analogous to this. The same analogy holds good for society' (Thompson, 1991, p. 360). If God is the being whose nature is intersubjectivity *par excellence*, then the human response to this divinely commissioned calling must be lived out as intersubjectivity. Jürgen Moltmann offers the most forceful narration of this position and, in doing so, clarifies the extent to which the model of God's mutual indwelling demands a transformation of perspective and identity for the individual Christian, the Church and (ultimately) the world.

> The unity of the triune God is no longer seen in the homogeneous divine subject nor in the identical divine subject, but in the eternal *perichoresis* of father, Son and Spirit. This insight has far-reaching consequences for the hermeneutics of the history of salvation and human experiences of God; for the doctrine of the image of God in human beings and the conception of a creation which corresponds to God; for the doctrine of the form and the unity of the church as the 'icon of the Trinity'; and not least for the eschatological expectation of a new, eternal community of creation. The monarchical, hierarchical and patriarchal ideas used to legitimate the concept of God are thus becoming obsolete. 'Communion', 'fellowship' is the purpose and nature of the triune God (Moltmann. 1991, p. xii).

It is clear that for Moltmann the ramifications of a perichoretic model of divine personhood move well beyond the revision of our idea of human personhood. The outcome of embracing a perichoretic, trinitarian conception of God only begins with the transformation of atomistic individualism into fellowship and communion. So the true conception of God transforms because the truth of personhood itself is revealed. 'The form and content of God's communication in salvation history is not that of an absolute, totalitarian ruler (monologue); it is an overspilling of the internal trinitarian process of communication' (McFadyen, 1992, p. 207). The fact that the trinitarian God, the God who is Word and whose nature is therefore one of communicative excess, gives himself and reveals himself to the world as a perichoretic inherence of persons, requires of Christians (and, indeed, all who are 'persons') that they live not as sovereign, discrete individuals for whom 'sociality' is only considered if it results in rewards such as status and power. For such a way of life is one of de-personalisation and de-humanisation. It is incompatible with the nature of the Christian God.

Communion, Community, Communication

If there is one area of theological enquiry where the ideas and proposals of the social modelists seem to make sense, it is in the domain of theological anthropology. Since the Enlightenment critique of a 'heteronomous' Christianity and the irrationality of the trinitarian doctrine, the human person has generally been ontologically, metaphysically and imaginatively cut adrift from ideas of the divine life. If the personhood of God had any impact at all on modern 'Man', it tended to convey a sense of authority and legitimacy to the human 'moral personality in its struggle towards lordship over the world' (Powell, 2001, p. 168). But here personhood – both divine and human – is understood in individual terms and as consisting or subsisting in discrete boundaries. Hence, lordship and sovereignty, those practices so despised by Moltmann, are not only normal but essential to the subject of modernity.

In contrast, we can witness something of a revolution in anthropological concepts due to the revolutionary formation of *hypostasis* within the Greek tradition of early Christianity. Parallel to a God who is a community of communicative love and freedom, an image of the human person is offered by a tradition that is ground-breaking in its form and its consequences. Yet, despite the excitement that such a 'society of divine persons' has generated within scholarly and more popular treatments of individual, church and society, the claims of the proponents of this anthropology require some analysis. It is incumbent upon us to consider the status of *hypostasis* within the Cappadocian doctrine of God, the concept of the human person that is said to evolve from this doctrine, and the importance and impact of those philosophical sources – especially personalism and a communicative ethic – that are used by the social modelists in their anthropological endeavours.

Chapter Four
The Question of Anthropology

The definition of the Trinity as persons-in-relationship has enabled the proponents of the social model to formulate and propagate a conception of the divine that is relevant to the needs and questions of modern men and women. It is a formulation of the doctrine of God that speaks to contemporary challenges, where the definitions of personhood are numerous. Today, we can choose from materialist, positivist, biological, bioinformatic, hereditary, psychological, psychoanalytic, deconstructive, cyborgic, and countless other classifications of the person or post-person. There no longer seems to be a point at which, or from which, persons might anchor their aspirations, needs and desires. Within this context of confusion, the claim that we have access to a notion of personhood 'after the pattern of the perichoretic divine life' (Grenz, 2001, p. 332) provides theologians and theology an authoritative, Christian alternative to the anthropological chaos of late-modernity. But the persuasive power of this model of the Trinity is not only found in its ability to resituate the self on solid (if transcendent) ground. The vision of God as an ontology of communion is an image which carries transformative potential for selves and societies. Theology, and theology alone, presents a genuine, revolutionary anthropology. In this view, it is theology, and not the social or human sciences, that offers a commanding and fruitful vision of what it is to be human.

The need to assess the significance of this recent strand of theological anthropology arises from the force of these claims. For the concept of person delineated in the light of the relational God is one that, despite its ultimate divine referent, is reliant on a commitment to three constructive tasks: the return to specific sources within the 'Cappadocian' tradition of theology for the description of a person as someone who exceeds individuality, as a being in communion; a formulation of a perichoretic or communicative concept of the relational self; and a presentation of the social or communal consequences of a divinely revealed anthropology. Each of these points of focus deserves some analysis if the bold claims of the social modelists are to be substantiated.

Person and Individual

The question of the relationship between antique Christian conceptions of the trinitarian 'person' and what we moderns understand by the term has long been a point of debate within the scholarly literature. In a work in which he assesses the patristic use of terms such as *persona* and *prosopon*, first published at the turn of the twentieth century, J.F. Bethune-Baker already warns of the problems which would arise if we were to accept too close a correlation between the various forms of usage. The terms *persona* or *prosopon*, within the lexicon of the Church Fathers, related to 'a person in particular circumstances; that is, it conveys the notion more of environment than of subject' (Bethune-Baker, 1903, p. 234). William Hill, likewise, has suggested that we must proceed with care when we translate the analogies of the Cappadocian fathers into a modern context. The Cappadocians, unlike the social modelists, seemed to be 'fully aware of the limits of their language' (Hill, 1982, p. 48). And more recently, Michel Barnes has argued that within Gregory of Nyssa's theological psychology, the category of 'person' does not rely on notions of personal relationship or consciousness, ideas that the social modelists all too often read into the ancient vocabularies (Barnes, 2002, p. 476). Each of these criticisms of the easy assimilation of anachronistic categories is both important and warranted. However, the most salient assessment of the distinction between the modern 'person' and the use of the concept in Cappdocian theology, at least for our purposes, is offered by Lucian Turcescu in a critical evaluation of the theological anthropology of John Zizioulas.

The focus of Tucescu's article is, at least in general terms, the tendency of the social modelists to assume that the idea of the human person has its origins in the theological articulation of the nature of trinitarian relations. As we have already seen, the view that the Cappadocian fathers introduced a new set of nuances and connotations by which the term *hypostasis* would be transformed into 'person' rather than substance is one that is uncontroversial. But the much bolder claim that the Cappadocians 'invented' the term person represents a statement of a quite different order. It is the accuracy of this profession of theological and historical truth, especially in the work of Zizioulas, that Tucescu wishes to examine.

Tucescu begins his assessment of Zizioulas's theology by examining the latter's assertion that the 'person' outlined in Cappadocian thought cannot be understood as 'a complex of qualities possessed by the individual' (Tucescu, 2002, p. 530). Drawing on those instances when Basil and Gregory of Nyssa *do* describe individuals as collections of properties (particularly St Peter and Job), and by outlining the influence of Porphyry's *Isagoge* on Gregory, Tucescu demonstrates that it is certainly not unknown for the Cappdocians to 'suggest that this person is individualised by putting together some of his characteristic marks' (p. 531). Indeed, Gregory himself explicitly confirms that this is the case: a *hypostasis* is also the concourse of the peculiar characteristics' (ibid.). It is the influence of a Neoplatonic conception of the individual that is at work here, an influence of which Zizioulas is unaware. It is obvious, then, that the description of the 'person' proffered within the patristic texts is at odds with the 'Cappadocians' of Zizioulas. Such a dissonance between the sources of theological anthropology and the modern use of these sources as a point of authoritative reference is also evident in Zizioulas's contention that a person can only be understood as ekstatic, emancipated from the limits and fetters of those concepts which inform and bound individualisation. By attending to the trinitarian theology of the Cappadocians, Tucescu illustrates how the 'concept of enumeration' was a significant ingredient in their development of the concept of person. In distinguishing between the three persons of the Trinity and the divine substance, Gregory of Nyssa argues that, although substance cannot 'be enumerated, individuals sharing the same substance (or nature) can be counted' (p. 532). In his rejection of this process of counting, Zizioulas has in fact departed from the tradition which forms the backdrop to his anthropology.

The most significant criticism outlined by Tucescu, at least in the context of the social modelists' understanding of personhood, is presented as a counterpoint to Zizioulas's tendency to denounce the individualism of Augustine and Boethius. These Latin theologians secure the individual through rational and substantive qualities; the Cappadocians offer a rendition of the idea of 'person' that is distinctive in its ekstatic and hypostatic transcendence of subjective boundaries. Once again, however, we must conclude that the formulation of a clear-cut Greek–Latin divide is something of a modern invention. The Cappadocians, Tucescu argues, 'were using person interchangeably with individual and did not have any problem with that. Theirs was a time when the notion of individual/person was only emerging. They were faced with other problems, trying to distinguish between substance (or nature) and person' (p. 533). This point is crucial: the emergence of a trinitarian vocabulary did not 'invent' the person as an alternative category or phenomenon to the individual. Nor did Gregory's approach to the trinitarian persons 'attempt to "nail" the meaning of divine hypostasis' (Coakley, 1999, p. 125). It is the social modelist who has invented this distinctive and novel class of personhood through an eisegetical foray into the texts of the Greek patristic era. It is for this reason that the confusion of Augustine and Boethius is significant; we are presented with an historical moment when the employment of the terms *persona* and *prosopon* covers a wide range of practical and theoretical territory: theatrical, juridical, philosophical and theological. Only out of this variety of contexts does the application of a series of trinitarian terms begin to gain an authority that we latecomers take for granted.

Person, Personality and Communication

Despite the textual, historical and hermeneutical problems associated with the social modelists' appropriation of Cappadocian technical vocabulary, the fact remains that the new conception of personhood has a significant heuristic function. The attempt to map notions of identity through the formulation of interpersonal and theological contours offers a constructive alternative to the atomisation of individuals within the context of modernity. Nonetheless, this processes itself raises a number of difficulties and problems concerning those modern sources upon which the proponents of the social model of the Trinity are liable to draw. In an effort to give content to an anthropology predicated on co-inherence or *perichoresis*, there is a temptation to utilise theories of personhood in a rather uncritical or unreflective manner.

A case in point is the ubiquitous application of personalistic philosophy as an anthropological tool, an instrument applied so that the theologian might expose and expound a concept of personhood that is adequate to the revealed nature of the divine life. Nonetheless, personalism is not without its opponents. It is a strand of philosophical reflection that has done much to demonstrate the shortcomings of modern notions of personal autonomy; in doing so, however, it is predisposed to retain the sovereign perspective of the modern subject.

While Buber, in particular, held that the I–Thou relation was the Relation *par excellence*, there remains something quite problematic in the procedure by which 'I' and the 'Thou' come to be in this specific mode of relation. The encounter which makes possible this relation and distinguishes it from relations of utility ('I–It') does not actually enable a true differentiation of the I and the Thou apart from the subjectivity of the 'I'. Buber's formalism here depends on a process by which the moment of consciousness of the Other is the point at which the I becomes 'I'. According to Emmanuel Levinas, because the self becomes an I in saying Thou, 'my position as a self depends on that of my correlate and the relation is no longer any different from other relations: it is tantamount to a spectator speaking of the I and Thou in the third person' (Levinas, 1989, p. 72). The Other, as with objects and things of use, is only the Other in that they constitute my consciousness of them, from which I am consequently formed. In the course of possessing myself the Other becomes a tool. Moreover, if there is to be a relation here, it cannot be an ethical relation of embodied creatures, only an abstract relation based on consciousness. The relation is one of disengaged abstraction. As John Milbank puts it:

> Personalism still too often suggests an impossible, ahistorical, encounter of absolute wills unmediated by a common spatial 'identity', or by signs which, through their indeterminacy must always 'defer', not only an absolute meeting with the other, but also our self-possession (Milbank, 1986, p. 220).

If we are to consider what kind of persons relate within the 'absolute meeting' of the I and the Thou, they are not persons we know or would want to know. The very abstraction from the terms and conditions of our worldly interaction suggests that the Idealism inherent in this concept of intersubjectivity would render such an encounter extraordinary rather than normal. In short, we have to wonder whether the I and Thou are 'persons' at all. Within the constitution of this kind of person is a tendency to bracket out the personality as an ontological ground; it has little or no relation to our activity, our relating, in everyday life. This point is made forcibly by Simone Weil who, in a critique of personalism written in 1943, demonstrated the perversity of this idea of the self. If I see a passer-by in the street, what would stop me from putting out his eyes? It is with this question that Weil highlights the irrelevance of personalism. For if the true self is the personality, as 'a blind man he would be exactly as much a human personality as before' (Weil, 1962, p. 9). What happens to be sacred in this Other is neither his 'person' nor his 'personality'. 'It is he. The whole of him. The arms, the eyes, the thoughts, everything' (ibid.). The demands of an ethical intersubjectivity far exceed the parameters defined by the nature of person or personality.

The Communicative Self

It is probably no coincidence that the abstract character of personalist philosophy, although prized by the social modelists, is often augmented with more embodied theories of a practical or linguistic kind These philosophical tools, especially those which emphasise communicative rationality, challenge contemporary theological anthropology to examine the framework for, and the processes by which, human intersubjective relations are actually formed. Moreover, through an explicit critique of postmodern attempts to resituate the self, these theoretical undertakings question a thorough-going dismissal of the modern project through a reassessment of reason, language and identity. Yet the constitution of the formal conditioning of the public realm and radical consensus is augmented theologically with an attempted retrieval of the doctrine of the trinity – it is the divine who can be said to provide the most fundamental representation of the possibility and conditions for non-dominant, peaceable intersubjectivity.

Because of the dependence of Alistair McFadyen's communicative-relational model of human interaction on the critical theory of Habermas, I will, for the most part, take it as read that criticisms of Habermas also challenge the force of the former's argument and the applicability of his hypothesis. It is at the point which McFadyen's work departs from Habermas, in his espousal of the social doctrine of the trinity, that his originality and distinctly theological credentials come into play. However, as we shall see, even this theological supplement rests on the theory of a communicative ethic.

While criticisms of Habermas's project are numerous, it is not possible to rehearse all of them here (see Thompson & Held, 1982). There are, however, two significant responses to the Habermasean project that it is essential to outline and comment on at some length. The terms upon which these responses will rest are, first, the place, purpose and status of embodiment in communicative rationality and, second, the role and standing of desire in intersubjective relations. Both of these important themes are deeply problematic in McFadyen's reconstructive, trinitarian enterprise.

The first response to the social reconstruction of the subject is prompted by Friedrich Nietzsche's suggestion in *The Antichrist* that one can distinguish between two forms of Christianity: the religion of holding to *belief* that is concerned with original sin, free will, judgement, heaven, hell and damnation and the *practical* religiosity that is evident in pre-Pauline practices of the development of character. Nietzsche ties the latter to Jesus and a pre-institutionalised faith:

> It is false to the point of absurdity to see in a 'belief', perchance the belief in
> redemption through Christ, the distinguishing characteristic of the Christian: Only
> Christian *practice*, a life such as he who died on the Cross *lived*, is Christian ...
> *Not* a belief but a doing, above all, a *not*-doing of many things, a different *being*
> ... States of consciousness, beliefs of any kind, holding something to be true, for
> example – every psychologist knows this – are a matter of complete indifference
> and of fifth rank compared to the values of the instincts ... 'Faith' has been at all
> times, with Luther for instance, only a cloak, a pretext, a screen, behind which
> the instincts played their game – a shrewd blindness to the dominance of certain
> instincts ... (Nietzsche, 1968, p. 151).

William Connolly, in his commentary on this passage (Connolly, 1998, pp. 27–29), suggests that 'instincts' here are not to be understood as a 'brutish, biologically fixed force'. Rather, what Nietzsche is proposing is that our thought operates across and through several registers and that in his advocacy of instincts he is demonstrating the importance of 'visceral modes of appraisal'. Connolly, following this Nietzschean lead, suggests that 'thinking and intersubjectivity operate on more than one register and that to work on the instinctive register of intersubjective judgement can also be to introduce new possibilities of thinking and being into life' (p. 27). These new possibilities are posited by Connolly on the basis that the visceral nature of intersubjective relations is fundamentally excluded by contemporary reassessments of rationality. Indeed, the visceral register is a dangerous outsider. Habermas is a case in point. He institutes a vision of the public realm that extracts public conflict at a cost: he demands submission to an 'infectious insistence upon an authoritative model of discourse from which the visceral element is subtracted' (p. 35). The point here is that Habermas, and McFadyen with him, ignores not only the visceral nature of human interaction but also the need for reflection on and experimentation with practices that relate to an 'ethic of cultivation' (p. 36). These are not practices that arise from the need for pragmatic responses to various political, social and intersubjective difficulties. On the contrary, they can be seen as arising from a generosity that accepts the place of others in the *agora*, the market place, as providing the context and opportunity for cultivation. Connolly calls this an 'ethos of engagement'.

An ethos of engagement does not eschew the fact of disagreement and the demands of agonistic pluralism. This is where attention to the visceral and contingent elements in our thinking and practice question the communicative rationality of Habermas and its theological application in a theory of personhood. Habermas claims to reject in his quasi-transcendental scheme the transcendental status of the Kantian supersensible. Yet, in accepting only a limited space for the contingent and finally imposing a firm foundation for intersubjectivity, he is taking one step forward and two back. Habermas claims that

> Transcendental thinking once concerned itself with a stable stock of forms
> for which there were no recognizable alternatives. Today, in contrast, the

experience of contingency is a whirlpool into which everything is pulled: everything could also be otherwise, the categories of the understanding, the principles of socialization and morals, the constitution of subjectivity, the foundation of rationality itself. There are good reasons for this. Communicative reason, too, treats almost everything as contingent, even the conditions for the emergence of its own linguistic medium. But for everything that claims validity *within* linguistically structured forms of life, the structures of possible mutual understanding in language constitute something that cannot be gotten around (Habermas, 1992, pp. 139–140).

It is the logic of linguistic performance that provides the ground for the assessment of validity claims and, thus, epistemological justification. There is a sense here that unless the condition of intersubjectivity can be judged and evaluated from an Archimedean point then any possibility of non-coercion is removed and the public realm, indeed politics, will dissolve. The consequence of this fearful stand is in fact – *contra* Habermas – a refusal of the public. It is, to borrow Gillian Rose's designation, 'Agoraphobia'. This familiar term is 'usually defined as fear of wide open space, but the word, more closely observed, is specific. *Agora* means the market-place, the place of assembly; it implies public, articulate space, space full of interconnections, with which you cannot enter into exchange' (Rose, 1995, p. 123). To be more accurate, Habermas is a *quasi*-agoraphobic: his fear of the market-place is only one side of the coin. He accepts contingency, flux and contestation but only on the basis that it can ultimately be filtered through a communicative rationality and transformed into a unidimensional institutional situation constituted by that filter. In this process, the embodied, visceral selves of the *agora* are reduced to epistemological pawns in the quest to remove any non-cognitive element. Not to do so would be to accept the 'irrationalism' of the postmoderns.

The case of Alistair McFadyen is even more difficult to uphold in the face of Connelly's Nietzsche-informed *apologia* for the visceral nature of thought and intersubjectivity. In place of bodily practices of faithful intersubjectivity, he asserts the priority of a secure, rationally sound theory of relationality. One wonders where existence, that is often so messy and difficult, meets a form of thought that is sanitised, and where it is that the visceral register comes into play in the context of faith. If theological anthropology ignores the multidimensional nature of being human and the investment in faith of the *viscera* then this subject is at the very least half-dead.

McFadyen, however, goes further than Habermas and modifies the latter's understanding of intersubjectivity in order to place the self, prior to and apart from communication, on a firmer footing. He claims that the self is 'internally centred' and that this centre is the very thing that makes interaction possible (McFadyen, 1992, p. 69). This reflexive, internal 'I' is the premise and foundation of any processes and practices of mutuality and communality. Again, Gillian Rose's reflections are apposite here. She rails against such a notion of subjectivity anterior to the world and the public realm:

> This self-reliance leaves us at the mercy of our own mercilessness; it keeps us infinitely sentimental about ourselves, but methodically ruthless towards others; it breeds sureness of self, not ready to be unsure; with an unconscious conviction of eternal but untried election. ... This *unrevealed* religion is the baroque excrescence of the Protestant ethic: hedonist, not ascetic, voluptuous, not austere, embellished, not plain, it devotes us to our own individual, inner-worldly authority, but with the loss of the inner as well as the outer mediator. This is an ethics without ethics, a religion without salvation (Rose, 1995, p. 127).

The univocal imposition of a personally-centred basis for intersubjectivity in fact destroys intersubjectivity. Truth, standards and validity begin from what is private and non-negotiable – the 'I'. For all his talk of sociality and community, McFadyen is universalising a form of cultural solipsism that is only deserted on the occasions that sentimentalism provokes this 'I' into giving and receiving. Indeed, self-understanding according to McFadyen is mediated by the other in that they provide a reflection of who I am. The other is a mirror; he, she or it is inert and unreal in itself, save that it provides a reflection of me, over there. Its only significance is that it provides an insight into who I am – Narcissus.

A second objection to Habermasean theory and its theological offspring is the role and status of desire within the quest for intersubjectivity. Central to this criticism is the argument that if one is striving to delineate the basis of and means for agreement then a variety of concerns and issues must be met. As Jane Braaten puts it, in relation to her anxiety that in Habermas epistemological 'justification is the foundation of all forms and dimensions of relationship', is it not the case that 'mimesis, sympathy, and affection have at least as much claim to this status'? (Braaten, 1995, p. 149). Braaten's point is that, as with the visceral, there are a number of 'registers' through and upon which thought and consensus are constituted. Agreements are embedded, to coin a Wittgensteinian phrase, in forms of life and procedures that engender consensus, and intersubjective communality only exists as a complex ensemble of practices, attitudes and theories. Desire is an indispensable element within any assessment of how human beings might communicate with and understand each other. And, in the projects of Habermas and McFadyen, the matter of desire is both included and excluded in a rather strange manner.

For Habermas, desire is little more than a matter of social utility. If, through the procedures of communicative rationality, desires converge, then all to the good. The status of desire here is that of a second order constituent of relations between subjects:

> [Habermas] at best regards desire as an external threat to the autonomy of the rational subject. As a result, the transformative potential of desire, its orientation

'beyond' that may be revealed in and through the recognition of concrete others, is lost; it is jettisoned as part of the sweeping critique of 'transcendental philosophy' (Cascardi, 1992, p, 271).

Habermas is committed to a theory and procedure of universalising rationality that underpins intersubjectivity. Selves do not move beyond themselves to another but are implicated in a model of mutual understanding. Other subjects are not people who we meet in desiring, bodily encounters in which we are taken beyond ourselves, but other subjects who share the capacity for rationality or the competence for argument that are the essential ingredients for public life. I am not for one moment dismissing these factors that Habermas has done so much to bring to the fore in contemporary social and political theory. I am simply questioning their priority and the concomitant exclusion of other registers (indeed others in general) which (or who) are surely part of the diverse fabric that constitutes subjectivity. This reductionism is highlighted by Anthony Cascardi:

> In resolving the characteristic antinomies of the subject in relation to a world of objects, Habermas has in essence reduced the Other to a merely empirical or 'perspectival' variation of the self, and this reduction is in turn symptomatic of the Habermasean attempt to reconstruct the totality of knowledge based on the accessibility of practical 'rules' to rational consciousness (ibid.).

The other is a reflection of social or practical positions and is seen, perspectively, only in retrospect. This problem of the other is the result of an understanding of subjectivity which is formed in the private sphere and is then – and only then – adequately prepared for, and capable of, engaging with others in the public sphere of communicative rationality. Desire is dangerous because it disrupts this neat division of discrete identities who meet in a clean, regulated forum. Desire is that which gives rise to contestation and the demand for recognition, not least of interests and goods that may be incommensurable.

The Social God

If there are significant problems with the application of a communicative ethic within the mundane realm of interpersonal relationships, then the consequences for the idea of a divine society must be addressed. If the sociality of the trinity – the perichoretic relationship or co-inherence of the three divine persons who exist in mutual communication – provides the church (and ultimately society at large) with a definitive model for intersubjectivity and peaceable living, what substantial proposals can be gleaned from this theoretical relationship? Can we really insist that adherence to a social doctrine of the trinity, and all that this model of God promises, will effectively transform the ways in which human beings will relate?

The theoretical context for this claim of the adherents of the social doctrine is the relationship between our two models of God and the crisis of subjectivity in a modern context. As with McFadyen's attempt to construct a notion of Christian personhood that is relational and social in character, the broad framework within which the social modelists work is that of a response to the autonomous subject of modernity and its rejection of an autocratic, totalitarian God. As Walter Kasper has admitted, the challenge facing trinitarian theology is to respond to the modern condition: 'Above all, the issue is how, in continuity with and yet also in opposition to the spirit of the modern age, the human person can be properly understood as the image of the trinitarian God' (Kasper, 1983, p. 286). Not surprisingly, in order to respond to (and against) a particular modern conception of the self, the social modelists are highly critical of an Augustinian psychological analogy in which God's identity is not found in a perichoretic relationship between the three persons of the Godhead but in three activities in the individual soul, a claim that is, at the very least, spurious. In place of this unitary, monolithic God, the social modelists champion a modification of the Cappadocian relational analogy in which, they claim, the emphasis lies with the unity of the three persons in their interrelation and coinherence within God. Nevertheless, the identity of these persons is suspiciously modern.

The notion of separate, distinct centres of various activities and attributes suggests that the selves who are trinitarian persons are disengaged, atomistic individuals *first* and from that position move into communality. This, it now seems rather clear, from the use of personalism to the employment of Habermasian theory, is the crisis of theological anthropology – an imposition of a particular model of the subject onto the Godhead and an idealist belief that if we say often enough that *these* persons are relational then human beings will follow suit. There is no struggle in McFadyen, Gunton, Moltmann, Boff or Thiselton to craft a theological response to a triune God that is appropriate for embodied, instinct-saturated human beings. There is, in short, no hard labour of love, no *paideia*. Moreover, there is no content to the human divine analogy but for a simplistic correlation. To suggest that the identity of God and the identity of human beings consists in their both being relational beings is vacuous to say the least. What is the content of 'relational'? Is it not true that human beings may be immersed in relations at every waking moment of their lives but these intersubjective moments can be violent and jealous and full of misunderstanding? It is a terrible fact that the perpetrator of domestic violence is a human-in-relation. Of course, this kind of relation deserves condemnation, but it is a form of relationship. And are not intersubjective relations embedded within communities who practise, shape and develop theology as well as vice versa? What is required in a theological examination of the subject is that these contexts are taken seriously and that hope is offered rather than a simplistic idealism. Consequently, an ethically responsible theological anthropology must take account of the violence and fragmentation of human interaction as well as the beautiful, the intimate and the loving that are part and parcel of life. It would also account for the dialectical and integral relationship between thought and practice, ideas and existence, a relationship which takes the questions and positions of power and authority very seriously indeed.

The relations that subjects are involved in and constituted by are, even in relation to the church and doctrine, constantly renewed, reconstructed and displaced in terms of a logic of repetition and difference that marks practice and thought. In consequence, relationality is then exposed as encompassing two dimensions: the synchronic (involving particular groups of subjects in time and space) and diachronic (involving the identity of subjects as realised in the context of tradition, change and textuality) with all the inevitable engagements, rhythms and collisions that living amidst the two entails. The logic of difference, however, does not proceed neatly and sequentially but can be characterised as layers of interpenetrating apertures and closures that give rise to a multifaceted relationality.

A second problem with an all too simplistic association of anthropological discourse with trinitarian models is closely related to the first. If the first failing of the social modelists is that they move too quickly to correlate the divine and human conditions, and follow with a far too bare analysis of the identity of both, then any distance between God and human beings is evacuated. The logic of correlation pursued by McFadyen and others results in the equivocal nature of analogy being either forgotten or ignored and the idealist account of the relationship between God and the world follows. For example, McFadyen suggests that 'In the provision of space for free human response to the divine address, the divine-human relationship is structured from God's side as a dialogue' (McFadyen, 1992, p. 19). In a footnote to this statement, McFadyen then provides a helpful explanation of what exactly he means by 'dialogue':

> Dialogue is a relationship in which the mutual orientation of the partners is based on their personal uniqueness and discreteness (independence from one another and their relation). It is therefore a bipolar interaction involving both distance and relation. Because it is based upon the unique identities of each and because these must remain unknowable in any final and complete sense by the other, each partner must make her or his own independent contribution to the relation (i.e. be a subject and originator of communication and communicate herself and himself) and give space and time for the other to do the same. So each partner will be passive and active, the subject (I) and object (Thou) of communication (p. 275, n. 2).

Of course, dialogue is central to relations between subjects and it would be churlish to dismiss the presence of dialogue in the human–divine relationship. However, there is an element within McFadyen's outline that seems to be all too clear-cut. There is no place for uncertainty, absence and misunderstanding on the part of human beings. If there is a desire to overcome the post-Kantian construction of an *absolute* distance between God and beings, then the desire itself is laudable. But McFadyen's understanding of divine–human dialogue, in its institution of perfect reciprocity, effectively annihilates almost any logic of difference between God and the world. Thanks to the divine structuring of dialogue, any distancing functions to ensure that dialogue is conducted between 'discrete' entities in a bipolar relation. There is not here any concession to the doctrine of creation and, accordingly, to the fact that the structure of divine–human dialogue might be understood as a gift that maintains a distance between God and humanity while, at the same time, enigmatically marks the immediacy of God. The distance and closeness of God is, of course, analogous to intersubjective dialogue but this analogy must incorporate the manifest dissimilarity of relations because of the status of the participants. In this sense, the commitment to the distinction between immanent and economic Trinities provides something more than a heuristic device: it offers something like the co-ordinates by which the earthly pilgrimage can be negotiated.

In contrast to an unproblematic correlation between human and human-divine dialogue, Hans Urs von Balthasar, in his study of the thought of Gregory of Nyssa, defines the distinction between the human and divine as 'diastemic' (Balthasar, 1995, pp. 27–31), dependent, that is, on a 'spacing' that is coextensive with creation. Yet this diastasis is not simply a static chasm between the human and the divine, between nature and grace, but a movement of transformation and alteration (p. 31). This movement is further (and concretely) exposed in Maurice Blondel's point that:

> To reach God, man must go through all of nature and find him under the veil where He hides Himself only to be accessible. Thus the whole natural order comes between God and man as a bond and as an obstacle, as a necessary means of union and as a necessary means of distinction (Blondel, 1984, p. 410).

Rather than establishing theological anthropology on grounds that emphasise the univocal relationship between human intersubjectivity and human–divine relations, Blondel elucidates both the inherent equivocation and the attendant discrimination that are required when situating the dialogue partners. Crucially, Blondel also establishes this dia-logic without positing an absolute rupture between God and the world.

From Perichoresis to Anthropological Reserve

The foregoing discussion forces us to consider an important question: should 'one renounce the very idea that the point' of the social doctrine, or model, of the Trinity 'is to give any insight into God'? (Kilby, 2000, p. 443). The model offers an Idealist relationship which, as part of a circular argument, enables concepts to determine how we ought to be. Commencing with a critical evaluation of modern (and postmodern) conceptions of the self, an alternative and acceptable theory of personhood is posited. This, in turn, acts as the theological basis for a description of the nature of the divine 'persons'. Finally, the character of the trinitarian persons is presented as the ideal to which we humans must aspire.

The most frustrating aspect of this theoretical procedure is its faith in the concept of person and the confidence with which the concept is delineated and employed. Is a sense of anthropological reserve too much to ask? As far as the social modelists are concerned, it is. To commit to such anthropological reservations is to submit to the 'violence' of the postmodern deconstruction of the self (Thiselton, 1995). But if one considers, for example, Jean-Luc Nancy's interrogation of the 'sense' of self or personhood, this accusation cannot be sustained. Nancy wishes to think of the person beyond value, as an entity or phenomenon which is 'without price' or invaluable (Nancy, 1997, p. 128). Any attempt to provide a description of the self which claims a certain adequacy is little more than an exhortation which rests, Nancy argues 'on a tacit and unquestioned consensus according to which one knows very well what "the person" is' (ibid.). While a consensus of this kind may well serve as a useful ideological weapon in political or social struggles, it is wont to obscure the excessive character of personhood. Being a person is not something possessed or mastered; it is, rather, a being-possessed by that which is immeasurable (p. 131).

The reserve with which Nancy approaches the question of the definition and description of the person, is not an attitude that is necessarily antithetical to Christian theology. Indeed, if we compare Gregory of Nyssa's account of the nature of human being with Nancy's anthropological hesitancy, the latter appears positively presumptuous. Gregory quotes, in the eleventh chapter of *On the Making of Man*, Paul's challenge concerning knowledge of God (Rom. 11:34):

> 'Who hath known the mind of the Lord?' the apostle asks; and I ask further, who has understood his own mind? Let those tell us who consider the nature of God to be within their comprehension, whether they understand themselves – if they know the nature of their own mind (Gregory of Nyssa, 1893, p. 396).

It is this kind of challenge that the social modelists cannot or will not accept. For if we are to truly understand what is sacred or divine-like within the human, we may have to look beyond the category of the person. As Simone Weil has argued, 'So far from its being his person, what is sacred in a human being is the impersonal in him' (Weil, 1962, p. 13). Even if we know the names of great artists, scientists or philosophers, even if we remember their great artefacts or inventions, their person or personality has disappeared. From this perspective, it is impossible to forge idols of persons (liberalism), communities (Leninism) and societies (fascism) that are somehow sacred and require our undying commitment. To forge an image of the church in these terms is nothing short of tragic.

It is to these more political questions that we must now give our attention. In addition to the theological and anthropological application of the doctrine of the Trinity, the social modelists have formulated a series of arguments for the application of a trinitarian image to wider issues of institutional and political form.

This is the point at which the social model draws a great deal of its popularity; in the context of economic injustice, poverty and war, the image of the Trinity is deemed to offer an alternative vision of a world of justice.

PART III
LIVING

Chapter Five
Trinitarian Politics

An important consequence of the trinitarian turn of the twentieth century is that the spheres of political and social identity are brought into the very heart of theological and doctrinal discourse, a productive innovation that cannot be ignored. Of course, this recent interest in the theologico-political nexus is not a sign of the emergence of a wholly new phenomenon within Christian theology, but the urgency and specificity with which a range of thinkers (both denominational and geographical) can share a point of departure is unprecedented. The doctrine of the Trinity is deemed to provide an ethic of political and social transformation that challenges both the presuppositions of our present (such as consensual realism and the politics of contingent pragmatism) and those ideologies that produce a conception of 'the good' which is detrimental to the majority of the world's population as well as the earth itself (such as boundless consumption and global economic injustice as the norm). Of course, it may seem rather strange that an apparently arcane and paradoxical doctrine can affect our estimation of those issues that appear to be to a great extent immanent and profane, but the proponents of the social model are quite clear as to the impact and significance of the mysterious doctrine.

> An unheard-of doctrine of God, beyond our conceiving, yields up the most radical possibility and authorization for liberated living in this world. In other words, God as Holy Trinity does not just permit, it positively requires a way of being human that is unimaginably *more* human than we can all desire (Kevern, 1997, p. 47).

The manner in which the unimaginable transformation of human individuals and communities is realised is dependent upon the doctrine in a quite straightforward manner. The Trinity points to an alternative mode of being-with: it offers a framework by which institutional structures might be enhanced or revolutionised for the good of all rather than the few; as a generative tenet, the doctrine brings to light an alternative route to the fulfilment of human potential and purpose. Nikolai Fedorov's adage – that 'The Holy Trinity is our social programme' – is commonly utilised in this regard because of its rhetorical force and its authorisation of a substantively different vision of the principles by which communal and political lives are to be lived. Indeed, for one important advocate of the socio-political relevance of the doctrine of the Trinity, Miroslav Volf, 'the question is not whether the Trinity should serve as a model for human community; the question is rather in which respects and to what extent it should do so' (Volf, 1998, p. 405). Volf's assertion is echoed in any number of evaluations which begin from a trinitarian perspective, of modern political types (and concomitant political theologies). These assessments seek a truly Christian reconfiguration of our social and political ends, but do so on the basis of a commitment to the priority of the trinitarian doctrine of God as a *practical* doctrine. And while there is certainly enough theoretical elasticity among and between the perspectives of the social modelists – a point that is especially evident when it comes to the question of 'in which respects and to what extent' the doctrine should impinge on our social and political reflections – there is a distinct theological conjunction at the points of critique and construction. In the various critiques of an array of totalitarian and hierarchical political forms, the underlying relationship between power and monotheism is unveiled and appraised in the light of trinitarian doctrine. In the construction of an alternative image of a transformed politico-social existence, the Trinity is employed in a way that engenders imaginative alternatives to the politics of the *status quo* in which injustice and inequality are an inevitable corollary. The doctrine of the Trinity enables, then, a twofold response to the socio-political conditions of the present; it acts as a critical resource in the face of inequity and a reserve for a constructive reformation of our social existence.

Monotheism and Totalitarianism

In line with the theological and cultural criticism that is stimulated by the focus upon the triunity of the Christian God, the socio-political explorations of the proponents of the social model begin with a criticism of monotheism and its status within the intellectual, practical and juridical traditions of the west. From the perspective of this source of dissatisfaction, a theologically informed criticism is required. According to Jürgen Moltmann, Christian theology must utilise all its analytical resources to question a strident and unapologetic monotheism that has led to a variety of significant but surmountable 'deformations of life' (Moltmann, 1985, p. 57). The western tradition has been littered with these distortions because of the persistence of the image of the *one* God and its intrinsic relationship to notions of power and sovereignty that are unitary and oppressive. In fact, the idea and ideal of the monotheistic God has not only endured. According to the trinitarian critics, it has occupied a privileged place in the Christian tradition and has comprehensively influenced, and often underpinned, tyrannical and hierarchical structures within both the church and the *saeculum*. Three examples, one taken from late-antique Christianity, one from the early-modern period, and the last drawn from the twentieth century, will clarify this historical persistence and its impact.

Perhaps the most famous example of the manner in which a unitary sovereignty, an imperial project and a monotheistic 'Christian' God fuse to generate a theological *apologia* for a historically specific, and thus contingent, political formation, is to be found in a text that is often cited by the critics of political monotheism. In Eusebius of Caesarea's *Life of Constantine*, written in 337, the Christian bishop presents a panegyric which salutes a Christian emperor whose Christian belief and practice is predicated on 'the one supreme God' (Eusebius, 1975, I.27). As Yves Congar has shown, the basic outlines of Eusebius's work, the first section of which was composed to celebrate the thirtieth anniversary of Constantine's accession, advance a conception of earthly political form that is little more than a mimetic representation of the divine life. In turn, the image of God acts to 'divinise' the imperial project. But what kind of God does Eusebius expose, and how does this divine image influence the type and manner of the emperor's political rule? As far as Congar is concerned, a theological vision and a political arrangement are unified in Eusebius's eulogy.

> When Eusebius speaks of monotheism, he is referring to the Father, who has no relationship with his creatures except through the *Logos*. He reigns like the Persian monarch, hidden in his palace. The *Logos* proceeds from him; he is *deuteros theos, secundus deus* (as he already was in Origen), as the river proceeds form its hidden source; he is the image of the Father, the one who orders and preserves creation. Through his work of 'economy', the incarnate *Logos* creates a terrestrial empire as an *eikôn*, an image of the heavenly empire. The Christian emperor, imitating the Logos-Christ-King, reproduces the image of the Father on earth. Constantine governs for the *Logos*, by a process of *Christomimesis*, as the *Logos* governs for the Father. So there can be only one emperor, just as there is only one Father (Congar, 1981, p. 33).

In line with this theology of representation, imitation and power, Constantine could establish for himself the motto that is fundamental to political monotheism: one god, one empire, one emperor (Eusebius, 1975, I.5. See also, Eusebius, 1902, III.3–6). A formidable bond holds together divine and earthly emperors and the fortunes of the empire are interpreted in this light. The authentic king of humanity upon earth is, in Eusebius' schema, modelled upon the Father through the mediation of the Logos, Christ (Eusebius, 1902, III, 6, and VI, 9). Accordingly, Constantine is the imitation of the divine Logos in that he prepares Christians for the heavenly Kingdom and subordinates the enemies of God (ibid., II, 1–5). As Eusebius himself makes clear, the sacral king (who also called himself a bishop),

> openly declared and confessed himself the servant and minister of the supreme king. And God forthwith rewarded him, by making him ruler and sovereign, and victorious to such a degree that he alone of all rulers pursued a continuous course of conquest, unsubdued and invincible, and through his trophies a greater ruler than tradition records ever to have been before. So dear was he to God, and so blessed; so pious and so fortunate in all he undertook, that with greatest facility he obtained authority over more nations than any who had preceded him, and yet retained his power, undisturbed, to the very close of his life (Eusebius, 1975, I.6).

The early Church historian outlines a relationship between mundane power and sacred identity which, according to Leonardo Boff, justifies, via a specific vision of God, the most distasteful of regimes (political and ecclesial), a justification that reinforces, through the successes of a singular political form, a problematic conception of the divine. 'There is a strange dialectic at work here: authoritarian theories can lead to acceptance of a rigid monotheism, just as theological visions of an a-trinitarian monotheism can serve as an ideological underpinning of power concentrated in one person: dictator, prince, monarch or religious leader' (Boff, 1988, p. 20). And we must not forget a crucial aspect of those imperial projects, like the emperor Constantine's, which are the progeny of a theologically sanctioned monarchianism. It would be impossible for us to claim, as Costas Carras reminds us, that these political arrangements are in any way 'humane' (Carras, 1989, p. 179); they are predicated on the customariness of divinely sanctioned violence.

The dialectic that Boff identifies serves not only to justify political deification and violence but also to rein in the revolutionary insights and demands of the gospels, the consequence of which is a fundamental distancing of God from the history and actuality of salvation. Both God and the emperor share a rule that is nothing less than, to borrow a phrase from Catherine Mowry LaCugna, the reign of 'the superordinate over the inferior subject' (LaCugna, 1991, p. 393). That is why an imperial 'refurbishment' of monotheism as a project central to historical Christianity shifts the point of emphasis in the construction of any kind of practical theological reflection. Such a theological imbalance is, according to many social modelists, discernible in the wake of Constantine's settlement, a point reflected in Aloys Grillmeier's contention that with Eusebius's work 'a *political* theology seems more and more to have gained the upper hand over a *doctrine of the economy* and a *theology of history*' (Grillmeier, 1975, p. 251). In short, not only is a monotheistic monarchianism theologically deficient (and, as we have seen in Chapter One, deemed alien to Christianity), but it is a theology that in turn overcomes and conceals the political and social implications of the incarnation and resurrection of Christ and the sending of the Holy Spirit.

Monotheism and Absolutism

Such a concession of the radical political possibilities that arose from the Christ-event, and the concomitant dilution of 'the radical teaching of Christ' (LaCugna, 1991, p. 392), is not a factor that is exclusive to the historical fate of early Christianity's coming of age with the conversion of Constantine. The early-modern period was to see the development of an absolute monarchy which arose at the moment that Europe began the process of evolving what we now call the nation state. The character and status of absolutism was determined by the fact that its identity was constituted by a strange amalgam of both feudal and modern (that is to say, innovative) themes and ideas. Consequently, the juridico-political attitude of many early-modern thinkers was rather confused in the face of a monarchy of this kind: John Calvin dedicated his *Institutes of the Christian Religion* of 1536 to Francis I of France and described the first absolute monarch as a minister of God (see Ahmed, 2004); Hugo Grotius was charged by his critics with an ambivalent attitude to absolutist states (see Tuck, 1979, pp. 63–64) But as far as the theological significance of absolutist monarchism is concerned, Leonardo Boff eloquently describes the social modelists' view of the implications of the tragic validation of untrammelled power.

> absolute monarchs were justified like this: the king enjoying absolute power is the image and likeness of the absolute God. Just as God is above all laws ('*Deus legibus solutus est*'), so the prince too is above all laws ('*princeps legibus solutus est*'). So laws come to depend on the will of the sovereign, not on truth or justice. Again, Christian absolute monarchs found a theological justification (Boff, 1988, p. 20).

In many respects, Boff is right, but one could actually suggest that his criticisms of absolutism do not go far enough. The problem with early-modern absolutism is not merely the fact that the monarch is established in a relationship of representation to the divine King, as with the Holy Roman Emperor, so that the monarch exceeds the limits of the law in a manner that is preceded and authorised by God. Rather, the absolute monarch's relationship to divine power is a more radical example of the modern tendency towards self-assertion. The monarch tends to actively apprehend divine power so that an equality of relation, as an alternative to a relation of dependence, is ascertained and instituted.

The evidence for this transformation of the relationship between divine and princely power is provided by a Florentine painter of the late-Renaissance period, Rosso Fiorentino, who was commissioned by Francis I to decorate the long gallery at his palace at Fontainebleau. Rosso's drawings and frescoes offer pictorial renditions of 'several ancient and modern stories' (Carroll, 1987, p. 224) such as the *Death of Adonis*, the *Funeral of Hector*, the *Education of Achilles*, the *Unity of the State* and *The Enlightenment of Francis I*. 'The general scheme of the iconography of the decorations of the Gallery of Francis I alludes', according to Eugene Carroll, 'to the person and power of the monarch' (ibid., p. 225). The depiction of power that this uninterrupted commentary on the absolute authority of Francis portrays is one that exceeds the terms of an uncomplicated return to pre-Christian paganism. Francis is figuratively and literally exposed as the heir of Greek wisdom and Roman imperial power or, in a rather different idiom, the Christian church without the scriptures. At the very least, Francis is constituted as a monarch whose very person represents a formal superiority and a substantive sublation of Christianity itself. It is for this reason that the image or vision of Francis is so important: the principle of authority that is inherently (though not completely) invisible for the church, is above all visible in absolutism – power as representation, iconography and ideology.

This decisive purpose of an absolutist monarchy is verified by a painting of Rosso's in the gallery of Francis I that is generally ignored by the historians and art historians (see also Béguin et al.; 1972, Franklin, 1994). At the very end of the gallery the viewer comes to the chapel doors, above which is installed the painting in question. Unlike so many of the pieces that adorn the gallery, with their classical and literary allusions, it is a very undemanding and unambiguous image. The painting portrays an altar covered with an altar cloth that descends almost to the bottom edge of the canvas. Upon the altar cloth there is no ornamentation except for the mighty and striking 'F' that is the monarch's coat of arms, a figure that is regularly depicted in a number of other works in the gallery. Anyone entering the chapel is reminded, then, of the status of the individual – the true monarch – that they are about to worship upon their admission to the consecrated area of the chateau. Francis had, in the light of this synecdochical depiction of himself, assumed a rank that was at least co-equal with the divine; in the image above the chapel doors a political representation notifies the keepers of the sacred of its and their own source of authority.

We must be careful, however, to avoid the mistake of supposing that this modern political development arises from, and is sustained by, individual monarchs themselves or a set of political systems in which theological voices are silenced or ineffectual. As Jürgen Moltmann explains, the valorisation and maintenance of the concept of absolutism was formally established by early-modern Christianity itself. Moltmann traces the doctrine of the state as it was developed in the wake of Francis I and the Reformation struggles for legitimacy, struggles that in many respects determined the status and meaning of the religio-political contours of Europe (Moltmann, 1981, pp. 195–196). After the failure of the Huguenot efforts to control their self-determination, and we should remember that Huguenots were associated quite early with utopian ideas and attitudes (see Manuel & Manuel, 1979, p. 369), a number of Calvinists broke from the resistance theories delineated most importantly by François Hotman in the 1560s.[1] The heart of resistance theory was encapsulated in the maxim that political institutions were not constructed for the benefits of citizens. Political life was, in contrast, a direct gift of God. With the break from resistance theory, it was to Jean Bodin's theory of the absolutist state that a number of influential Calvinists turned, and a modern *raison d'état* was fashioned in which the monarch stood above the community of humanity 'because he occupied the place of God on earth' (Moltmann, 1981, p. 196). Thus we have a theological constitution of the monarchy which substantiates and makes legitimate the profane larceny of divine power. Even if, as Moltmann avers, theologians continued to establish the ultimate sovereignty of God, not least as a safeguard against unlimited human ambition, the consequences of the early-modern conflation of supernatural and natural power in the person

---

[1]   For the importance of these resistance theories and the contribution of Hotman, see Tuck, 1979, pp. 42–44.

of the King brought dire consequences for political and theological contexts in western modernity.

> Theoretically, the union of the highest power and the highest law in God excludes earthly tyranny; but in actual practice the ruler's lack of accountability to anyone else puts him outside the law and 'above the constitution.' All that remains is Thomas Hobbes' brutal principle: *Auctoritas, non veritas facit legem* (ibid.).[2]

It is unrestricted power – let us remember that Hobbes makes 'the *summa potestas* into *summa auctoritas*' (Schmitt, 1996a, p. 45) – that marks the far-reaching course of the historical vicissitudes of a unified monarchical God. Theology and politics co-inhere in the theory and practice of the absolute monarch and the absolute state. The story of the significance and force of this history, however, is not exhausted with the acquisition of unqualified power in absolutism.

Monotheism and Sovereignty

The problems associated with the colonisation of a monotheistic theology, a theology which finds its apotheosis in the early-modern conception of absolutist monarchy, should be seen as more than contingent hindrances that serve to encourage a rightly-understood Christianity to seek, as an alternative, a truly biblical and more just orientation. That is because the manifestation of monarchical power in its sacred and mundane semblances is not concluded at the threshold of modernity. A more thoroughgoing secularisation of political monotheism is conspicuous in the totalitarianisms of the twentieth century where the sovereign decision of the divine monarch is made wholly and completely immanent in the decisive moment of judgement performed by the earthly sovereign. It was this complete redistribution of power – from the theological realm to the restricted and undivided authority of the *saeculum* – that prompted an important and influential treatise that underlies so many of the critical interrogations of monotheism by the advocates of the social model. It was the threat, actualisation and aftermath of a new kind of absolute power and its ramifications that compelled theologians to reassess the significance and influence of a monolithic political theology. Principal in this critical interrogation was Erik Peterson who directed his attention to this problem in the 1930s.

Peterson's influential work, *Monotheism as a Political Problem*, first published in 1935 and so often cited by recent critics of political monotheism, is a powerful intervention in the context of both fascism and a newly configured notion of 'political theology' (Peterson, 1994). Ostensibly, Peterson's tract demonstrated the grave effects that a 'strict monotheism' had upon early Christianity. Indeed, many of the analyses by Christian theologians of Eusebius's portrayal of the *pax Augustana*

---

[2] 'Authority, not truth, makes the law.'

and the life of Constantine (that we considered above) are deeply influenced by Peterson's powerful denunciation of the relationship between theological concepts and political identity (see, for example, Congar, 1981; Lochman, 1975; Moltmann, 1981). But as a cursory glance at the social modelists' use of Peterson reveals, the actual target of this assessment of monotheism within the early Christian church is the important essay, *Political Theology*, penned by the famous jurist Carl Schmitt and published in 1922.

The power of Schmitt's work resides in the fact that he asserted that the relationship between theology and state sovereignty was based not only upon a chronological correlation but upon 'fundamental systematic and methodological analogies' (Schmitt, 1985, p. 37). Thus, he can claim that,

> All significant concepts of the modern theory of the state are secularized theological concepts not only because of their historical development – in which they were transferred from theology to the theory of the state, whereby, for example, the omnipotent God became the omnipotent lawgiver – but also because of their systematic structure, the recognition of which is necessary for a sociological consideration of these concepts (ibid., p. 36).

In so many respects, we might consider this statement as an authoritative feature of modern thought in which socio-political models are but secularised versions of what were once theologically-informed conceptions. But Schmitt continues with a statement that takes the reader to the heart of what constitutes a *political* theology: 'The exception in jurisprudence is analogous to the miracle in theology. Only by being aware of this analogy can we appreciate the manner in which the philosophical ideas of the state developed in the last centuries' (ibid.). The miracle in theology and the exception in law are distinguished from all other related principles of order because of their similitude. But what does this mean? The answer is given by Schmitt in the opening line of the first chapter of his book: 'Sovereign is he who decides on the exception' (ibid., p. 5).

The exception is the borderline concept that defines the status and substance of sovereign power. Only the sovereign can suspend the normal operation of the law and it is this juridical fact that determines the norm. What Schmitt is suggesting is that just as the miracle is a general concept in theology – the fact that God intervenes in the lives of human beings and the processes of nature is the sign and performance of rule and sovereignty – so with the theory of the state, the exception is more than 'a construct applied to any emergency decree or state of siege' (ibid.). The exception that is situated at the margins of normality is the basis upon which normality stands. The sovereign is located, therefore, both outside and within the law and only the sovereign possesses the powers to abrogate the normal situation.

The structural analogy between divine and state sovereignty that is delineated by Schmitt is, of itself, a significant contribution to modern jurisprudence (to which we shall return in Chapter Six). However, its significance for Peterson, and for Christian theology in the 1930s and beyond, is that this theory of sovereignty legitimates a pure form of power that exceeds the rule of law and is truly totalitarian. Much of Schmitt's analysis returns to Article 48 of the Weimar Constitution which enabled the sovereign to suspend at will the normal workings of legal and political structures in Germany. It is more than noteworthy that from 1933 to the end of the Second World War Article 48 was in constant force. Within the context of the permanent removal of the norm and the constancy of the exception, therefore, it made perfect sense for Adolf Eichmann to declare that 'the words of the Führer have the force of law' (Agamben, 2005b, p. 38).

This is the context in which Peterson's denunciation of political theology in antiquity finds its modern relevance, and why his 'reply' to Schmitt was only published over a decade after the appearance of the latter's *Political Theology*. The unfettered and voluntaristic authority of a state sovereign without a (legal) state, whose actions and words were recurrently 'miraculous', prompted Peterson to destabilise and undercut the force of its theological significance. In his confrontation with the diachronically persistent phenomenon of political monotheism and its historical origins, he was compelled to provide more than an intellectually and critically stimulating genealogy of the sources and significance of the problem itself. The times in which Peterson lived and wrote demanded a rejoinder that was founded on an authentically Christian paradigm, a God whose revelation and identity could never justify totalitarian politics of any kind. This academic and existential responsibility was carried out with a contribution that has become an authoritative rejoinder to the problem of political monotheism; and this rejoinder finds its authoritative ground in the doctrine of the Trinity. Peterson presented the trinitarian God as a theoretical and dogmatic adversary, in the face of which 'divine monarchy was bound to run aground' (Peterson, 1935, p. 105). In addition, trinitarianism meant 'in principle that a final and fundamental breach with every "political theology" which misuses the Christian proclamation for the justification of a political situation was effected' (ibid.). This sentiment, which refuses any distorted or deficient association between political power within a given situation and the Christian faith, on the basis of the latter's primary theological resource, the doctrine of the Trinity, is taken up and elaborated by the proponents of the social model. The doctrine of the Trinity, in this light, provides 'the contours of the ultimate normative end toward which all social programmes should strive' (Volf, 1998, p. 406).

Trinitarian Politics

The constructive theological labour that is both authorised via, and made possible by, the critical analysis of political monotheism, requires an assessment of the manner in which a correctly understood doctrine of God will allow Christians to re-imagine forms of political and communal life. If there is a direct correlation between the divine (monotheistic) monarch and earthly domination, then, surely, a divine (trinitarian) God of mutual relations and freedom will bestow an alternative foundation for societal structures and their principles of formation. It is to this task, in the wake of the attack upon unitarian conceptions of the divine, that our social modelists have committed themselves. Exemplary here is Jürgen Moltmann:

> Religiously motivated political monotheism has always been used in order to legitimate domination, from the emperor cults of the ancient world, Byzantium and the absolute ideologies of the seventeenth century, down to the dictatorships of the twentieth. The doctrine of the Trinity which, on the contrary, is developed as a theological doctrine of freedom must for its part point towards a community of men and women without supremacy and without subjection (Moltmann, 1981, p. 192)

A politics that is realised as a corollary to the triune God does anything but legitimise oppressive and hierarchical structures. The social model of the Trinity is, therefore, 'the negation of the negation of communion' (Parker, 1980, p. 179).

If the monotheistic conception of God unequivocally sanctions a rigidly constructed hierarchical formation of power relations, then the doctrine of the Trinity provides the tools for a reconstruction of political life predicated on a distinctive conception of the self-in-relation and the complementary principle of radical freedom. The Trinity, in contrast to the totalitarian impulses of the western religio-political tradition offers a vision of communal life that eschews the norms of dominance, supremacy and subjection. In short, the doctrine offers an egalitarian ethic and an anti-hierarchical politics that, once these possibilities are taken seriously, would transform our understanding and practice of communal relations and formations.

> The doctrine of the Trinity has the potential of playing a liberating role in the political and economic struggles of our time by exposing the idolatry of monarchical power and the control and consumption of the world's resources by a few at the expense of the many. Trinitarian faith tends in the direction of political and economic theory based on mutuality, participation, and the distribution of power and wealth (Migliore, 1980, p. 493).

If this vision of politics appears to be little more than an unadulterated Marxism, it certainly shares some elements of the communitarian and egalitarian sources of European socialism. Given that such rudiments of communism are frequently espoused by proponents of the social model of the Trinity, it is tempting to ask how the 'permanent utopia' (Boff, 1988, p. 151) envisaged in the triunity of God might be distinguished from the state-bureaucratic systems which, for the most part, disappeared after 1989. The answer lies in the dialectical relationship between individualism and collectivism that is challenged and overcome by image of God that triunity generates.

In the first place, it is quite evident that the politics of liberal individualism and liberal capitalism are inappropriate in the light of a trinitarian ethic. Capitalism and liberalism share the logic of political monotheism; that is, both promote 'domination based on the One' (ibid., p. 150). Liberal individualism is constituted through a one-sided emphasis on identity and integrity as the prior property of the individual. Isolation and atomisation are the key predicates of the political form that dominated, and continues to dominate, so-called advanced societies. Rights of the individual are considered outside their place and relation to societal relations. These tendencies are reinforced, or even intensified, in the context of capitalism, an international structural reality that imposes the 'concentration of power in the hands of an elite', and which creates the marginalisation of the vast majority of the world's population. The effect of the adoption and practice of capitalist values is that difference gives way to the hegemony of the one: 'one all-embracing capital, one market, one world of consumer, one legitimate view of the world, one way of relating to nature, one way of meeting the Absolute' (ibid.).

If the homogeneity that is provoked by liberalism and capitalism is to be refused from the perspective of a social trinitarianism, it is just as certain that the tendency towards an impersonal collectivism and communitarianism within socialism is similarly erroneous in the light of the doctrine of God. According to Leonardo Boff, the principles upon which socialist regimes are erected are fundamentally sound. That is because socialism acknowledges that communion is the central and vital ingredient of society, as is the involvement of all within the means of production (ibid.). But, once again, the thrust of this social form is towards homogeneity and conformity, as the mediation of communion is hierarchical. It is still the Party or the elites who organise and determine social form, and divergence and variation are not to be tolerated. It is no surprise, then, that Boff is equally critical of the socialist agenda. 'Bureaucratic imposition of the social dimension does not produce a society of equality within the bounds of respect for differences, but one of collectivization with elements of massification' (ibid., pp. 150–151).

As a radical counterpoint to these dominant positions within modern political thought and practice, positions that share an exclusionary logic, the responsibility of the theologian of the Trinity is to construct a version of political form which safeguards against uniformity and marginalisation. In line with this aspiration, Moltmann attempts to break the divisions created by coercion in capitalism and the invariability constituted by force in communism. His vision of a Trinity-inspired society endeavours to overcome these false poles of the human visions of the modern that have dictated the nature of political affairs and the landscape of social identity for over a century: 'Social personalism (individualism) and personalist socialism (collectivism) could, with the help of the trinitarian doctrine, be brought theologically to converge' (Moltmann, 1983, p. 56; see also Moltmann, 1981, p 199). Moltmann's point is that the dignity of the unique individual and the necessity of interrelation that are core elements of individualism and communism are reconfigured in a productive and fruitful manner in the trinitarian vision. As part of their respective social frameworks, these ciphers have contributed to the politics of distortion; in a trinitarian relation of mutual recognition, they signify liberation and harmony.

In his emphasis on the value of a sense of equilibrium, Moltmann is placing himself and Christian theology within a specific idea of political change. Freedom and the benefits of a reciprocal intercommunion, both concepts grounded in the 'inviting picture of the triune God on earth' (Moltmann, 1985, p. 57) and in consequence founded on love, necessitate a transformation of the *status quo*.

> The one-sided patterns of domination and subjection are replaced by forms of community based on free agreement. At the grass-roots the Church consists of and in such communities and exists through them. This also means the democratisation of the process of decision in political and economic life. It can also lead to the decentralisation of political and economic power, to the extent that better systems of communication are built to link together into a single network the individual communities in which one can keep track of what is going on (ibid).

The conception of church and world that is delineated by Moltmann refuses the ubiquitous norms of subjection and those forms of injustice that arise from an exclusionary politics. Hierarchy is dismissed as constructing an asymmetrical world of the power and frameworks of society in which indulgence of the few and the oppression and disenfranchisement of the many are actively promoted. That is why social equality and decentralisation are movements that free and empower. And the authorisation of this democratic communion is the doctrine of the Trinity.

The Pitfalls of Patriarchy

In a similar tone and with a comparable resolve, Catherine Mowry LaCugna criticises hierarchy *as* power (LaCugna, 1991, p. 396). Her examination of the historical development and modern utilisation of the doctrine of the Trinity reminds us that if we seriously embrace the social model of the Trinity we can overcome the '*disastrous political results*' (ibid., p. 392) that emerge from the monarchical paradigm, the dominance of which is, in practical terms, the 'theological defeat' of trinitarianism (ibid.). An important and enduring outcome of this 'defeat' is the way in which patriarchal conceptions of human nature have been unshakable within the church and wider society. From the perspective of the community of the triune God, however, a reconstitution of our presuppositions is imperative: 'As the revised doctrine of the Trinity makes plain, subordination is not natural but decidedly *un*natural because it violates *both* the nature of God *and* the nature of persons created in the image of God' (ibid., p. 398). This reconception of divine and human natures takes its bearings from the mutual co-inherence of the God of love, whose challenge in the face of subjection and subordination relates to the very character of human being and being-with. It is a confrontation that probes the nature of our true purpose and the nature of our misunderstanding of the qualities and characteristics of humanity in all its variety. In response, however, we need to expend more than our thought and imagination. The social doctrine of the Trinity defies the contingent norms of history and offers us a very different kind of communal achievement. 'Man's patriarchal privileges and the deformation of woman they bring about are overcome. The trinitarian community is a community of brothers and sisters and can become the model of a human community' (Moltmann, 1985, p. 57). The contours of the programme that is bestowed by the relational doctrine of God suggest that Christians must form and sustain communities in which equality and just interaction eradicate patriarchal rule. The possibility of creating this human replication of divine love and communion – in other words, the actualisation of the Trinity as a social programme – has been most purposefully pursued in the arena of sexual politics within Christian theology, and the attempts of feminist theologians to think creatively in terms of a new sociality has contributed significantly to the challenge of reflecting upon the nature of God and its political implications.

With an acceptance that 'we are relational beings' (Soskice, 1994, p. 138) has come the possibility of altering our dominant images of God which, in so many ways, reflect the sexist assumptions of the transcendent, detached God-male of sovereign disengagement. A number of feminist authors have demonstrated how the dominance of gender-bias theological interests has thoroughly damaged our ability to think of the nature of God beyond its monolithic form. However, because women 'do not extricate themselves from their environment as transcendent beings, but remain contextually integrated (Hein, 1983, p. 138), the force of the social model of the Trinity is that it questions an ethic of disengagement, especially through the insistence that the internally engaged relations of persons are also a constant of God's economy. As a consequence, it is clear that a 'revitalized trinitarian theology of God' offers us a very different conception of the divine nature to that propagated on the foundation of a masculine monarch: 'the idea of the *archē* of God is not the enemy of mutuality, equality, and a non-hierarchical social order, but its only sure foundation' (LaCugna, 1991, p. 399).

Once again, the need for a theological reorientation is due to the constancy of a doctrine of God in which the triunity of the divine is overshadowed and replaced by a dubious monotheistic concept. Consequently, the presentation of a Son and Spirit who are indistinct 'clones' of, and interchangeable with, the Father is the norm. Rosemary Radford Ruether describes this tendency as the production of a deity in which the 'three are the triune multiplication of the one and single male divine identity' (Ruether, 1985, p. 22). The habitual constitution of this multiple male serves to subject woman to the position of the other of the divine, a division that actively functions as the ground of a whole set of dualisms in which masculine principles take precedence. As Mary Grey insists, the conception of the social model of the Trinity assists the attempt 'to break out of patriarchal space, that is, out of harmful dualistic interpretations of transcendence / immanence, spiritual / material, mortal / immortal, infinite / finite' (Grey, 1990, p. 366). In each of these binaries it is the female who is consigned to the space of the immanent, not least because of the continued theological dominance of a negative assessment of those forms of identity which are characterised as relating to, and engaging with, the changing and immediate flux of existence. As a counterpoint to the correlation of the disengaged male and the disinterested, patrician God, trinitarian sociality promotes a conception of human and divine natures in which the 'diversity among the divine persons is a principle for the affirmation of the diversity within creation' (Wilson-Kastner, 1983, p. 124). The importance and cogency of this reconstruction of theological anthropology is evident in the fact that the gap between theology and a political ethic is bridged through the reappraisal of the nature of the triune God.

A Political God

The political critique of the social modelists is provoked by what is seen as the ascendancy within the Christian tradition of a univocal portrayal of the divine as unitarian. The alternative political vision of the social modelists is provoked by the requirement to counter the disastrous ramifications of this perverse theological arrangement for social and political life. For this reason alone, the social model of the Trinity is good news. And it is especially good news for those who have suffered and continue to endure the injustices of political frameworks in which subjection and subordination are the norm. As Boff argues, 'If the Trinity is good news it is so particularly for the oppressed and those condemned to solitude' (Boff, 1988, p. 158). For all these critics of the global arrangements of the present, the trinitarian figure of God alerts us to the fact that oppressive structures, as with their related divine image, are contingent and can be revised. The challenge of the triune God is nothing less than the transformation of patriarchal and hierarchical structures 'in the light of the open and egalitarian relationships that obtain in the communion of the Trinity, the goal of social and historical progress' (ibid.). The practical framework of trinitarian theology transfigures our conceptions of economic and political exchange; of bodies, of nature, of cultures. In doing so, it presents a fundamental alternative to our petty preoccupations and demands attention to the question of what it is to be a Christian. In this light, Miroslav Volf's view of the body of Christ is compelling: 'a people whose social vision and social practices image the Triune God's coming down in self-emptying passion in order to take human beings into the perfect cycle of exchanges in which they give themselves to each other and receive themselves back ever anew in love' (Volf, 1998, pp. 418–419).

Forceful and persuasive as this 'vision' might be, it is important that we consider the assertions and claims of the social modelists in relation to what is possible politically, and in what sense and to what extent we can use the vigour of a new imaginary to fulfil the aims of social transformation. These reflection are vital because, more then ever, we see a world driven by political violence, injustice and hopelessness. More than ever, we see a world that requires a new political vision and the concrete hope of political transformation. More than ever, we see legal and international institutions by-passed in the quest for power and hegemony. But the stakes of our hope in the social model are high; if the 'social programme' fails to offer substantial structural change, then the product of an alternative representation of God may well be despair and desolation.

Chapter Six

The Political Ideal

It is indisputable that the social modelists have triggered an important debate concerning the relationship between theology and politics. The manner in which particular structures of oppression have been questioned on the basis of gospel imperatives and the character of divine life has stimulated a rethinking of the role of Christian thought and practice in its engagement with the world in which we live. The constructive analyses of post-patriarchal and anti-hierarchical social forms have enabled the recognition and interrogation of sexual, cultural and economic difference. The social model of the Trinity offers, as a communal heuristic and motivating paradigm, an inspiring model for human community and for social transformation. One way of characterising the restitution of a bridge between concepts that derive from scripture and tradition and ideas and formulations of social life – a conduit that is reconstituted by the work of the social modelists – is that the horizon which transcends humanity in the loving interaction of the persons of the Trinity is a horizon that is donated to the Church and ultimately the world. And it is this horizon which must not be refused. Another method of depicting this restoration is to 'propose a social knowledge based on the doctrine of the Trinity' (Volf, 1998, p. 415). In other words, the self-donation of God constitutes a powerful and perpetual point of reference for the enactment of the gospels in Christian self-donation and the life of the Church. Whichever route we take, one cannot but praise the passion and commitment of the proponents of the social model and welcome their endeavour in constructing what is an essential bridge if theology is to remain in any way relevant.

As we have seen, from the outset of the Introduction to this book, it is the very question of relevance that dominates modern theology in its apologetic and constructive forms. And it is this factor which must be borne in mind when we come to assess the relationship between the social model of the Trinity and its application to political critique and social reconstruction. At every turn, the social modelists tune into and utilise the liberationist and egalitarian language of western modernity. Of course, that is not necessarily a bad thing and such discourse and sentiment is to be positively embraced if and when it empowers and frees. The difficulty arises when we consider the ways in which historically, geographically and incessantly the modern has actually produced inequality and suppression. In the face of this fact it is appropriate to ask whether the social model is able to provide a 'social programme' that will succeed where liberalism has itself failed. It is this question that we shall attempt to interrogate most fully in this chapter. Before doing so, however, we must attend to two basic problems with the sources used and the assertions made concerning monotheism and its dire political influence. The underlying purpose of these historical and hermeneutical analyses is a consideration of the veracity of the social modelists' claim that a rightly imagined doctrine of God presents us with a radically different conception and practice of political and social life. So it is right and proper that we assess, as we did with the theological and cultural claims of the social modelists, the question of Christian monotheism and its impact upon the manner in which the political realm is vividly imagined and authoritatively constituted.

The Trouble with Monotheism

It is undoubtedly the case that at the heart of the critical project of the proponents of the social model of the Trinity lies the effort to reveal and recognise the appropriation of a specific, monotheistic idea of the divine. Accordingly, we charted a process of the seizure of the characteristics of the unified, transcendent sovereign and their relocation within a mundane political order and its orders of legitimation and representation. The types of political theology that dictate the Church's legitimation of political power, often to the extent of deifying the monarch, are disclosed – and in turn evaluated – as aberrations both theologically and politically. The existence and persistence of these bonds between profane and sacred orders is not in dispute; the tendency of a whole range of theological voices within the tradition towards the universalisation of the contingent is widely and irrefutably documented. The questions we must ask, however, are whether this evidence is sufficient to condemn and repudiate the monotheistic impulse within Christian theology; and, as a counterpoint, whether it is incontrovertible that the relational, trinitarian conception of God offers a truly alternative basis for political thought and action.

It is noteworthy that Erik Peterson's essay *Monotheism as a Political Problem* is the common reference point for the critical anti-monotheism which was outlined in the previous chapter. The reliance on Peterson's work does not simply mark a move on the part of the social modelists from anthropological concerns to those of political community. On the basis of Peterson's intervention, a hermeneutic of suspicion regarding the effects of monotheism is intensified with the declaration that monotheism encourages the politics and policies of intolerance by shrouding them with the quality of the sacrosanct. Yet, as any close scrutiny of Peterson's *Monotheism* essay will confirm, the use of certain antique examples of political theology does not constitute an essential or even general link between a unitarian notion of God and totalitarian politics. That is why Guiseppe Ruggieri can say, of a volume of essays dedicated to Peterson's influential treatise, that their 'conclusions are devastating' (Ruggieri, 1985, p. 18; see Schindler, 1978). In terms of historical argument and 'systematic generalizations' (Schindler, 1978, p. 12), the alleged intrinsic relation between monotheism and totalitarianism, on the one hand, and the affirmation of the connection between trinitarianism and the overcoming of such politico-theological arrangements, on the other, are shown to be without any solid foundations. An illustrative example of the difficulties associated with Peterson's generalisations is offered by Ruggieri in his thoughtful evaluation of contemporary anti-monotheism:

> Not only monotheism, but trinitarian belief too has *in fact* been linked to a political theology used to justify the existing political order. Eusebius himself justified the fact that Constantine had three successors as an imitation of the Trinity. ... And the history of the Byzantine Empire includes the famous acclamation of Heraclius and Tiberius as co-rulers with Constantine IV Pogonatus: 'We believe in the Trinity; we here crown the three' (Ruggieri, 1985, pp. 18–19).

In the first of these instances, we are reminded that Eusebius described the 'pious sons' of Constantine – Constantine II, Constantius and Constans – as 'a Trinity', a description that is nothing less than an unequivocal and explicit modelling of their natures and authority on the nature and authority of the triune God (Eusebius, 1975, IV, 40). Their sovereignty is guaranteed by an interrelatedness and a unity (they share the same origin) along with an inherent co-equality that transcends the purely natural realm. Nevertheless, they retain distinct identities and purposes. The trinitarian glorification of the emperor's offspring may well be just as distasteful as any univocal identification of the emperor himself with the unified and sovereign Godhead. And it is not a isolated example. One could also mention the construction of a temporal alternative to theology and church undertaken by Frederick II, the Holy Roman Emperor, in the thirteenth century: 'Law-Order-Humanity – typified in the three Caesar figures, a trinity that embraces the function of the State' (Kantorowicz, 1931, p. 227). These cases alert us to the fact that it is the utilisation of a conception of the divine that is problematic; of secondary concern is the nature of the God upon whom political form is modelled.

The example of Eusebius prompts us to consider the manner in which Peterson's thesis is specific to its time, that is to say, to Germany in the mid-1930s, a context in which the Führer had assumed a quasi-theological status. In that situation, the repudiation of political theologies makes absolute sense, although Peterson's contention that there 'can be something like a "political theology" only on the ground of Judaism and paganism' might seem rather irresponsible in the context of rabid anti-Semitism (Peterson, 1994, p.59).

The case of Eusebius's divinisation of the sons of Constantine also alerts us to the danger evident in Peterson's proposal that the Cappadocian reconfiguration of divine *archē* is antithetical to political monotheisms and their attendant political theologies. Peterson's case is overstated and, as any number of commentators have made clear, historically shaky[1]. Nonetheless, it is an opinion that has attained the status of canonical truth among the political trinitarians. Thus, for Leonardo

---

[1]   It is rather surprising, then, to find Catherine Mowry LaCugna citing Alfred Schindler's collection of critical essays after referring to Peterson's 'classic study', as if the former had no bearing on her utilisation of the latter. See LaCugna, 1991, p. 414 n. 46.

Boff, Peterson's thesis has direct political connotations and the latter's trinitarian conclusions have substantial consequences for the method of understanding exactly what political configurations can be drawn directly from the status of the triune God: 'Dictators and tyrants could never draw arguments to legitimize their absolutism from the God-Trinity, because this is not the oneness of a single source, but the unity of three divine Persons, eternally involved in full communion, with no distinction between them on grounds of prevalence of one over the others' (Boff, 1988, p. 22). Boff portrays an ignorance of the use of trinitarian models of God for the legitimation of forms of political power, models that are routinely adverse to the establishment of egalitarian and emancipatory social structures. Given that the nuances of trinitarian theology are seldom debated by the political elites, let alone the average Christian, it is no surprise that Boff's contention attracts both shock and stinging criticism. 'A military triumvirate might very well do this!' exclaims David Nicholls (1993, p. 20). And even a theologian as sympathetic to the 'plurality' model of the Trinity as David Brown cannot control his surprise at the naïve way in which the social modelists – and here the target is Jürgen Moltmann – move recklessly from a model of God to grand statements concerning their constructive political application:

> Moltmann has an extraordinary chapter … in which he argues that the unity model has reinforced patriarchy and dominance within society rather than encouraged mutual cooperation and respect. Whether this is true historically is questionable, but, even if true, the plurality model would not necessarily lead to the latter objectives. After all, three man juntas are almost as common in the world as one-man dictatorships. One hopes that such thoughts played no significant part in leading Moltmann to advocate the latter model (Brown, 1985, p. 308).

It might seem that a 'correctly' understood conception of the triune God enables us to think differently and positively about alternative socio-political arrangements. However, the exposition of the Trinity as a 'social programme' runs aground at the point of correlation between the God imagined and the forms of politics proposed. It is this idealism – the belief that, if only we have appropriate concepts at our disposal, then the world can, and will, be changed – that is found wanting, not least because of the refusal of theologians to consider the multifarious ways in which theologians have, and must, utilise the association between God and politics in both negative *and* positive fashion (see Nicholls, 1989, pp. 233–234).

Only on this basis does it become possible to comprehend the power and significance of the critique of National Socialism that might be, and actually is, inspired by monotheism. Take, for instance, George Steiner's exploration of the sources of, and reasons for, the rampant anti-Semitism within Germany during the 1930s and its culmination in the horror of the death camps. As a complement to the well-worn, and possibly over-determined, historical and sociological reasons for the genesis and development of the Holocaust, Steiner explores a hitherto ignored possibility: that for National Socialist ideology 'the requirements of absolute monotheism proved all but intolerable' (Steiner, 1971, p. 37). The (monotheistic) God of Judaism did not divinely legitimate, however indirectly, the totalitarianism, subjection and subordination of the Hitler regime. On the contrary, this God provoked and in some senses bore its violence because of his monotheistic identity, and the identity of God's people was to be effaced because of their relationship with this One God. For, insofar as Steiner offers a 'reason' for this brutality, it is obvious that the relationship between a particular political arrangements and a monotheistic God that he uncovers shatters to the core the crude and one-dimensional theses of the social modelists.

> By killing the Jews, Western culture would eradicate those who had 'invented' God, who had, however imperfectly, however restively, been the declarers of His unbearable Absence. The holocaust is a reflex, the more complete for being long-inhibited, of natural sensory consciousness, of instinctual polytheistic and animistic needs (ibid., p. 38).

To claim that it is polytheism or animistic religions which 'caused' the Holocaust – and, of course, this is *not* what Steiner is claiming – is as emphatically preposterous as constructing a unified theory of the emancipatory prospects of a trinitarian theology. What Steiner's proposition does serve to elucidate is the complex character of politico-theological associations and it further confirms that the canonical connection between monotheism and totalitarianism is not only untenable but quite absurd.

The incongruous nature of the social modelists' view of the appalling ramifications that ensue with any allegiance to the monotheistic, sovereign conception of God is also disclosed as dubious if we take into account Karl Barth's stance on the opposition between state formations and the sovereignty of God, especially during the 1940s. As Waite Willis suggests, this opposition was not the outcome of a particular prejudice regarding mundane politics but was a necessary conclusion to Barth's conception of the unfettered rule of God. For Barth, then, the state 'stands under the judgement of God' and no other (Willis, 1987, p. 98). The significance of Barth's delineation of the relationship between the state and the divine is, quite understandably, influenced, though never quite determined by, the context in which he wrote. His commentary and gloss on Calvin's catechism, presented as lectures between 1940 and 1943, corroborates this fact. In the lectures, Barth constantly refers to the sovereignty of God over history and, in doing so, ensures that the appropriate distance is maintained between God and the world. But this distance serves not only to preserve the usual (Barthian) Otherness of God. In the context of the 1940s, it is essential to ask 'Where do I stand vis-à-vis God the master' (Barth, 1960b, p. 86). Indeed, even when Barth considers the Ascension of Jesus, the commentary fails to evoke a sense of equality and freedom that naturally evolves from the event of the resurrection and the reality of the Trinity. On the contrary, Barth retains the element of radical difference so that we are clear, and that totalitarian governments are assured, that 'every man is under the dominion of Christ, whether he knows it or does not know it' (ibid., p. 94). In the confidence of this assertion we have a remarkable example where a hierarchical conception of the Godhead proffers an opportunity for the critical negation of domineering and violent politics. That is not to say that Barth's conception of God must act as a permanent feature of a theological consideration of the political situation. It *is* to suggest, however, that this is a conception that is always available – in the scriptures and the tradition – when our mundane presuppositions take on the air and authority of divine proclamation.

On the grounds of these difficulties with the univocal and monological theses of the social modelists, the case for their critical and constructive proposals is certainly weakened. But there is a more serious failure on their part, a failure that questions the principles around which the proponents of political trinitarianism construct an alternative vision of socio-political promise. The social modelists simply do not grasp the metaphysical doctrines upon which modern politics is grounded, a politics that they extol in their constructive enterprise, and, just as crucially, they refuse to consider the point at which, and the means by which, politics and theology coalesce.

Political Theology

It is worth remembering how Immanuel Kant employed the Trinitarian persons as the juridico-theological precondition of the truly ethical commonwealth, a theme we exposed and interrogated in the Introduction to this study. Even more revelatory for an examination of the nature of the politico-theological nexus, however, is the famous copper engraving that adorned the first edition of Thomas Hobbes' *Leviathan*. Within the very heart of this book, a work that withholds any role for the church in the regulation of religious as well as temporal affairs (Hobbes, 1996, pp. 342–346), we are presented with a portrayal of the unification of the plurality of wills in one 'Person'.[2] Seldom appreciated is the fact that the sovereign's power and authority is represented in a rather peculiar fashion: he holds a bishop's crook and a sword in a manner that reveals the status of modern sovereignty. As Jacob Taubes has argued, the fact that the figure holds the crook in his left hand and the sword in his right is no accident (Taubes, 1980, p. 572). It is a conscious reversal, and therefore a repudiation, of the medieval version of papal power. Inverting the relationship between spiritual and temporal power, the frontispiece confirms that the earthly city has acquired an authority that is nothing less than a *plenitudo potestatis* (fullness of power). If we are prepared to take seriously the implications of Hobbes' concept of sovereignty, then we must conclude that the modern state is not simply a phenomenon that is predicated on the *separation* of religious and

---

[2]   For Hobbes' own explication of the status of this 'Person', see Hobbes, 1996, p. 120.

secular authority. Modern politics is only possible because of its *acquisition* of sacred power.[3]

Far from being a solitary and atypical episode, this tendency is also evident when we chart the ramifications of a process that produces a realm of material reality that is ultimately transformed for theological reflection and experience. The split between nature and grace is consummated in their conflation. For this reason, one of the least ambiguous – and best known – illustrations of the seizure of the supernatural within the realm of immanence surfaces with Benedict de Spinoza's 'pantheistic' metaphysics. The most renowned element of Spinoza's naturalisation of metaphysics is his identification, in the *Ethics*, of God and Nature, the absolutely infinite substance. Spinoza not only revolutionised the late-medieval conception of the univocity of Being, 'freeing it from the indifference and neutrality to which it had been confined by the theory of a divine creation' (Deleuze, 1986, p. 58). In an even more radical step, he creates a theology in which God is effectively naturalised.

> Since nothing is necessarily true except by the divine decree alone, it follows quite clearly from this that the Universal laws of Nature are nothing but decrees of God, which follow from the necessity and perfection of the divine nature. Therefore, if anything were to happen in Nature contrary to her universal laws, it would also necessarily be contrary to the divine decree, intellect and nature ... We could also show the same thing from the fact that the power of nature is the divine power and virtue itself. Moreover, the divine power is the very essence of God (Spinoza, 1989, vi.8–9).

The consequence of this profane apprehension of divine power and identity is that such a monism, *Deus, sive Natura*, represents the relation between the mental and the physical as no more than one of a difference of attributes. With the creation of an essentially unified pantheistic system, Spinoza succeeded in making 'a religion out of science by divinizing nature, and a science out of religion by naturalising the divine' (Beiser, 2003, p. 134). God is intelligible to the intellect in unmediated form and all knowledge is knowledge of God. Of course, within Spinoza's system there are subtle and important distinctions which partially secure an apparently discrete divinity, but the margin of difference is threadlike. Eternity is supposed as separate from (historical) duration and (measurable) time but because 'motion and rest is an eternal mode of infinite extended substance, and motion is relative change of position in time' (Donagan, 1996, p. 355), the divine is no longer timeless but is drawn into the tangled knot of quotidian history. Nature consumes supernature and the time of the latter is rendered historical.

Over a century after the posthumous publication of the *Ethics*, Hegel brought this process of the subjugation of the sacred by the profane to an historical finale.

---

[3] For a more thoroughgoing analysis of the significance of this acquisition of sacred power, see Fletcher 2004a.

Hegel, as the beneficiary of a vulgar reception of Spinoza via Jacobi and the Jena Romantics, transposed a metaphysics that developed its categories by interpreting reality as substance or by dissecting and evaluating the concept of nature – whether in its ancient or modern guises – into the more immediate idiom and categories of Spirit. The nature of the order of Being as it is given or created is erased in the system. This transcendental move is, therefore, also the anthropological move *par excellence*, as creation and its creator are no longer meta-physical norms. The creative production of Man or, more exactly, History is placed above even natural, as well as supernatural, categories and co-ordinates (see Taubes, 1963, p. 152).

In the 'Preface' to his *Phenomenology of Spirit*, Hegel plots the enactment of this '*panological pathos of perfection* with its eternally completed final word pushed back undifferentiatedly into the empirical' (Bloch, 2000, p. 181). The fate of this pathos is intrinsically linked to the destiny of the Subject: 'In my view, which can be justified only by the exposition of the system itself, everything turns on grasping and expressing the True, not only as *Substance*, but equally as *Subject*' (Hegel, 1977, pp. 9–10). The nature of Spirit that is unfolded and charted by Hegel begets a unification of history as action and an eschatological ideal within the radical presuppositions and parameters of the system. 'That the True is actual only as a system, or that Substance is essentially Subject, is expressed in the representation of the Absolute as *Spirit* – the most sublime Notion and the one which belongs to the modern age and its religion' (ibid., p. 14). This notion of Spirit as Subject brings together two concepts that are indebted to Christianity but its truth is neither disclosed nor progresses in relation to the *civitas dei* or as a feature of the life and purpose of the church. Christianity is sidelined by Hegel who, in his description of the realm and purpose of Spirit, presents a thoroughly secular history from the Greek *polis* to the French Revolution, before analysing the Terror and, via Napoleon, the Prussian state. As a consequence, a temporality that was once reliant on creation, providence and an integral relation to another time and space of consummation, has now itself become Absolute in history.

As for God, he is not simply subsumed into the system in a dialectical process of sublation and perfection. It is quite apparent, in the *Phenomenology* at least, that the destruction of the divine is an essential stage on the way of the dialectical advancement of consciousness. In Hegel's reflection on the death of Christ, this murder of God is simply a phase in the march of *Geist* to its fulfilment. It is noteworthy that the *Phenomenology* concludes with Golgotha as the finite and the infinite find unity without resurrection.[4]

What we see – relentlessly performed – in these modern appropriations of the power and authority of the divine is not the construction of a historically specific or generalised conception of politics which, in turn, is dependent upon an

---

[4]   See also Hegel's contention in the 'Preface' to the *Phenomenology* that 'the life of the spirit is not the life that shrinks from death and protects itself from it, but the life that endures death and maintains itself in it. It wins its truth only when, in its utter laceration, it finds itself' (Hegel, 1977, p. 19).

unwavering concept of the monarchical God. Nor do we just witness a simplistic representation of a unitary divine within particular political settlements. We have, more decisively, a refusal of Christian eschatology and its significance for the earthly activity of both church and world. The modern, in its range of political pretensions, is a time of the refusal of what *is* the very time in which Christians live and the time that makes the church possible. Modern political theology or, as Leo Strauss terms it, the 'theologico-political predicament' of modernity (Strauss, 1997, p. 1), seeks to capture the power and force of the transcendent through its relocation within the immanent as history, event, nature, sovereignty or subject. These modern attempts to refigure sacred and profane space mark the end of eschatology through the acquisition of its very force and authority.

From this perspective, we can appreciate that the modern history of time is one in which gradually but eventually the time of the end is evacuated from history. Eschatology is eviscerated to the extent that its threat, in the weakest sense of the word, is eliminated and its historical force is domesticated. This untying of time from its end, and the definitive marginalisation of a Christian conception of the world in temporal terms, is clearly demonstrated by the war of words that commenced with the publication in 1966 of Hans Blumenberg's *The Legitimacy of the Modern Age* (1983). One of Blumenberg's primary targets in this work (for there were many opponents found wanting at the bar of historical reason) was Karl Löwith's *Meaning in History* (1949) (or, in the German, *World History and Saving Event*). Despite the fundamental differences in their respective theses (see Wallace 1981), Blumenberg and Löwith shared a common premise concerning the status of history and its meaning and significance: the irreconcilable difference between modernity and eschatology, that is, *in nuce*, a Christian conception of time. In both of these reflections the Christian conception of time oriented towards the eschatological end was obsolete due to its incompatibility with the modern experience of time.

Is it any surprise then, that, if we return to Peterson and his critics, we find that the significance of the famous essay on monotheism does not lie with the cursory dismissal of all unitarian conceptions of God? Rather, the focus of the work is actually the critique of de-eschatologisation (*enteschatologisierung*) that Peterson unveils in a range of historical circumstances, a refusal of eschatology that is the generative principle of all political theologies (see Badewein, 1978, p. 46). Again, Giuseppe Ruggieri concisely summarises this point when he argues that

> if one reads the essay on monotheism carefully, the true force of Peterson's argument, that which can reasonably be said to demonstrate an effective connection between acquiescence in the political situation and the teaching of Eusebius, does not lie in the field of trinitarian doctrine but in that of eschatology. The process by which Eusebius utilises the concept of divine kingship to attribute a privileged role in Christian economy to Constantine becomes secondary to the process of 'de-eschatologization' in Eusebius' thought: that the prophetic

promise is realised in the peace brought about by the empire (Ruggieri, 1985, pp. 19–20).

Destructive and hierarchical politics is not created in the image of a deviant God, although a convergence might occur contingently. The tendency within political theologies is towards a realisation or historicisation of eschatology in which the divine is acquired as a metaphysical and historical foundation of authority and power. Sacralised temporality is the norm of the politico-theological alliance and it is on this basis that we must treat the simplistic claims of the political trinitarians with caution, if not antipathy. The propagation of the monotheistic thesis and its trinitarian counterpart distract us from the actual and essential relationship which remains at the core of political projects, even today. As a consequence it is no surprise to find that Peterson, within a text that held on tenaciously to this view, presents the reader with a text from Gregory of Elvira in which it is maintained that the those who wish to realise the divine monarchy on earth would be akin to the Antichrist for 'it is he who alone will be the monarch of the whole earth (*ipse solus toto orbe monarchiam habiturus est*)' (Peterson, 1994, p. 47). The predicament encountered in Peterson's challenging essay is that the conjunction of any political arrangement with a theological legitimation is more than problematic: eschatology disqualifies any legitimate, mundane identity between the *saeculum* and the Kingdom of God.

Just as crucially, the reproduction of the contours of a trinitarian political theology also neglects a range of criticisms of political theology engendered by a monotheistic ethic, such as the prophetic tradition within Judaism, a tradition that 'severely criticised the exploitation of the poor on the basis of the sovereignty of God' (O'Donnell, 1988, p. 22). It is not monotheism that is constitutive of the predicament of political theology but the use of models of God (of any kind) which secures divine legitimation for the orders of the profane *in time*.[5]

The Deified *Saeculum*

The consequence of this de-eschatologisation of Christianity, a project that constitutes the nucleus of modern politics, is the levelling out of the sacred, the marginalisation of doctrine and the creation of an ontological premise for human relations of equality and fraternity. This is, of course, the world in which we live and a world that is celebrated in Moltmann's contention that 'Social personalism (individualism) and personalistic socialism (collectivism) could, with the help of the trinitarian doctrine, be brought theologically to converge' (Moltmann, 1983, p. 56). It would be as well to accept that Moltmann's vision is one that seeks the propitious overcoming of the divisions, both ideological and practical, between liberal individualism and state socialism. However, from the context of the third

---

[5]   We shall return to this theme of 'de-eschatologisation' in Chapter Eight.

millennium, we have seen Moltmann's desire fulfilled in the 'third way', a concept espoused by Bill Clinton and Tony Blair and given intellectual weight by Anthony Giddens (see Giddens, 1998). The trinitarian vision has been (very easily) realised in the post-political vision of a neo-liberal capitalism tempered by social justice (or at least an aspiration for the latter). And why should the politicians not profit, if they so desired, by giving the 'third way' a trinitarian badge of authority?

Notwithstanding the bizarre identity of a perfected trinitarian politics, Moltmann is repeating the very catastrophe for which he condemns the political monotheists. He is authorising particular political arrangements on the basis of a theological concept, and through a generalised judgement as to the integrity or otherwise of this concept. As long as the structure of the political matches the character and profile of the concept it is admirable. But in the process of this idealist construction of the apposite form of the political community he is repeating the Hegelian move whereby a virtuous religious ideal is interlaced with the perfect state structure in the very act of refusing eschatology and its challenges. For his part, Hegel was just as explicit in the pursuit of this Idealism, as we can see from his reflections on religion and the State in the *Lectures on the Philosophy of Religion*:

> In general, religion and the foundation of the state are one and the same thing – they are *identical in and for themselves.*

> [A] people which has a bad concept of God also has a bad state, a bad government, and bad laws (Hegel, 1999, p. 225).

At least with Hegel, we *could* assess these statements as speculative rather than positive propositions, that is to say, statements that concern the unity which religion and the state share, but a unity that is only to be realised teleologically in the realisation of Absolute Spirit and the cessation of alienation. We cannot provide Moltmann with such a justification. His flattening out of theological politics mirrors the acquisition of the sacred within the modern period and the definitive removal of an eschatological notion of fulfilment. That is why Moltmann's gift of the sanction of the divine to the politics of the present completes the critique of religion which began with the masters of suspicion and which finds its faultless definition in Theodor Adorno's assertion that 'Nothing of theological content will persist without being transformed; every content will have to put itself to the test of migrating into the realm of the secular, the profane' (Adorno, 1998, p. 136). The sacred is thus subsumed into the proximate; the historical and the *saeculum* are deified and *kairos* is historicised and naturalised as the completion and fulfilment of history.

The failure here, a failure that is shared by the majority of the social modelists, is that they believe that if only we can build upon the desire for change and transformation then politics will continue to flatten out with the removal of subjection and subordination. While the Trinity is the pivotal figure for the conception and performance of this revolutionary politics, it is actualised on the terms, and within the parameters, of the modern view of political systems and identities. What is missing in the midst of all this hope and anticipation is a thoroughgoing examination of what happens when the struggles in mundane politics are overcome and equilibrium is reached and maintained. What if the actualisation of balance produces a form of politics that meets the requirements of egalitarianism but does so in a way that is a perversion of politics itself? Instead of mutuality, balance and equality, modern liberal politics has been fulfilled in the return to animality and the triumph of biopolitics, the flattening out of hierarchy *par excellence*. The end of history and the redefinition of politics as the sovereignty over life itself is the consequence of a de-eschatologisation which weaves the threads of a time of fulfilment in accordance with the event of the present time. And it is via the political philosophy of Alexandre Kojève that we might track the magnitude of this transformation and the perfection of the modern capture of sacrality.

The Biopolitics of Modernity

Between 1933 and 1939 Kojève lectured on Hegel at the Ecole Pratique des Hautes Etudes in Paris. Kojève placed the dialectic of Master and Slave at the centre of, and as the key to understanding, what he considered to be the most significant of the '*écrits hégéliens*', the *Phenomenology of Spirit* (Kojève, 1947).[6] It is the fight for recognition that is essential to the political process and to becoming a self – an 'I' (Kojève, 1980, p. 7). Kojève, like Hegel (Hegel, 1977, pp. 109–110), posited a distinction between the desire to fulfil instinctual needs or 'appetites' and a higher Desire. This higher Desire *is* human desire and must win out over the purely animal desire. Human Desire, however, is not, as is animal desire, simply instinctual:

> Desire is human only if the one desires, not the body, but the Desire of the other; if he wants 'to possess' or 'to assimilate' the Desire taken as Desire – that is to say, if he wants to be 'desired' or 'loved', or, rather, 'recognised' in his human value, in his reality as a human individual (Kojève, 1980, p. 6).

This 'recognition' is not simply a matter of some supplementary status that sorts the masters from the slaves – it is an essential characteristic of human identity. As Kojève declares, 'the human being is *formed* only in terms of a Desire directed towards another Desire, that is – finally – in terms of a desire for recognition' (ibid., p. 7). Thus Kojève, in positing the fight for recognition as pivotal, proposes a reading of the *Phenomenology* in which we are presented with an 'account of universal history in which bloody strife – and not 'reason' – is responsible for the

---

[6]   An abridged version is available in translation (Kojève, 1980), which I shall use where possible.

progress towards the happy conclusion' (Descombes, 1980, p. 13). The conclusion being, of course, Absolute knowledge and the End of History. Kojève bequeathed to his readers '*a terrorist conception of history*' (ibid., p. 14). For Desire to be Desire, then, *Thanatos* must be its precondition in an economy of becoming that is sacrificial and where death only has meaning to the extent that its meaninglessness is wagered.

While commentators and critics have repeatedly emphasised this violent element of Kojève's legacy, there is an often-ignored factor that is central to the realisation of the consummation of desire: happiness *is* the ultimate goal of history, conflict and Man. This point is of the utmost importance not least because the once-certain distinction between human and animal disappears on reaching happiness – the End of History – and desire is once again transformed.

> The *Selbst* – that is, Man properly so-called or the free Individual, *is* Time and Time is History, and *only* History. … And Man is essentially *Negativity*, for Time is *Becoming* – that is, the *annihilation* of Being or Space. Therefore Man is a *Nothingness* that nihilates and that preserves itself in (spatial) Being only by *negating* being, this Negation being Action. Now, if Man is Negativity – that is, Time – he is not eternal. He is born and he dies as Man. He is '*das Negativ seiner selbst*,' Hegel says. And we know what that means: Man overcomes himself as Action (or *Selbst*) by ceasing to *oppose* himself to the World, after creating in it the universal and homogeneous State; or to put it otherwise, on the cognitive level: Man overcomes himself as *Error* (or 'Subject' *opposed* to the Object) after creating the Truth of 'Science' (Kojève, 1980, p. 160).

The ends of Man can be discerned with the coming of the 'universal and homogeneous state' and the closure of ideology. At this point, when Man is no longer, 'life is purely biological' (Kojève, 1947, p. 387). Man is once again pure animality and, in a footnote to the first edition of his *Introduction* in 1947, Kojève confirms and affirms this *telos* of the human: Man becomes an animal who is 'in *harmony* with Nature of given Being' (Kojève, 1980, p. 158). Although this 'annihilation of Man' brings about the end of philosophy and wisdom, there is sufficient consolation in this 'state' of being animal: 'art, love, play, etc., etc' (ibid., p. 159). Nevertheless, Kojève's vision is fundamentally horrific: human life has become what we might call 'lifestyle as biopolitics', where biopolitics is the constitution of life as little more than 'birth, death, production, illness, and so on' (Foucault, 2003, p. 243). Mere survival of the flesh is the logic of the biopolitical era in which traditional sovereign power – to make die and let live – has been superseded by biopower – to make live and let die (ibid., p. 241).

In the second edition of *Introduction à la lecture de Hegel* (published in 1959), Kojève returned to this biopolitical footnote with a change of mind. The animality of the post-historical human that is so persuasively delineated in the first edition is abandoned in the midst of a complete reappraisal of a culture after History:

If Man becomes an animal again, his acts, his loves, and his play must also become purely 'natural' again. Hence it would have to be admitted that after the end of History, men would construct their edifices and works of art as birds build their nests and spiders spin their webs, would perform musical concerts after the fashion of frogs and cicadas, would play like young animals, and would indulge in love like adult beasts. But one cannot then say that all this 'makes Man *happy.*' One would have to say that post-historical animals of the species *Homo sapiens* (which would live amidst abundance and complete security) will be *content* as a result of their artistic, erotic, and playful behaviour, inasmuch as, by definition, they will be contented with it. But there is more. 'The *definitive_ annihilation* of Man *properly so-called*' also means the definitive disappearance of human Discourse (*Logos*) in the strict sense. Animals of the species *Homo sapiens* would react by conditioned reflexes to vocal signals or sign 'language,' and thus their so-called 'discourses' would be like what is supposed to be the 'language' of bees. What would disappear, then, is not only Philosophy or the search for discursive Wisdom, but also that Wisdom itself. For in these post-historical animals, there would no longer be any '[discursive] understanding of the World and of the self' (Kojève, 1980, pp. 159–160).

In the wake of pure animality comes pure formalism and the refusal of reflexivity – Japanese aristocratic snobbery is the exemplar of post-History. But Kojève is being disingenuous here. Animal desire, as the merely sentient condition of human desire, is characterised by Kojève as lacking the essential reflexivity or ability to dis-quiet Man (ibid., pp. 3–4). This, in turn, remains the very status of post-historical humanity even in its revision as formalism (Kojève, 1947, p. 387). Notwithstanding his reservations, Kojève cannot escape the biopolitical implications of his analysis – political action is no longer possible or commendable and desire is always aligned to the mores of the 'universal state' in which the human is a refugee (ibid.). The universal state is now realised as global liberal governance and the latter is enforced, for the most part, by multi-national corporations and trans-national agencies.

A vision of this kind, in which a perfected humanity reaches a pure form of egalitarianism, is a product of the manner in which modern political form is theomorphic. The power over life itself is no longer an eschatological affair. The last judgement is now a judgement in this life, in the here and now, as part of the immanent manipulation of naked animality. But it is also a political judgement that is couched in the terms of the mythologemes of management, security and morality, terms that cannot be questioned in a context where even the Christian church has moved from eschatological indifference to a complete disavowal of the eschatological principle. The church is no longer a remnant but a collection of bodies who must disclaim the 'arousing restlessness' of the religious life (Rose, 1992, p. 157).

The Rule of the Exception

This may well be a vision of the end of history that is somewhat odious and repugnant, but that is no reason to excuse the political naïveté of the proponents of the social model and the continued belief in the transformation of the present on the basis of a concept – albeit a positive concept – of God. This form of politics, the politics of biopolitics, is a central and constant factor in the constitution of the modern. Politics of security, territories and populations, in which 'life' as a biological fact is managed and controlled, are part and parcel of the modern contexts in which the social modelists have composed their political visions. But the real danger arises out of the fact that our political theologians are divinely sanctioning the present, even if they do so unwittingly and even if they would tend to refuse its results. That is one reason why an accurate diagnosis of the present, where life is reduced to its biological elements, is urgently required. Another reason is that this transformation which *is* modern politics radically alters the status of forms of life, of which the church is one. The conclusion that we must draw is that material, naked existence, the very 'stuff' which Kojève located at the fulfilment of history, has now become everything, and the body alone is the 'substance' of politics and power.

This refiguration of the body politic – biopolitics – constitutes, then, 'the decisive event of modernity and signals a radical transformation of the political-philosophical categories of classical thought' (Agamben, 1998, p. 4). The break with the political philosophies of Plato, Aristotle and the *Respublica Christiana* is categorically exposed in our context in which the life of the *polis* is constrained by the removal and reformulation of the soul and the violent displacement of that eschatological time which constitutes the very end and meaning of the body of the Church. But a reflection on the manner in which the nature of contemporary political subjectivity is distinct from classical and Christian models may well help us to reflect on the ramifications of the evacuation of the theological from the material. In his account of modern political sovereignty, Giorgio Agamben does just this. He begins with the classical Greek distinction between two forms of life: *zoé*, 'which expressed the simple fact of living common to all living beings', and *bios*, political life or 'the form or way of life proper to an individual or a group' (ibid., p. 1). Life as *zoé* – what Agamben calls 'bare life', which signifies mere reproductive existence – is excluded from the city yet is of necessity included in the constitution of modern sovereign power. Indeed, there is in modernity a gradual coincidence of bare life and the political realm. 'If anything characterises modern democracy as opposed to classical democracy ... it is that modern democracy presents itself from the beginning as a vindication and liberation of *zoé*, and that it is constantly trying to transform its own bare life into a way of life and to find, so to speak, the *bios* of *zoé*' (ibid., p. 9). In the modern period, according to Agamben, bare life has *become* political existence and has effected the blurring of juridico-institutional life and biological existence through the indifferentiation of right and fact and inside and outside.

The protagonist who, as it were, embodies this change in political identity is a rather peculiar subject of archaic Roman law: *homo sacer*. He is the sacred man, who may be killed but not sacrificed: 'The sacred man is the one whom the people have judged on account of a crime. It is not permitted to sacrifice this man, yet he who kills him will not be condemned for homicide' (ibid., p. 71). *Homo sacer* stands outside both human and divine law and as such is the exception whose very exteriority is instantiated within the law outside of which he stands. However, there is another character that shares this logic of the exception – the sovereign. Taking his lead from Carl Schmitt's assertion that the sovereign is at the same time inside and outside the juridical order (see Schmitt, 1985, p. 19), Agamben points to the paradox of sovereign power: 'the sovereign, having the legal power to suspend the validity of the law, legally places himself outside the law' (Agamben, 1998, p. 15). The sovereign is the mirror image of *homo sacer*, the exceptional figure. 'At the two limits of the order, the sovereign and *homo sacer* present two symmetrical figures that have the same structure and are correlative: the sovereign is the one with respect to whom all men are *homines sacri*, and *homo sacer* is the one with respect to whom all men act as sovereigns' (ibid., p. 84). The supreme power of sovereignty is established by the capacity to constitute '*oneself and others as life that may be killed but not sacrificed*' (ibid., p. 101). Sovereign power, then, like the figure of *homo sacer*, subsists in an area of indistinction between nature and culture. This is evident in Hobbes' understanding of sovereign power where the state of nature is the state of exception not as the war of all against all but, 'more precisely, a condition in which everyone is bare life and a *homo sacer* for everyone else' (ibid., p. 106). As the condition of possibility of modern politics, this sacred life is that which is the very subject of (and subject to) sovereign decision. While it might well be rights and free will and social contracts that constitute the political realm for the citizen, for the sovereign it is bare life which is given over to him in return for peaceable living.

Agamben's analysis of the figure of *homo sacer* and the status of sovereign power from the Roman Empire to the modern period, via conceptions of the 'ban' and myths of the werewolf, is a most impressive exercise in the history of the development of political forms of power. His aim, however, is not simply historical. Indeed, the historical material is but the necessary prolegomena to a shocking conclusion – the exception (*homo sacer*) has become the rule. In coming to such a conclusion, Agamben is drawing on the opening lines of the eighth of Walter Benjamin's so-called 'Theses on the Philosophy of History' (Benjamin, 1973, pp. 248–249).[7] There Benjamin suggests that 'The tradition of the oppressed teaches us that the "state of exception (*Ausnahmezustand*)" in which we live is not the exception but the rule' (ibid., p. 248). The exception as the rule is made evident

---

[7]   Although Zohn translates *Ausnahmezustand* as 'state of emergency', I will use the term 'state of exception' as the more common German term for the state of emergency is *Ernstfall*. Furthermore, 'exception' is the more common translation used by students of both Benjamin and Carl Schmitt. Cf. the original in Benjamin, 1974, p. 697.

by the fact that 'there is no longer any one clear figure of the sacred man' because 'we are all virtually *homines sacri*' (Agamben, 1998, p. 115). The outcome of the ubiquity of the exception is that the death camp becomes the *nomos* of the modern. The reason for the paradigmatic status of the camp is because the Jew living under Nazism is

> the privileged referent of the new biopolitical sovereignty and is, as such, a flagrant case of a homo sacer in the sense of a life that may be killed but not sacrificed. His killing therefore constitutes ... neither capital punishment nor a sacrifice, but simply the actualisation of a mere 'capacity to be killed' inherent in the condition of the Jew as such. The truth – which is difficult for the victims to face, but which we must have the courage not to cover with sacrificial veils – is that the Jews were exterminated not in a mad and giant holocaust but exactly as Hitler had announced, 'as lice', which is to say, as bare life. The dimension in which the extermination took place is neither religion nor law, but biopolitics (ibid., p. 114).

This 'capacity to be killed' is the principle of formation of the modern political body of the west. 'Equality', claims Hobbes, arises only in one context: with the ability to 'do the greatest thing (namely kill)' (Hobbes, 1983, p. 124). This conception of equality is possible only when identity is predicated on natural life and the 'subject' is transformed into a 'citizen' whose birth (that is, bare natural life) 'becomes ... the immediate bearer of sovereignty' (Agamben, 1998, p. 128). The epitome of this movement is Nazism which 'made of natural life the exemplary place of the sovereign decision': National Socialist ideology is, as such, captured by the syntagm 'blood and soil' (*Blut und Boden*) (ibid., p. 129). Such a conflation of bare life and juridical rule is now a norm that is rarely revealed. For this reason, Agamben considers the recent fate of refugees, human guinea pigs (*Versuchspersonen*) and the comatose person as figures who reveal – in their status as persons on the threshold – that it is bare life which is the foundation of contemporary juridico-politics. The camp has become the model of contemporary existence.

Agamben's conclusions are shocking, but we should not be surprised. We see all around us a de-politicisation that is predicated on the importance of consumption, well-being, lifestyle and longevity to the extent that sovereignty's function – to make live and let die – is integrated in the processes and procedures of everyday life. The significance of modern biopolitics for the Christian church, of the statistical and functional reduction of existence to measure, is that the body of Christ is a biopolitical body, a body that is identifiable, tractable and quantifiable. Furthermore, the fact that this condition of the human is produced through the suspension of the law reminds us that biopolitics has a logic that is perversely parallel to, or is even a profane and illegitimate anticipation of, the *eschaton*. In contrast to the body of the church becoming transformed through redemption, however, our bodies are juridico-politically distorted so that they resemble 'the fellowship of buried lives (*symparanekromenoi*)' (Kierkegaard, 1971, Vol. 1, p. 450, n. 1). And it is not with the social model of the Trinity that we find the resources to question, undermine and transform this context of impotence. Nor is there the prospect of unearthing the source of a practical and political response to the ideology of global liberal governance in the tropes of relationality and equality. That is because the trinitarian theologians glibly evoke the images and desires of a liberal political settlement which is, *de facto* and *de jure*, dependent upon a refusal that there is more to life than its survival.

It is a curious fact, although one that in no way produces an incompatibility, that an age that has wagered its future on equality and freedom should have invested so heavily in the inscription of life at its material base. But with the recognition that at the very ground of modern politics lies an onto-zoological principle there must come a realisation that theology and politics have very different ends and purposes. The drive of humanistic politics has dislocated and finally refused the theological axiom that donation is at the foundation of living life itself and that being alive is a gift that proceeds towards a different end than the securing and management of species-life. This very point is reinforced in Hannah Arendt's reflection on modern politics as a rupture with its classical and Christian antecedents.

> Since we have made life our supreme and foremost concern, we have no room left for an activity based on contempt for one's own self-interest. Selflessness may still be a religious or a moral virtue; it can hardly be a political one (Arendt, 1961, pp. 52–53).

One can see, in Arendt's perceptive comment, that the political pursuit of theological ends is impossible, unless (as is generally the case) this quest is undertaken within the constraints of a deracinated, privatised and moralised theology, not least because of the incommensurability of the distinct practices and discourses that are pursued in biopolitics and within the purview of the church. Yet there is a family resemblance between the two. In the demands of liberal biopolitics, with its management of materiality and its shepherding of self-interest, and the Christian theological emphasis upon a life that is enabled by a grace that cannot be economised upon, there is a prominence afforded to the theme of ineluctable surrender. In both cases, the life that is lived is predicated on the nonautarchy of the human being, the giving up of what is promised in each discourse – life itself. But the kind of life that is demanded by the promptings of grace will never lead to the biopolitical dream of *pax et securitas*; it begets, on the contrary, the paradox that a compromise with life for the sake of life will end in death. The two discourses and practices cannot concede ground to each other or they lose their very identities. Yet what we observe at every turn is that theology has yielded its very ground and purpose to the biopolitics of the present through acquiescence or the nostalgic retrieval of a metaphysics that is anatopistic. The present requires more than the gentle 'critique' of political 'reality' or the passionate exposition of the aesthetic majesty of those magnificent artefacts in the theological museum.

In the face of this theological failure, what can be achieved is the construction of a point of departure from which we might begin again the (always provisional and preliminary) task of sketching a vision of another politics, an alternative account of being-with. Today, on the basis of the bankruptcy of a whole range of political theologies, the nature of our starting point is an honest and candid attempt to re-conceptualise the status and parameters of a temporal category that shatters the pretensions, and questions the purpose, of the modern endeavours to heal the theologico-political predicament. This is an undertaking in which eschatology impinges on the present in a mode that is far more substantial than the usual declarations of the absolute future as fulfilment. Only on such a basis might we begin a task that is more than wishful thinking. Only then might our hope be established upon a firm footing, rather than upon the ethereal idealism of a particular – if important – conception of God. That is the task we shall undertake in Chapter Eight. In the meantime, an interlude is fitting.

PART IV
END MATTERS:
OR THE MATTER OF THE END

Chapter Seven

Anatopism

It is worth reflecting for a few moments on where our analysis of the social model of the Trinity has led us. In doing so, it is important to account for those significant markers that designate the type and nature of the exploration we have engaged in. The substantive expositions and critical assessments of the threefold identity and character of the claims of the proponents of the social model – theological, cultural and political – were prefaced with a narrative which recounted the dislocation of the Christian doctrinal tradition. The value of this narrative investigation lies not only in its contextualising function but also in its exposition of what is at stake in the very composition of a constructive theological project. What I hope to have shown is the manner in which the social model of the Trinity is an attempted *relocation* of doctrine but one which, in almost every aspect of its claims and applicability, fails.

There is little point in reviewing the specific reasons for the failure of this particular relocation of doctrine (I hope by now that they are crystal clear), but it might be helpful, at this stage, to reflect upon some general themes and problems that account for what is a *necessary* failure of the model. These topics are by no means exhaustive but they also serve to create a bridge between the critical project undertaken hitherto and the challenge of providing a constructive theological politics in the next chapter.

Most crucially of all, these themes and problems are highlighted not in order to dismiss modern theology or its general attempt to engage with the contexts of its formulation. Rather, the rationale for underscoring these particular theological tendencies is that, by interrogating the points at which the social model of the Trinity breaks down, we may understand why the task of theology as a practical discipline must itself be pursued in a different key. This process requires that we understand the failures of our theological heritage *and* that we appreciate the basic and far-reaching pretensions of modern forms of life and governance within which Christians are immersed and, indeed, that Christians actually perform and renew, even if unwittingly. Only on this basis might we actually compose a theological politics that is sensitive both to the inadequacy of such an undertaking and, at the same time, to its vital role in re-imagining the status and meaning of the body of Christ.

1. The social model of the Trinity is an exemplary case of what Hans Urs von Balthasar has termed 'a Christianity which would know too much' (Balthasar, 1982, p. 185). When the doctrine of God is so fully disclosed to the point of its immanent bareness – a theological operation that is simply the requisition of the unqualified

revelation of God in God's own activity as Persons in history – the very status of God as divine is close to being irrevocably lost. The social modelists constantly and purposefully refuse the mystery of God (see Gunton, 1991, p. 31) in order to save doctrine from meaninglessness or because one fundamental root of western atheism, it is claimed, is the undue emphasis upon the unknowability of the divine. It is a task that is stimulated by a virtuous and honest concern. The proponents of the social model are looking to break beyond the confines of the apologetic corner. However, this task ends in the definitive failure and irrelevance of theology. Its modern status is only confirmed rather than confounded. The predisposition to the demands of relevance, and the incapacity to question the implications of these predispositions, establishes theology as *the* science of quiescence *par excellence*. The weight and importance of doctrine is predicated on its elasticity in the face of the onslaught of the modern tropes of 'the human', of 'history' and of 'immanence'. Theology then becomes, because of (rather than despite) this flexibility, beholden to those very tropes. Consequently, if theologians are to renew a commitment to doctrine, by which its role and purpose challenge our presuppositions and excite an alternative vision of practical and ecclesial possibilities, it is important to listen to a range of voices who question the incessant drift towards the total exposition of the meaning and status of doctrine, especially the doctrine of God.

The weight and importance of doctrine begins not with its transparency but its indispensable opacity. In this light, it is worth reflecting on Fergus Kerr's argument that it is erroneous and misguided to regard doctrine as having an 'explanatory force'. Correctly understood, doctrine 'does not *explain* but rather *protects* the mystery' of God's being (Kerr, 1999, p. 119). The force of unknowability and mystery resides, however, in more than the conviction that human beings are essentially ignorant of divine things. In addition, it actively engenders a dynamic refusal to chart a path through which the Trinity is rendered mundane and, thence, flattened out by the inducements of the pertinence and utilisation of doctrinal content. The protection of mystery which is proffered by doctrinal formulations demands, in contrast to the constant modern temptation to make visible and utile, a process of prayerful discernment and a labour of love and dedication. These commitments are, in themselves, the performative contradiction of those processes and dispositions from which an unproblematic and transparent interrogation of articles of faith begins. In this context, Rowan Williams' indication of the role of doctrine makes perfect sense: 'Good doctrine teaches silence, watchfulness, and the expectation of the Spirit's drastic appearance in judgement, recognition, conversion, for us and for the whole world' (Williams, 2000, p. 43). The active passivity of the expectant, the demanding quest of the spiritual exercise, may speak to a sometimes obscure but essential need to question the parameters of our certainty.

2. The social model remains caught in the same confined space to which theology was restricted with the arrival of the Copernican Revolutions of the early-modern period. The apologetic corner continues to sustain a theological venture that longs for relevance. The very conditions for the relevance of modern theology

determine that theology is anatopistic, that is to say, out of place, unless it accepts the principles of the modern as *the* principles of theological formation *per se*.

As we have already seen, notions of hierarchy, the substantial meaning of analogy and the bearing of particular species of theological metaphysics are fundamentally destabilised with the ontocosmological transformations of the sixteenth century. In the place of gradations of being and an integrated cosmos, the modern world occludes the merit of theological discourse within the principles and planes of immanence. As Jacob Taubes suggests, with regard to the spiritual practices of the modern period:

> If the cosmological order presupposes the division between heaven and earth, then a bold statement that heaven is in man's heart translates the cosmological into an *ordre du coeur*. But if the *ordre du coeur* has no correlative in the external order of the cosmos, then its 'logic' only proves that heaven is lost. In Copernican cosmology the basic category of medieval theology becomes meaningless: the principle of analogy between below and above, natural and supernatural, and there remains only a dialectic of identity between Creator and creation (pantheistic tradition) or a dialectic of their irreparable alienation (Luther, Pascal, Kierkegaard, Barth) (Taubes, 1954b, p. 115).

The translation of theological categories into an idiom of immanence, even if that idiom attests to the impossibility of the proximity of natural and supernatural, is a realignment that enables Søren Kierkegaard to suggest that 'the only consistent position outside Christianity is that of pantheism' (Kierkegaard, 1941, p. 203). And a distinctive characteristic of the historicisation of God within the work of many of the social modelists relies on the fusion of Christianity and a version of pantheism that secures a relationship of nature and grace in theological terms, with regard to the relationship between God and humanity and, finally, socio-politically. The reason this course is taken is because the metaphysics of grace and nature, once they have lost their natural, ontocosmological home, are flattened in accordance with a metaphysics of 'balance' or 'history'.

3. The social model of the Trinity is predicated on a historical principle that is largely alien to theological categories. For much of what constitutes antique and medieval Christianity, the significance of history is to be found in the fact that human, earthly existence is transient. Time's passing signifies the *cor inquietum*, the experience that discloses the truth that human hearts are restless until, according to Augustine, they find their peace in God (see Augustine, 1961, Bk. I.1, p. 21). History, as a modern dynamic principle of becoming and teleology, transfers the condition of fulfilment – or, to use Augustine's idiom, the peace for which the heart yearns – to the realm of the historical.

It is the Enlightenment which manufactures, in a style that is familiar to us, this historicisation of our satisfaction, of our redemption in a humanist key. And it is no surprise that in his developmental treatment of knowledge, G.E. Lessing, the father of the Enlightenment, evokes the *evangelium aeternum* (the 'eternal gospel') of Joachim of Fiore (Lessing, 1956, p. 96). This allusion to the Calabrian abbot is pursued in Lessing's delineation of 'education as revelation' (ibid., p. 83), an education that finds its fulfilment in 'the time of perfecting' – 'It will come' (ibid., p. 96). And it is no accident that both Joachim's reconception of history and Lessing's *The Education of the Human Race* are formative influences on Hegel's definitive historicisation of the eschatological imperative of Christianity (see Taubes, 1991, pp. 79–88).

It is predictable, in the light of this 'relocation' of grace within time, as a divinised philosophy of history, that Joachim's theological framework is utilised as a means of grounding, in time, the significance of the social model. Jürgen Moltmann, in particular, wishes to overcome monotheistic perversion of Christianity, through a return to Joachim's 'trinitarian view of history' (Moltmann, 1981, p. 203).[1] The importance of Joachim's turn to history is, for Moltmann, due to the former's unification of Augustine's eschatology – 'the kingdom of endless glory' (ibid., p. 204) – and the Cappadocian idea that the 'kingdom of God ... takes on particular forms in history corresponding to the unique nature of the Trinitarian Persons' (ibid.). What Moltmann fails to mention, however, is that in Joachim's schema we are beseeched to look towards the overcoming of Christ *historically* in terms of the goal of history itself, the Holy Spirit. Thus, the Trinity is actually relativised and, indeed, divided – historically. The age of the Father and the age of the Son are overtaken historically in a qualitatively new, transcending temporality of the Spirit. The Trinity is flattened and history is deified.[2]

4. The fact that so many of the advocates of the social model begin their critical and constructive analyses from a location made possible by Karl Barth is to be expected. Barth is the giant of twentieth-century theology and his work deserves to stand alongside that of the greats of the history of Christianity. However, in many respects, the very theoretical space that Barth clears, and from which his work begins, and to which it always returns, is fundamentally problematic: the dialectic, as a theology of negation and as a theology of reconciliation, is the sphere into which modern theology has been forcibly squeezed.

The theoretical aperture through which the extent of the problem is evident, and because of which its character can be gauged, is Barth's insistence that the

---

[1]   Indeed, in a letter to Karl Barth, the contents of which he celebrates in a comparative analysis of the work of Joachim and Thomas Aquinas, Moltmann claimed that 'Joachim is more alive today than Augustine' (Moltmann, 1991, p. 92). Moltmann is most certainly correct in his assertion, but that is why theology is thinned out in the context of modernity. See also Leonardo Boff's attempt, on the one hand, to distance himself from Joachim but, on the other, to historicise 'the particular presence' of each of the trinitarian Persons 'in particular events' (Boff, 1988, p. 228).

[2]   For a remarkable overview of Joachim's theology of history, see McGinn, 1985, pp. 161–203.

analogia entis is 'the invention of Antichrist' (Barth, 1975, p. xiii). As we have already seen (in the Introduction), this disavowal of an analogy of being actually indicates that there can be no return to (or restoration of) an ontocosmological theology in which concepts such as hierarchy, gradation and participation make perfect sense. In the process of this rejection of an ontocosmology, something that he never explicitly acknowledges, Barth is restricting all modern Christian theology to the determinate categories of the modern. That is not to say, as one would with Hegel's translation of the eschatological terms of the faith into a historical category, that Barth's theology is synthetic from beginning to end. The problem, however, is that Barth's theology *is* synthetic, *even if* only at the end.

Many of Barth's early critics were aware of this fact. In the midst of the early dialectic of creature and Creator lies the 'original identity between the divine and the human' (Taubes, 1954b, p. 237). In Barth's negative schema,

> There is no Fall from God in Adam and no judgement of death that does not have its origin at the point where man, already reconciled to God in Christ, has been promised life. ... Dialectics is a movement of the second moment against the first, the turning or reorientation of the first to the second, the victory of the second over the first (Barth, 1933, p. 143).

Despite the fact that Barth always keeps intact the divine Otherness, there is always a commitment to the priority of reconciliation, even if this is only and always the activity of God. This propensity for resolution becomes all the more apparent as Barth moves from a theology of crisis to the fulfilment of his life's work in a doctrine of reconciliation. That it why Barth is unambiguous in his insistence that it is only 'through redemption that man knows that he lives in separation' (Taubes, 1954b, p. 238). Now we must give Barth his due. His conception of reconciliation is most certainly different from Hegel's absolute synthesis (just as his understanding and use of negation is evidently distinct from Kierkegaard's absolute repudiation of synthesis). But, as Hans Urs von Balthasar suggests, the tone with which Barth considers the goal of redemption 'veritably thrums with a hymnic certainty of eventual victory' (Balthasar, 1992, p. 354).

The rationale for Barth's life-long movement between the poles of negation and affirmation is quite simple: with the loss of a cosmos, of the *analogia entis*, of natural theology, dialectic is the only principle that theology has at its disposal in the modern world. So, while he is most definitely distinct from the dialectics of Kierkegaard and Hegel, Barth still works within their temporal-historical framework. Jacob Taubes offers a mathematical simile that nicely illustrates Barth's place within the antithetical and synthetical extremities of dialectic.

> A plane passing through a cone parallel to the base always cuts a circle. If, however, the plane is tilted it cuts an ellipse, and, as the plane is increasingly tilted, one focus of the ellipse becomes more and more eccentric until the curve changes from an ellipse to a parabola. The basic dialectic between the human

and the divine remains the same in the antithetical and synthetical dialectic, and
it is only a question of how far the plane is tilted. In the synthetical dialectic
the plane is almost parallel to the base (the circle is the mathematical figure
of Hegel). In the antithetical dialectic the plane is tilted until it shifts from an
ellipse to a parabola (the open parabola is the mathematical figure of Karl Barth)
(Taubes, 1954a, p. 117).

The mathematical image that Taubes deploys is not to be taken as a fundamental
critique of Barth's application of a dialectic schema. To make such an assumption
is to miss the point. The illustration of the proximity of Barth's work to that of
Kierkegaard and Hegel is not intended to suggest that Barth is, for instance, a
secret Hegelian (although he may be haunted by Hegel's spectre). Instead, Taubes
recognises that Barth cannot escape this modern dialectical configuration because
he is a modern theologian, a theologian for whom the cosmos is no longer a home
and for whom analogy is ruined. Anatopistic theology *is* dialectical; it is required
to operate immanently, constrained by the flattening of the world. This fact
remains true even if, like the open parabola, Barth's dialectical theology exceeds
the parameters and boundaries of the synthetic 'theology' of Hegel.

To highlight the manner in which this is not exclusively a Barthian problem,
but a predicament that is inherent to any post-Copernican composition of
theology, consider Catherine Pickstock's efforts to restore a liturgical order. There
is no doubting the sophistication of her approach, with its abundant nuances
and creative re-readings of canonical and paracentral texts. Her exposition
and employment of the Roman rite certainly does prompt a reconception of
the doxologic status of creation and, moreover, raises important questions and
challenges in the face of the dominance of *mathesis* as a world historical task.
However, the very project of regenerating a litugical 'displacement' of the
discretely 'quarantined realms of earthly and transcendent' – a displacement
inaugurated with the Roman rite – requires a cosmology that is no longer extant
(Pickstock, 1998, p. 211). The 'displacement' she identifies within a Christian
liturgical performance requires a world in which the placement and interrelation
of nature and grace find a fitting context in which *exitus* and *reditus*, a movement
of grace within and beyond natural and ontological gradations, is both possible
and integral. But a more disturbing displacement occurred with the cosmological
revolutions, a dislocation that rendered the liturgy, theology and language
anatopistic and which leaves metaphysical and liturgical theologies of this kind
in search of a new home.

5. The proponents of the social model of the Trinity present us with a facile and
banal version of political theology, a version that has little political import and a
modest theological significance. A very good example is the definition of 'political
theology' offered by Dorothy Soelle. She presents a conception of political theology
that neatly captures the conceptions and purpose of the political use of theological
categories as they are presented through a trinitarian schema.

> Political theology is … a theological hermeneutic which, in distinction from
> a theology that interprets reality from an ontological or existentialist point of
> view, holds open a horizon of interpretation in which politics is understood as
> the comprehensive and decisive sphere in which Christian truth should become
> praxis (Soelle, 1974, p. 59).

In some respects, Soelle offers a vision of Christian practice that is unproblematic
and hopeful. It is a vision, however, that simultaneously presents the world as a
horizon of Christian potentiality and forgets the manner in which the political
realm itself is already a performative scene of the fusion of religious and secular
categories. And Soelle overlooks the fact, a fact that is just as important as the
interrelation of religious and secular categories, that the political sphere is also
the context for the critical attempt to control and separate the relationship between
theology and politics. A consideration of the origins of political theology may well
help to elucidate this point.

The term political theology, although as old as Stoicism, receives its definitive
examination in the sixth book of Augustine's *City of God* (Augustine, 1972).
There Augustine exposes and scrutinises the *Antiquitates rerum humanarum et
divinarum* (History of Human and Divine Concerns) of M. Terentius Varro, an
influential figure of Roman politics and letters in the first century BC and extolled
by Cicero as the most learned of men. Briefly put, Varro divides theology into
three kinds (*theologia tripertita*): mythical, natural or physical, and civil or
political (p. 236). The content of the first type of theology is myth or fable and is
most fully exposed in the arts of poetry and drama. Natural or physical theology,
much loved and respected by Varro, is the intellectual horizon of the philosophers.
The object of civil or political theology, the 'special relevance' of which 'is to
the city' (Varro in Augustine, 1972, p. 236), is the proper practice of civic piety
and for Varro this is more essential to the strength and continuity of the political
order than doctrine, myth or contemplation. For Augustine, the Christian bishop,
cultic worship of these 'gods of human institution' occasions a political spectacle
of pure performance which is, like mythical theology, 'fabulous' in character (see
Augustine, 1972, p. 237 & p. 243). Nonetheless, the performance of the *religio
licita* (legal religion) provides political coherence, a homogeneous identity and
the constant benefit of self-authentication. Political theology provides the means
for constructing the supreme form of 'imagined community' and for this reason
Augustine resolutely confronts the generative, theological principle of the *civitas
terrena* with what he contends is the revelation of the true *Imperium*, the *civitas dei*.
On the basis of revelation Augustine displays a preference for natural theology and
a distaste for the Roman reliance on a purely theatrical or liturgical understanding
of the religious life. Liturgy here means, of course, *leitos ergos*; public works that
one performs in relation to one's standing in the political community (so paying
for a few days of games in the Roman colosseum is as much a liturgical act as is

paying for forty bulls to be sacrificed to Venus).[3] Despite his criticisms of Varro, Augustine accepts that the relationship between the metaphysical ordering of life and political identity is one of interdependent reciprocation. It is this aspect of Varro's exposition of political theology in the *Antiquitates*, and Augustine's rejoinder, that remains valid for us today.

If the underlying authority of political governance is theological it is not because of the manner in which scripture or dogma is espoused or reconfigured – the opposite is largely true of the liberal tradition – but the ways in which the mundane political order is dependent on a (now recurrently unavowed) transcendent order of things. This means, ultimately, that in order to think of the contemporary manifestations of the correlation of politics and theology, one must consider the question of authority and power and *not* the status of church in relation to state or the significance of theological hermeneutics. What is at stake in contemporary manifestations of political theology is the significance of a particular species of secularisation which, in contradistinction to the common explication of this term in which politics is freed from the fetters of dogmatism and superstition, actively sacralises the *polis*.

The force and significance of 'political theology' is, then, 'nothing less than man becoming man in the face of God becoming man', a perversion of the incarnation that is replayed by so many Christian political theologies (Taubes, 1980, p. 574). In fact, it is this compromise of theology with the power of the state to define the role and scope of the theological task – of what it is that constitutes 'God becoming man' – that leads Jacob Taubes to call the (dominant) modern political theologies of Johann Baptist Metz and Jürgen Moltmann 'trivialized versions' of the genre (Taubes, 1987, p. 21). If we are to consider a less trivial conception of political theology, one that more faithfully represents the character and compass of its intentions and imperatives, we might look to the definition of Jan Assmann:

> Political theology concerns the reciprocal relations between political community and religious order, in short: between rule and salvation. It arises there, where this relation becomes a problem. It is *practiced* [*betrieben*] by those who take a certain position, and it is *described* [*beschrieben*] by those who are interested in the history of the problem, the positions taken and the solutions found (Assmann, 1992, p. 24).

There is, in Assmann's delineation, a helpful portrayal of the critical and practical elements of political theology. It is a definition that demonstrates the manner in

---

[3]   Hence Augustine's antipathy towards Seneca who, on the one hand, provided an unqualified rejection of political theology in his (no longer extant) work *Against Superstitions* but then, on the other, counselled the wise man to worship the gods in accordance with the customs of the city. According to Augustine, Seneca 'worshipped what he criticized, performed acts which he reprehended, venerated what he condemned'; see Augustine, 1972, p. 251. Seneca's case clarifies the fact that, for the Roman citizen, the *crimen laesae religionis* (impiety or lax devotion) was anything but an intellectual or theoretical matter and only came into force where there was evidence of practical disregard for the required observance of the cult.

which theology can be co-opted in service of a divine politics, no matter how 'secular' or immanent the purview of that politics. To persist with the attempt to construct a relevant or topical political theology is to forget or ignore that 'as to its essence, political theology is not a part of theology, but of political thought' (Peterson, 1983, p. 174). Accordingly, we must be candid and openly admit that a responsible theology can never be a political theology. The latter, as a world-historical political task, attempts to eliminate negativity and construct a flattened and narrowed politico-theological schema which co-opts the future as horizon and hope: this is theology as politics. Consequently, all that a political theology can offer the theologian is a demarcation of the ways in which, and the extent to which, a *theological politics* must circumvent, negate or radically redefine the *topos* of the modern appropriation of the divine.

All of these theses demonstrate the way in which a Christian world is lost for any theological enterprise. They also serve to highlight the challenges that face any constructive theological endeavour in our dislocated setting. They alert us to the fact that modern philosophy, politics and history have taken for themselves the space of significance, the topography, in which theology finds its appropriate co-ordinates. But this scenario remains hopeful. Theology cannot retrieve its world (although a theological reassessment of the post-Copernican status of the universe is a necessary and long-overdue task). Theology cannot find itself another world (although the significance of the theological re-imagination of the world should not be underestimated). What theology can accomplish is the work of reconstitution of the ecclesial body in which, and through which, a form of life might be composed which is *impolitical*, that is to say, a form of life that cannot be acquired and appropriated by the political because it is unsuitable for the ends of politics and will not be employed in the theologisation of political purposes. An impolitical theology is only fitting for the end of theology: the kingdom.

The mode of this form of life is eschatological, not least because there is a fissure that is situated at the heart of western modernity. Modernity itself attempts to paper over and appropriate the importance and substance of this fissure by means of a vulgar historicism and its utopian myths (so often shared by the social modelists). Yet, in the wake of the death of God, a crisis which founds the modern as such, there arises an ineluctable quandary for the modern, a predicament that can never be expurgated or refused. As Eric Santner reminds us, when immanence becomes the degree zero of modern possibility and aspiration – which it does with the murder of the divine – 'the entire problematic of transcendence actually exerts its force in a far more powerful way in the fabric of everyday life. What is *more* than life turns out to be … immanent to and constitutive of life itself' (Santner, 2001, p. 10). In the space exposed by this basic impasse it is possible to refigure Christian thought and practice but in a manner which is antithetical (and antipathetic) to the domesticated forms of eschatology that have dominated recent theological research.

Chapter Eight

End Matters: Towards a Theological Politics

When there's no future, how can there be sin?

Sex Pistols, 'God Save the Queen'

From at least the fifth century BC, in Sophocles' *Philoctetes* and the plays of Euripides, dramaturgy was transformed by the introduction of a peculiar theatrical device. Resolution of crisis and a closure of the oscillations of chance and necessity were effected by means of divine intervention. The god who gatecrashed the tragedy, however, was no ordinary deity: the divine descended from Olympus via 'machinery' – a crane. Thus the *deus ex machina* was born. The mechanical god represents, in one sense, the metaphysics of certitude and the security offered by the 'real' in the midst of the turmoil of the natural. Resolution is divinely performed in the very process of the lowering of the god and the Law is returned to the city. As a scene of a dramatic overcoming of the violence, folly and irrationality of the human or, more crucially, of the triumph of (transcendent) order over pure contingency, the god-machine offers an authoritative spectacle of the victory of the theological over the political.

In the context of recent liberal theology, eschatology as a principle of theological completion has replaced the mechanical deity as the mythologeme which carries with it the force to prevail over the machinations of the mundane. Despite the fact that the political and social visions of a variety of political theologians are parasitic upon the beliefs and desires of liberal politics, even the greatest imaginable future offered by liberal progress is inadequate to the eschatological consummation of humanity and nature. Monika Hellwig confirms this peculiarly modern status of eschatology in a fairly standard overview of the significance and content of eschatology as a theological category. Hellwig reminds us that 'In our times the focus of eschatology is on the realisation of the promised reign of God in all human experience and in all creation' (Hellwig, 1991, p. 350). Eschatology does not simply bring with it connotations of a radically distinct temporality. Rather, it suggests a fusing of historical purpose, futurity and the Kingdom of God in a manner that gestures towards a very real possibility of the transformation of the violence, inequality and suffering of the present. Eschatology has become 'the absolute future' as 'fulfilment' (ibid., p. 352).

Since the publication of Jürgen Moltmann's *Theology of Hope*, in 1964, it has become all too common for theologians to outline this kind of eschatological resolution, along with its attendant socio-political ramifications, as *the* indispensable feature of a Christian imagination, an imagination, that is, which surpasses the social and political pretensions – and failures – of mundane institutions and their conceptions of the world's nature. Theologians (rightly) wish to affirm the 'determinate negation' (Metz, 1970, p. 37) of socio-political conditions that such an eschatological imperative implies. However, the underlying logic of the function of the eschatological imperative is enacted in a formally identical manner to the *deus ex machina*. In response to the damage and disconnection of world history, all will be well, but in a future that is (always) yet to come. The arrival of this future marks a comprehensive triumph of a theological vision. The effect of such a thoroughgoing eschatological gamble is that the *status quo* is preserved (even if reformed), only to be undercut, transformed or revolutionised at the time of the end of things. But this largely unqualified deferral of the significance of eschatology is the very reason why Jacob Taubes was forced to conclude that recent Christian formulations of political theology are but 'trivialised' versions. They have little, if anything, to say in (and to) the present. In order to substantiate this claim, I will consider the contributions to a Christian eschatology made by Moltmann and some less prominent, but nonetheless important, theological voices. As a counterpoint to what I consider to be the failings of these versions of eschatology, I will present an alternative delineation of the significance of eschatology that begins from a very different conception of temporality.

The Remedy of Hope

There is no doubt that Richard Bauckham is right to maintain that *The Theology of Hope* 'changed the way Christian eschatology was understood over a wide spectrum of contemporary theology, quite apart from its mediated influence far beyond the bounds of academic theology' (Bauckham, 2001, p. xiii). Moltmann brought eschatology to the forefront of Christian consciousness in the midst of the increasingly chilly atmosphere of the Cold War and neatly theologised the shoots of hope that ran as a counter-current to the nihilistic forces that culminated in the arms race. As is well known, the philosophical catalyst for Moltmann's recovery of a distinctively Christian hope is the work of Ernst Bloch and, in particular, his three volume presentation of 'heroic optimism', to borrow Richard Roberts' phrase, *The Principle of Hope* (see Roberts, 1990, p. 28, n. 3). In his *magnum opus* Bloch outlines a dynamic conception of the Not-Yet-Being [*Noch-Nicht-Sein*] as a vision of a comprehensive blossoming of the possibilities of a hopeful life that is predicated on a metaphysics of openness to the future:

> Only with the farewell to the closed, static concept of being does the real dimension of hope open. Instead, the world is full of propensity towards something, and this intended something means fulfilment of the intending. It means a world which is more adequate for us, without degrading suffering, anxiety, self-alienation, nothingness (Bloch, 1986, Vol. 1, p. 18).

An important ingredient in the constitution of an open, expectant concept of being is, as for Moltmann, the element of faith in what is possible: 'Unbelief weakens the soul, which no longer finds any clues to the blossoming, the phototropism and the fullness elemental in itself' (Bloch, 2000, p. 167) Faith is a central ingredient in enabling the forward movement of an active anticipation that is more than simply the drive of a desire which is predicated on lack. Unrest is constitutive of this faith in hope, of a penetration of the promise into a stagnant present, a theme that is radically reconfigured in Moltmann's Christological schema.

> Faith, wherever it develops into hope, causes not rest but unrest, not patience but impatience. It does not calm the unquiet heart in man. Those who hope in Christ can no longer put up with reality as it is, but begin to suffer under it, to contradict it. Peace with God means conflict with the world, for the goal of the promised future stabs inexorably into the flesh of every unfulfilled present (Moltmann, 1967, p. 21).

With an admixture of faith and hope, and in the light of the community of love that is the Kingdom of God, Moltmann boldly attempts a complete realignment of theology along an eschatological trajectory. Thus his famous declaration which, *in nuce*, summarises the direction and intention of a theology of hope: 'From first to last, and not merely in the epilogue, Christianity is eschatology, is hope, forward looking and forward moving, and therefore also revolutionising and transforming the present' (ibid., p. 16).

The trajectory of this eschatological schema, even in its application to the challenges of the present, is always futural. Moltmann has fashioned a doctrine of eschatology – from *Theology of Hope* to *The Coming of God* – that is premised on 'the promissory history of God' (Moltmann, 1975, p. 8). But the promise and person of God is not to be found in the distant realm of the heavenly or in the deepest depths of our hearts; God is 'ahead of us in the horizons of the future opened up to us in his promises. ... the "future" must be considered as a mode of God's being' (Moltmann, 1970, p. 10). In *The Future of Creation*, Moltmann further develops this ontology of the future in terms of an *adventus* in which the future meets the world (Moltmann, 1979, pp. 29–31). The future 'is coming', a future which, he notifies us in his most recent treatise on eschatology, includes the consummation of history *in* history (Moltmann, 1996, p. 199).

This millennial strand in Moltmann's thought makes perfect sense because of the necessary participation of humanity in the fulfilment that is the New Creation. Moltmann's Hegelianism remains so strong at this point that he thinks of the eschatological 'rupture' as (at the very least) a consummation and completion, that is to say, a futural realisation of the coming of God, as an impending historical fact. Yet it is clear that Moltmann's eschatology is a qualified or modified Hegelianism. The conception of temporality which Moltmann outlines is rhythmic (ibid., p. 138). It is a temporality that refuses the overwrought linear trajectory of modern historical time; rather than being directed towards a specific goal or target, history shudders in the wake of its future. 'In the expectation, time vibrates and dances' (ibid., p. 138). The end or the future of eschatology pulsates into the present time, 'qualifying' past and future in the experience of the now.

Considering the Future

As a mode of eschatological thinking, Moltmann's three-decades-long construction of a conception of Christian temporality is unsurpassed. Not only has his *opus* provoked a wide-ranging reconception of the status of Christian eschatology, it has stimulated a thoroughgoing analysis of the purpose and significance of theology more generally, especially in relation to its present contexts. It is not, however, without its flaws. According to Miroslav Volf, because Moltmann's project remains a distinctly modern undertaking, it shares many of the problems and predicaments of the modern concept of history and its political utilisation. This is especially true of Moltmann's 'millenarian eschatology' in which the consummation of historical time is effected historically. This approach to fulfilment can, for Volf, easily and unavoidably slip into an historical millenarianism that constitutes little more than a unified and unidirectional temporality, a chronology which effectively totalises identities and repudiates diverse historical experiences (Volf, 1999, p. 234). Moltmann unwittingly performs the kind of conceptual exclusion that is antithetical to the inclusive nature of his theological intentions. But there is another fundamental problem with the orientation of this eschatological endeavour. The very character of a future-oriented utopia, in practical terms and as a necessity, also tends to leave the present relatively untouched. The experience of the 'to come' is beautifully and powerfully imagined but the status and nature of the actual involvement of Christian communities in this millennium is conspicuously unclear. Hence the problem identified by Adrian Cunningham: that there is little content and substance, little in the way of existing and impending activity, with which to dynamically disrupt the *status quo*.

> There is ... in Moltmann a certain fudging of the terms 'fulfilment' and 'participation' (a pervasive feature of the 1960s ...), human participation tending to be seen as acquiescence in the right sort of future rather than an active achievement of it (Cunningham, 1970, p. 259).

The quotidian is reduced to a foretaste or substandard type of existence that takes its measure from the promise that will come. The horizon of fulfilment is always there – it *is* to come – and we utilise a principle of a 'Yes to life' (Moltmann, 1996, p. 234) in the face of the torpid politics of power. Until the realisation of the rule of God, we have but a horizon, a hope which, *de facto*, instils compliance; the impact of the future on the present is always tangential, always contestable, always indeterminate, always (as Volf demonstrates) guesswork.

Moltmann remains a modern utopian, despite the many nuances that characterise his thought and the many criticisms of modern utopian and historicist tendencies that scatter his writings. This is particularly evident in his penchant for completions of projects that are temporally drawn into, and along by, the slipstream of the historical consummation of the end. In this light, Volf's production of a trio of alternative theses concerning the status and character of eschatology deserves our attention, not least because they derive from a direct criticism of this modernist Moltmann.

Volf's challenge to Moltmann's millennial imperative is developed in accord with his desire to embrace the pluralities of the present and to disclaim any attempt towards the unification of cultural and historical difference in the present on the basis of a unified eschatological *telos*. He exposes three areas where an essential reconfiguration of the quality and bearing of eschatology is required. In the first of these substitutional proposals, Volf directly counters any kind of historical eschatology, even of the millennial kind: 'Christian eschatology should give up the notion that the goal of history lies in history' (Volf, 1999, p. 257). The imposition of the singularity of the eschatological event, when brought to bear on historical time, results in a totalising compression of 'multiple histories' and is inconsistent with the life of God as Trinity in history. In the place of this deficient historicising of the *eschaton*, Volf recommends that we think more in the direction of the 'eternal home of histories' (ibid.). In addition, 'Christian eschatology should give up the notion that the problem of history can be resolved by a process of "completion"' (ibid.). The concept of completion is inadequate to the thought of eschatology because history not only progresses but spoils and devastates as it drives along its inexorable trail. History is the creator of wreckage (and here Volf refers to Walter Benjamin's 'Theses on the Concept of History') that is deposited rather than perfected.[1] A univocal conception of history elides the multiple sufferings and subjections that are inherent in the dynamic historical process. Consequently, this belief in the 'completion of history' should be supplanted, Volf tells us, by a more adequate term, 'redemption of histories' (ibid).

Finally, Volf is distinctly critical of the constant referral to the future as the generative principle of the present. 'Christian eschatology should,' he argues, 'leave attempts to "narrate the future in the present" or "think the unity of the past from the perspective of the future" to futurologists or philosophers' (ibid.). The

---

[1]   Unfortunately, Volf offers a distinctly myopic reading of Benjamin's text. The wreckage that is so vividly presented in Thesis IX must be read in the light of Thesis II where Benjamin offers an analysis of envy as a political affect. Envy arises in the wake of histories which did not occur, histories that demand redemption in the present. Thus, it is not simply 'multiple histories' that are to be redeemed in messianic time but those possibilities that were passed over and which make history possible in the first place. A summary of Benjamin's position in the 'Theses' is provided in his notes on Baudelaire where he argues: 'The further the mind goes back into the past, the more the mass of that increases which has not yet become history at all' (Benjamin, 1977a, p. 1175).

speculation, or 'guesswork', that is required to identify the character of the future prevents a full and active participation in the creation of that future and contributes to the formation of a Christian who is quiescent, an onlooker. As a result, Volf suggests that 'eschatology should take on the prophetic task of explicating the hope for the ultimate redemption and reading and changing the present in the light of that hope' (ibid.). The illumination and elucidation of that which is in store for a world constituted by diverse (and often dissimilar) histories is – ultimately – the task laid at the feet of the eschatological theologian. The undertaking that we are invited to pursue is one in which Christian eschatology demands a prophetic and not a predictive disposition. And if we look to an attempt by Volf to define and delineate the character of this kind of eschatology, we can see more clearly how this 'prophetic task' impinges on Christian conduct in the present.

Critique of the Present

In a piece in which he reflects upon 'the social dimension of the eschatological transition' (Volf, 2000a), Volf portrays the problem and challenge of eschatology in uncompromisingly vatic terms. 'Sometime between a shadowy history and eternity bathed in light,' he declares, 'somewhere between this world and the coming world of perfect love, a transformation of persons and their complex relationships needs to take place' (ibid., pp. 91–92). It is this need that leads Volf to consider the nature of transformation and the role of an eschatological vision of hope in the process of this profound redemption of histories.

In the first place, the course of transformation has to be imagined as a two-fold event. Not only is the 'eschatological transition' to be perceived as 'a divine act towards human beings'; it is also to be imagined as a thoroughly '*social event between human beings*, more precisely, a divine act towards human beings which is also a social event between them' (ibid., p. 93, Volf's emphasis). The provision of this social dimension of eschatology in the conception of an ultimate transformation is reflected in the 'anthropological' dimension of the coming of the eternal home of diverse histories. As far as Volf is concerned, because identity 'is constructed in a social process,' then it is altogether clear that 'one should expect that the transition to a world of love will not circumvent a social process' (ibid., p. 99). That much is clear, but when it comes to the contemporary social processes and a Christian reflection on their status and nature, Volf intuits an influence and bearing of the ultimate figure of redemption upon our present, a forceful impression which positively informs the prophetic task.

> The final reconciliation is the eschatological side of the vision of the social transformation contained in the movement of the Triune God towards sinful humanity to take them up into the circle of divine communal love. The notion of the final reconciliation strengthens that vision and thus shapes social practices (ibid., p. 108).

There is a confidence in Volf's claim that the image of the final reconciliation will, indeed does, impinge upon Christian practice in social contexts and offers a prophetic horizon – a kind of theological *mise en scène* – in the light of which this practice makes sense. But how is it that the eschatological vision might affect or mould the social practice of Christians? What does it mean to say that a vision of an eschatological kind might shape practice? Are we once again in the realms of an insipid philosophical idealism?

Thankfully, Volf offers many clues as to the socio-political applicability of a Christian vocation in the wider world in that his analyses of justice and peace are predicated on a Christian utopianism. In a recent article, Volf suggests that the Christian tradition, in its declaration of the God of indiscriminate love and the narrative of the cross, offers the basis for the cultivation of a particular kind of Christian activism: 'Nurture people in the tradition and educate them about it, and if you get militants, they will be militants for peace' (Volf, 2000b, p. 866). The kind of militancy that Volf is looking to is one that eschews 'cheap reconciliation' and offers four visions and practices of justice. First, Volf outlines the 'primacy of the will to embrace the other' as an obligation to radically modify our disposition towards others. Consequently, Christians will give themselves 'prior to any judgement about others, except that of identifying them in their humanity' (ibid., p. 872). Second, attending to justice is a precondition of actual embrace. There is no room in this vision for a forgetfulness in which the struggle for freedom is lost in the midst of the embrace (ibid., p. 873). Third, and concomitant, the will to embrace actively pursues a framework for the search for justice (ibid.). And finally, the embrace acts as the horizon of the struggle for justice, that is to say, a horizon that is a teleology which culminates in the embrace.

As a framework for the pursuit of justice, the drive towards the event of the just and transformative embrace seems at first glance to be a commendable model. However, in the subtitle to his piece, Volf claims that this reflection is a 'theological contribution to a more peaceful social environment'. But how is this vision *different* from a humanistic vision of justice that seeks to avoid easy compromises and is committed to the difficult challenge of building a lasting peace predicated on justice? In short, it is not. And this depressing truth highlights how for Volf, as for Moltmann, the 'eschatological imperative' is *in practice* definitively petrified. The principles upon which a more just social context is built depend more on the categories of liberal humanism, juridicalism and politics than it does on the messianic intention of the church. In presenting a possible Christian contribution to peaceable living in the idiom of 'values' or 'aspirations', rather than on its own terms, Volf has surrendered the social and physical bodies of church and individual to the State and to the horizons of possibility that are essential to the continued renewal of forms of liberal governance, despite the continued injustice and violence carried out in the name of the latter. Indeed, this is a common theological move, where a specifically Christian horizon – and if this is not eschatological it amounts to nothing – is moralised and, as a consequence, compressed and constricted until it becomes a suitable Christian complement to a plane of immanence (see, for example, Webster, 2000, p. 27). What this amounts to is an acceptance of the liberal 'thinning out' of the content of tradition so that religious life and practice become acceptable, even edifying, to a liberal audience. While this move may well make Christianity palatable to its cultured despisers, it also transforms the faith in a most remarkable manner. Eschatology is defaced as it is reduced to a theological Jack-in-the-Box that really has no discernible impact on the practice of the present. The *status quo* is unchanged and eschatology only remains significant to the extent that it highlights the fragility of the human in the face of the unknown. In Kant's terms, the end of all time 'is frighteningly sublime partly because it is obscure, for the imagination works harder in darkness than it does in bright light' (Kant, 1995, p. 195). But its force and substance are abandoned in the present.

Obviously, an example to support this claim would be helpful and, in order to illustrate the importance of this accommodation with the modern, let us consider those ways in which the contemporary eschatologists might differ from the aspirations of that *doyen* of atheistic humanists, the Marquis de Condorcet. In his most famous work, the *Esquisse d'un tableau historique des progress de l'esprit humain,* first published in 1794, Condorcet provides an outstanding example of the pretensions of modern Man and the hopes upon which the self-sovereign subject of modernity places his confidence in the future.

> Our aspirations for the future condition of the human species can be summarised in three concerns: the abolition of inequality between nations; the progress of equality within each nation; the true perfection of mankind (Condorcet, 1966, p. 253).

The only manner in which Moltmann, Volf and any number of theologians might part from Condorcet is with the definition of the 'true' perfection of the species. Yet, even here, the vision of a hopeful future in which inequality, suffering and poverty would be overcome is shared by all, secular and Christian alike. Where the theologians do diverge from Condorcet's techno-utopian vision is with the eschatological promise of absolute triumph. The theologians have in their possession a wholly transcendent temporality which, although sadly lacking the melodrama of the *deus ex machina,* they will place on the worldly table at the very last moment (whenever it comes) and clear up. Until then, when the moment of the *echaton* brings an end to the norm of *chronos,* the world is very much the locale of those who espouse immanent necessity and the world is devoid of all but hope. And, yet, the high priesthood of progressive scientific intervention into life – the descendents of Condorcet's vision – are practising the promise of fulfilment in direct opposition to the theological vision of consummation. The river out of Eden (Genesis 2:10) is now dammed and utilised by instrumental reason. It carries within it a message 'that is an altogether more worthy testament to our life explosion than anything in Genesis' (Dawkins, 1995, p. 187). Whether we like it or not, the proponents of modern scientific progress have, in the wake of Enlightenment and its opposition to a Christian metaphysics, achieved the coincidence of participation and fulfilment, a conjunction that is but the hope of those who hope. The importance of such a modern transformation of the locale of discourses of accomplishment and realisation rests in the insight that the judgements concerning who is to live and who is to die are not deferred until the arrival of the end of all things – it is a verdict pronounced in this world rather than the next.[2]

The distressing status of theological discourse and practice – its lack of significance or force in the face of the world in which Christians are pilgrims – is further demonstrated in an example that discloses the full significance of the theological challenges at hand. In his review of Daniel Bell's critical engagement with liberation theology in a post-Marxist context (see Bell, 2001), Volf provides a number of important challenges concerning the relationship between theology and politics. One such challenge arises in the context of Bell's passionate and caustic questioning of the perverse logic of capitalism. In response, Volf cautiously admonishes his junior colleague and implies that, while there are evidently grave abuses within the capitalist arena, one might perceive certain goods within liberal, capitalist states. But in a moment of concession Volf does grant that in the hour of capitalism's triumph it requires 'a critique' (Volf, 2003, p. 265).

It is exactly this kind of disposition that is at the heart of capitalism's ability to renew itself in a process of constant metamorphosis. Volf seems to understand capitalism as a machine that misfires in its abuses although, ultimately, it is a machine that can be tamed or humanised through the strategic application of a theological critique. He is wrong. Capital is a machine which, and even Marx could only grasp this point inadequately, feeds not only on its misfiring but on the work of criticism that follows each misfire. One only has to think of the importance of the environmental critique of capital that began to influence and inform national and international policy strategies in the late 1970s and 1980s. It is not that this critical engagement 'humanised' the processes and procedures of capitalism – although this did occur as a by-product. Capital renewed itself on the very grounds opened up by the critical intervention itself. Consequently, if one walks into any supermarket in the western world, one can purchase both the ideologically sound, fair-trade, organic bananas harvested on a co-operative plantation in the Windward Isles *and* the ideologically challenging bananas from a major transnational corporation that offers no more than starvation wages to plantation workers, removes their contracts on the basis of a whim and is proud that it offers little in the way of social provision for its employees. Once, all we could 'choose' was the latter but the critique of capital reproduced capital; and the profit margins on our middle-class fruits and vegetables are much, much more lucrative than those procured through the sale of the intensively farmed varieties. (In any case, 'caring capitalism' is now more concerned with brand loyalty and 'product intimacy' than it is with profit margins because the former drives the

---

[2]   For a sustained analysis of these judgements, see Fletcher, 2004b.

latter.) The same logic applies to those wonderful recent inventions of capital: corporate social responsibility, ethical investments, and any number of morally positive initiatives which serve to reterritorialise capital. The critical reformation of capital is a capitalist precept.

The problem with so many recent assessments of the relationship between eschatology and the present, a problem that we must face with honesty, is that theology is unveiled as impotent. It is a discipline that is fundamentally eviscerated, irrelevant even as it searches for relevance. Hope is inadequate in the context of global liberal governance, a point that is hauntingly whispered by Franz Kafka in his observation that 'There is a goal, but no way; what we call a way is hesitation' (Kafka, 1954, p. 40). Hope is a performance of this hesitation; theology has relinquished its commitment to participating in the goal. All that remains is an ever-distant, indistinct point that can only be adequately characterised in terms of its utter division from our time and our world. Despite the fact that eschatology is an increasingly popular and important theological topic, its very status as an ultimate and unsurpassed future has resulted in the translation of its transformative force into nothing but a promissory trope. It is as if theology has thinned itself out historically as a discourse of expectation in which the nostalgia for the future tears the present moment from its fulfilment. In large part, this state of affairs has arisen because theology does not recognise the logics of the world in which we live, a world in which we are inclined to put up with anything while finding everything intolerable, a world that feeds upon the meagre fare of theological criticism.

Capitalism as Religion

That which seems a sensible and appropriate response to capital is the very strategy that fosters and sustains the capitalist project. Moreover, the de-eschatologisation of theology, a process that occurs when the significance and status of eschatology is located in almost every respect in the unqualified future, is mirrored by a capitalist acquisition of eschatology, a process which hollows out eschatology in its reconfiguration as pure imminence. Management scientists and analysts are more than happy to co-opt and refigure the status of eschatology in order to put its very incommensurability with the 'profane' to work in the service of more open and creative forms of capitalism, a task that attempts to re-enchant the world. This undertaking is one that projects a vision of hope into the present with such confidence that it puts our theologians to shame. For example, consumer research has recently perceived that its own purpose and methodologies are in crisis and it requires new formulations and concepts in order to revitalise its purpose and functions. By using the work of Moltmann, Metz, Tillich, Gutierrez, Bloch and others, Helen Woodruffe outlines how the principles of consumption and their theorisation might be reconstituted within a framework that improves upon the established and well-worn empirical methodologies. The model chosen is rooted in eschatology as 'the epiphany of the eternal present' (Woodruffe, 1997,

p. 617), a model that pursues a pluralistic and emancipatory relationship between marketing research and the lives of consumers. For this reason, marketing, indeed capital itself, must realise that we live in a kairological context: 'an old age is dying and a new one is waiting to be born' (ibid., p. 674). In contrast to the eschatological fudging of the theologians, the champions of capital wish to instantiate eschatology as a principle of renewal and remuneration, as a bridging of participation and fulfilment in the performance of consumption. Eschatology offers renewal because it is fundamental to capital that it inhabits the future – the promissory –rather than the present. In the present desire is unfulfilled, deferred until that moment in the future when the promise might be realised. And, of course, capitalism's fecundity arises from the fact that the promise is *never* fulfilled. Its renewal and reproducibility are predicated on the deferral of satiety into a future of possibility. The end will (never) come (see Brown et al., 1996). The eschatology of our theologians and the eschatology of capital are a mirror image of each other, except for the important fact that the arborescent structure of debt and command are ubiquitous in capitalism and remind us that we inhabit not the Kingdom of God but these immanent networks of economic and desiring flows.

If this requisition of eschatology were no more than a playful experiment in thought, it would be appropriate to respond with scorn or laughter. But the disclosure in management theory of a religiosity at the heart of capital has to be taken with utmost seriousness. Capital is a religion; it is a form of life that defiantly engulfs the futures and horizons of Christianity to the extent that theologians accept it as a (permanent) norm that will only be surpassed in the (unforeseeable) future. What is more, capitalism does not loudly proclaim its future as finality – as another form of the *deus ex machina* – but as promise. And despite the fact that all consumers understand that the promise will never be satisfied, we require, need and desire the promise. In the process of this dual logic of the chimera and the guarantee, the tasks of which are never complete, capitalism marks the point at which a Christian imaginary becomes dependent on the logic of an unmatchable but deficient form of redemption.

In the context of the analysis of western modernity and the emergence of a distinctly capitalistic socio-cultural system, this claim seems at first glance to be more than extravagant. We are all aware that, in Max Weber's classic study of the correlation of Protestant Christianity and the spirit of capitalism, the two fundamental elements of his survey come together in a historically complex, nondeterministic manner. The relationship between Christianity and capitalism is, as it were, that of an elective affinity. And this reading of a historical bond between Protestantism and capital has gained canonical status to the extent that even the philosopher of eschatological revolution, Ernst Bloch, could claim that the Reformation 'introduced elements of a new "religion": that of capitalism as religion and the Church of Mammon' (Bloch, 1962, p. 143). Bloch posits, in his Weberian assessment of the background and significance of the Radical Reformation, a loss of true and authentic Christianity in the development of capitalism. Capitalism triumphed as true Christianity waned. But in a remarkable fragment, written in

1922 although unpublished in his lifetime, Walter Benjamin radicalises this thesis when he charts the character of capitalism as *the* modern religion *par excellence*. Benjamin turns the assessment of the historical and sociological correlation of capitalism and Christianity undertaken by Weber and Bloch into a relationship of identity: 'The Christianity of the Reformation period did not favour the growth of capitalism; instead it transformed itself into capitalism' (Benjamin, 1996, p. 290). Capitalism is the religion of the modern context and it 'serves essentially to allay the same anxieties, torment, and disturbances to which the so–called religions offered answers' (ibid., p. 288). The religion of capitalism is one that organises, systematises and enchants the guilt-and-debt nexus of life and the lives of those who live within this matrix of reward and punishment.

There are, according to Benjamin's analysis, three distinctive characteristics intrinsic to this religiosity that 'may be discerned in capitalism': the purely cultic nature of this religion, the permanence of this cult, and the pervasive nature of guilt engendered by the purely cultic form of capital. Capitalism as pure cult implies that 'things only have a meaning in their relationship to the cult; capitalism has no specific dogma, no theology'. In other words, capitalism is *the* religion devoid of any content; it is the pure manifestation of a religion that fits the imploded space of the apologetic corner, of a Christianity which has relinquished the world. Moreover, in relation to Benjamin's second point, capitalism 'is the celebration of a cult *sans trêve et sans merci* [without rest or mercy]'.[3] Capitalism is a religion of unremitting demand, of permanent duration, and within its count and measure there are no 'weekdays', only the incessant feast day or holiday where the consecration of the profane (and thus the profanation of the consecrated) – that is to say, the eschatological completion *in toto* – is realised in the divine venture of capital (see Agamben, 2005a, p. 102). It is this insubstantial yet permanent nature of capital, its status as unqualified system, which yields both its success and its consequence – guilt. This third distinguishing mark of capitalism as religion has, in its wake, even engulfed God:

> A vast sense of guilt that is unable to find relief seizes on the cult, not to atone for this guilt but to make it universal, to hammer it into the conscious mind, so as once and for all to include God in the system of guilt and thereby awaken in Him an interest in the process of atonement. This atonement cannot then be expected from the cult itself, or from the reformation of this religion (which would need to be able to have recourse to some stable element in it), or even from the complete renouncement of this religion (Benjamin, 1996, p. 288–289).

---

[3]   There is an important philological issue here, first raised by Uwe Steiner (1998, p. 157, n. 25). The phrase is given, in both the *Gesammelte Schriften* and the English translation, as *sans rêve et sans merci*, without dream or mercy, but this makes little sense. The phrase *sans trêve et sans merci* is taken from Baudelaire's poem, 'Le Crépuscule du soir', the translation of which, as Samuel Weber informs us, was finally completed by Benjamin in the same year as he wrote 'Capitalism as Religion'. See Weber, 2005, p. 144, n. 4.

There are a number of remarkable points in this passage. Capitalism is a systemic religion of deficit in which means and ends converge. It is not as if this religion has an end – an atonement – for even the divine is implicated in its restrictive benevolence or *Schuld* – guilt and debt. God is no longer transcendent, nor the possible point of reference for an authentic form of existence; God is inscribed and incarcerated within the immanent demands of a structure that claims his compensation. In Werner Hamacher's terms, the system of this capitalistic religion is not simply pantheistic, a full realisation of Spinoza's conjunction of nature and divinity. It is, rather, an intensification of the logic of immanence 'to the exact point' that the system is 'schizo-theistic: the world and every human in it *is* God in His despair' (Hamacher, 2002, p. 96). God, like every unit or individual, is guilty and indebted to the immanent logic of capital. 'God's transcendence is at an end. But he is not dead; he has been incorporated into human existence' (Benjamin, 1996, p. 289). What Benjamin sketches, then, is a religion in which measure is not something that stands to be so thoroughly comprehended or grasped but is an excessiveness in which the human individual is located (in fact, dis-located) in the context of the 'absolute loneliness of his trajectory'.

As a form of life that actively expropriates life in the midst of (irredeemable) guilt, capital depotentiates individuals, communities and every mediating institution to the extent that the only future that can be imagined besides the imperatives of capital is the daydream, an immanent form of promissory hope in the midst of a despair which capital happens to produce. And we might even suggest that the positioning of eschatology as absolute future is in effect another of those daydreams that enables capital to run its course – except, that is, for those occasions when an eschatological perspective provides the grounds for a critique that serves to humanise and renew its processes and procedures. In this context, the challenge for theology is quite simple. How is it that a different form of life might be possible, a form of life that resists co-option and appropriation? To answer this question requires an honest assessment of those strategies that will necessarily fail. Those approaches that we have considered thus far – the social model of the Trinity and an eschatology predicated on hope – fail because they sadly reproduce and sanction a liberal-capitalist hegemony when they concede, in every way, the topography of this world to the myths and narratives of immanent salvation. They constitute no more than attempts to reform the Reformation, to 'humanise' guilt and its incessant logic. The eschatological narrative of an always future transformation only serves to intensify and elevate the logic of guilt that is the present. The form of this alternative is just as 'secret' as the deity of capital (Benjamin, 1996, p. 289). Its hiddenness is its key; its enigma is beyond representation even if, and when, it is a historical event. [4]

---

[4]   It is also worth considering Kojin Karatani's contention that 'It is absolutely impossible to control capitalism from the metalevel, because capitalism itself is deconstructive'. See Karatani, 1995, p. 71.

The purely cultic nature of capitalism, its permanence, and its pervasive guilt all find their vitality in the bosom of this secrecy. For this reason dogma cannot be allied to the capitalistic project. As we saw in the last chapter, dogma as such has no explanatory power, a fact that ensures a relationship of separation between divine and mundane orders. Just as in a post-Copernican universe, where there is no separation between the heavens and the earth and so no analogy is possible between above and below, so in capitalism a new relationship between the sacred and profane is revealed. 'In its most extreme form,' suggests Giorgio Agamben, 'capitalist religion realises separation as pure form, without separating anything anymore' (Agamben, 2005, p. 102). Dogma is by definition anatopistic within a capitalistic context (and so, in our time, within the entire world) and finds itself redundant not because of its illiberal tone or its antiquated language but because its inner principle no longer makes sense where the deity of *Schuld* is *absolutely* profane.

If then we are to embark upon another course, we must start with the recognition that all the platitudes of Christian theology, especially those assertions of faith in the effects of an atonement that are to come, have been grafted onto the logic of *Schuld* which dominates global liberal governance as a religious precept. That is why it is not simply the organisation of mundane affairs that is captured in the nexus of guilt and debt. A point has been reached 'where Christianity's history is essentially that of a parasite – that is to say, of capitalism' (Benjamin, 1996, p. 289). From this perspective, the 'critique' of capital is as desperate and as misleading a theological task as the illusion of founding an ecclesial possibility on the basis of the historical future, in a time and space that is free of guilt. Christianity, in the midst of its occupation by capitalism or, which is the same thing, its anti-eschatological accommodation with the ascendancy of guilt, is dependent on the horizons of possibility and significance that are (as with the constant recourse to the future) only tangible in their promised effects. As a counterpoint to this disastrous theological position, we must begin the activity of identifying and reconstructing a genuinely Christian form of temporal existence, an undertaking which begins from the point at which the God of capital is not only identified but from which the practice of giftedness and kenosis is intensified within the very heart of the dream-world of the system.

This liberal-capitalist system thrives on its dreaminess, its promissory character, and it flourishes when it is confronted with its failures. In part, that is because of the 'secrecy' of its deity that Benjamin isolates. The form and character of liberal governance is always immature and must remain so if it is to thrive. In order to respond to our present in a manner that will neither serve to revitalise capitalism by critique nor seek to escape the accounting of guilt by fleeing into history to come, it is imperative that we conceive of an alternative task at the point at which capitalism exhausts itself in the perfection of its intensity. In concrete terms, this requires the theologian to resist the obvious temptation of playing the trump card, the *deus ex machina*. In terms of the labour of thought, this task entails practical concepts and possibilities that relinquish the desire that capital be brought to account. In short, we must attempt to provide an alternative, if provisional and preliminary, *topos* to the surreptitious religion which dominates the context of late-modernity. Such a *topos* must nevertheless be sought at the very centre of our times. It can only be located within the midst of the barbarism of the capitalist machine and in the bounds of its redemption of (commodity) value.

A Reconception of Time

A good place to begin the exploration of a theoretical *topos* of this kind is with conceptions of time, not least because temporality is so integral to notions of hope, expectation, fulfilment and eschatology. But as soon as we begin to analyse the status of time, we encounter a peculiarly modern problem. The foundations of temporal experience, as opposed to those of historical knowledge and purpose, have become atrophied in the modern period. It fell to Friedrich Nietzsche to illustrate, with his familiar mixture of perspicacious insight and uninhibited polemic, that when history gains a degree of excess in bestowing upon life its meaning and substance 'life crumbles and degenerates' (Nietzsche, 1983, p. 67). History settles accounts with life. In a manner analogous to capitalism, it offers a philistine constitution of the complexity of human experience in accordance with the demands of a security – in this case as knowledge or pure science – for the future.[5] The only unambiguous knowledge of the application of norms which has authority for human action and purpose is the knowledge of actions and purposes that have taken place in the past. The delineation of the future is not to be based on tradition, eternal ideas or revelation but upon human intervention as a dynamic process which offers the principal source and resource for the transformation of the time that is always upon us. And, moreover, it is always possible that the singularity of an event is interminably malleable according to its variable significance in the dynamic progress of history *per se* (see Koselleck, 1985, p. 250). This is as true for Romantic and revolutionary politics as it is for consequentialist ethics and the now ubiquitous discourse of risk assessment.

In contrast to the supremacy of historical truth, a temporality of human existence is spent. That is why our age is obsessed with the retrieval of such a time. The quest for a time that is neither crudely purposeful nor historically determined – along with the haunting desire for all the attendant attributes of authenticity and destiny – is a pervasive feature of popular cultural discourses of the present as well as the horizon of those over-familiar tag-lines associated with the cosmetic arts. And the more that time is lost, the more life becomes meaningless and inscrutable.

---

[5]   A point that finds its mirror image in Albert Schweitzer's dismissive understanding of the psycho-political purpose of an anticipation of the end, a perspective that might applied with pertinence to our eschatological theologians: '"Assurance of salvation" in a time of eschatological expectation demanded some kind of security for the future of which the earnest could be possessed in the present.' See Schweitzer, 1954, p. 376.

In this context, is it any surprise that those with the requisite means yield to the necessity of therapeutic time or personal time, to a time that is spatially secured from the processes that guarantee its demise? But this bourgeois time is necessarily myopic; it is a quintessential example of, to borrow a phrase from Ernst Bloch, '*the darkness of experiencing in itself*' (Bloch, 2000, p. 199).[6] It is little more than an attempt to escape history and to evoke an experience that is already lifeless.

There are, however, always traces of the experience of a temporality that is resolutely other-than-historical-time and which, because of their nature, tend to elude history as purpose. We are all aware of the manner in which winks and blinks, play and orgasms create discontinuities in time, along with so many forms of gesture which are not, at least in the first instance, predominantly purposeful (see Casey, 1999, pp. 80–83; Agamben, 2000a, pp. 49–60). Along with Søren Kierkegaard we can perceive the manner in which these temporal displacements reveal the destructive promise of the eternal instant. In his analysis of time, Kierkegaard's chief target is the philosophy of G.W.F. Hegel in which, because of the pre-eminence of the system, the event, the moment or the unforeseeable time of experience is little more than the ground of History's becoming. Hegel, it should be noted, had domesticated the Romantic conception of the truly aesthetic event that was deemed terrifying and terrible. Kierkegaard seems to have had in mind a quality of the event similar to the Romantics', but this time with regard to *interested* subjective time rather than art, when he contrasted the 'present' with the 'instant' (Kierkegaard, 1980, pp. 87–88). The instant is intrinsically related to eternity and, as a consequence, destruction. Its status is one that is outside normal time but is, nonetheless, temporal in a curious way. The instant, according to Kierkegaard, 'is a figurative expression, and therefore is not easy to deal with'. As the editors of the translation of *The Concept of Anxiety* inform us, Kierkegaard is referring to the fact that, as with the German *Augenblick*, the instant is captured in the figurative term, *Øiblikket*, a word that is coined from the actuality of 'a blink of the eye' (ibid., p. 245, n. 21). A blink is 'a designation of time, but mark well, of time in the fateful conflict when it is touched by eternity' (ibid., p. 87). It is also a designation of gift, of a spontaneity that opens oneself to a world that is other than an object. Moreover, a random remark that Kierkegaard makes in a footnote to his analysis of the instant discloses the theological significance of this experience of time. With reference to St Paul (ibid., p. 88, note), he describes the manner in which 'the instant of destruction' is said to express 'eternity at the same instant'. Kierkegaard resolutely underlines the commensurability of eternity and the instant, a relation which eludes historical determination as fate, strategy or fortune.

The transformative quality of the instant finds its specific and efficacious character at the point of the convergence of immediacy and ultimacy. There is no

---

[6]   See also Walter Benjamin's essay of 1933, 'Experience and Poverty': 'never has experience been contradicted more thoroughly,' he claims, than in the modern period (Benjamin, 1999, p. 732).

doubt that Kierkegaard has disclosed a central, formal attribute that is constitutive of a distinctly Christian experience of time. But Kierkegaard unquestionably tends towards the limitation of the significance and consequence of this time when he insists that its impact is primarily located within the domain of a *subjective* experience. True inwardness is the fundamental (subjective) category of the modernity of which Kierkegaard was so critical, but of which he was also part and through which he found many of the basic elements of his re-conception of time. Yet it is possible and essential to broaden the context within which the intensity and fecundity of this time might ramify. If we are to analyse the modes in which the sheer urgency of eternity impacts upon the temporal, we can fully comprehend the manner in which the time itself is marked by the moment of destruction. (And here, it ought to be noted, destruction in no way denotes an experience that is bloody, diminishing or violent. Its force is transformative.) That is because eternity has, as it were, a double intention that cannot be accounted for within the promise of capitalistic guilt or contained in history. It is a time in which we are confronted with an old and a new beginning, a time between history and its end. And it is a time, most crucially, that is given as a communal, political experience which renders the selves and communities of this time 'out of order'. It is the instantiation of eternity as a form of temporality that undermines the classic modern distinction of time as conceivable and eternity as unthinkable: the phenomenon of eternity is only to be validly represented either as a quantitative extension of *chronos* (as Thomas Hobbes demands; see Hobbes, 1996, pp. 466–467) or in exclusively negative terms (see, for example, Kant, 1995, p. 195).[7] In short, this time is an opening into time of the lapse of time as an omission of time – it does not add up, no calculable *telos* is installed within it and it demands no returns in an economy of knowledge or exchange.

It is generally accepted that Kierkegaard's conception of eternal time as an essential aspect of the identity of the instant or moment was highly influential on Karl Barth's assessment of that peculiar and very particular time in the knowledge of which the work of love is to be undertaken. 'Between the past and the future – between the times – there is a "Moment" that is no movement in time. This "Moment" is the eternal Moment – the *Now* – when the past and the future stand still, when the former ceases its going and the latter its coming' (Barth, 1933, p. 497). Barth, after Kierkegaard, pushes the logic of eschatological promise to its temporal extreme. That is to say, Barth identifies a point where the prevailing accommodation of modern Christianity with history is overwhelmed by the irruption of another time, the Moment. The force and significance of his account of the Pauline message, the non-sequential character of which is highlighted in

---

[7]   Indeed, in *The Concept of Anxiety* (1980, p. 77), Kierkegaard expressly condemns the depiction of eternity as 'an infinitely long time, as infinite succession' because such a representation is nothing but a 'parody' of the eternal. Of course, as parody, the imagery is comedic; hence, Woody Allen's contention that 'Eternity is a very long time, particularly at the end'.

Barth's passionate refiguration of its contextual significance, is that it enables us to think outside and ahead of the dominant characterisation of eschatology in historical terms. It is essential, of course, that we must never deny that the impress of eschatology on history derives from its distinctiveness, its incongruity: that of the absolute future *as* fulfilment. But, as we have seen, there is a sense in which the admixture of a reverent agnosticism concerning the time of the *parousia* and the unqualified yearning for participation in that future constitutes a Christian comportment that is marked by *stasis* and stagnation. Barth's vertical turn displaces this problem through the interception of time by eternity; time remains, even in its crisis, the point of the emergence of the matchless potential and discontinuous dynamic of eschatology.

There remains, nonetheless, something dissatisfying about Barth's conception of the manner in which time and its ending converge in the moment, a problem that is also true of Kierkegaard's understanding of the destructive force of the instant. It is clear, as so many commentators have remarked, that both Barth and Kierkegaard draw out what history refuses and it is similarly true that they also intuit the manner in which a Christian conception of time questions, undermines and devastates the pretensions of history and its attempt to account for all phenomena, whether immanent or transcendent. Yet, from the context of a form of life that is ecclesial and political, there is something distinctly arbitrary about the manner in which this time is operative and efficacious. It is for this reason that they must both seek to anchor God's time to some point of security: with Kierkegaard this point of fixity and security is located in the subjective experience of the instant; with Barth in the otherness and dissimilarity which qualifies every instant and aspect of time because the moment carries with it its transcendental significance. Barth defines this temporal bequest as the 'unborn secret of revelation' (ibid.).

For a more precise perception of the significance of the *eschaton* and its relation to history, we must do more than keep this impression of the end within the present in mind. It is imperative that we acknowledge the way in which the moment of the experience of time is marked as a time *between* time as history and its fulfilment. The experience of the New Testament church and the temporal context in which the church lives can be characterised in terms of this 'time between'; it is first and foremost 'an experience of time and history as interval [*Frist*], as a stay of execution [*Galgenfrist*]' (Taubes, 1987, p. 22).

In this light, Hans Urs von Balthasar's attempt to configure eschatology as an integral aspect of Christology is pertinent here. There is little point, Balthasar argues, in considering the *eschata* as accessible to thought, as if they could be studied and comprehended in the same manner, and with the same disposition, as mundane events (Balthasar, 1965, pp. 152–153). This temptation, frequently yielded to in the history of Christianity, is also the target of Günther Bornkamm's assessment of the Pauline corpus.

Eschatology has left such a deep impress on Paul's gospel that it will not do – as was common in the later church – to gather together his teachings 'on last things'

into a body and then make out of it a kind of summary appendix assembling all
that the apostle ever said or thought about the death of the individual and the end
of the world (Bornkamm, 1971, p. 197).

Instead of constructing eschatology as a posthumous or temporal addendum
to dogmatics or systematic theology, we should consider the manner in which
rooting eschatology in Christology rather than history offers a series of essential
insights into the status and nature of past, present and (ultimate) future. Balthasar
begins this task by contemplating the way in which the Chalcedonean definition
carries with it a biblical and patristic theology of history. Here he draws on Jean
Daniélou's reflections on the 'hypostatic union of the two natures' in which the
argument is made that the Christological formula announces that Christ is 'the
Eschaton which governs the time both of the promise and of the fulfilment, and
essentially, as he who has come, is the one coming and the one who fulfils all'
(Balthasar, 1965, p. 154, n. 3). In response to this Christological source of an
eschatological theology Balthasar goes on to offer an important depiction of
the manner in which a Christian time is an interlude, as both intervention and
expectation. He suggests that,

> new light may be thrown on the whole complex of ideas, already known to the
> fathers, concerning the time of promise and time of fulfilment, in fact between
> the three times of mere promise (the Old Testament), of fulfilled promise along
> with fulfilment promised (the Church of the New Testament), and complete
> fulfilment (eschatology). Dodd's 'realised eschatology' and, opposed to it,
> Cullmann's 'preparatory [*vorlaufende*] time' help, by their mutual dialectic,
> towards an understanding of the biblical idea of time (ibid., p. 168).

As neither mere promise nor unreserved fulfilment, as neither complete
realisation nor fragile prelude, this 'dialectic' of time reveals a certain specificity,
if insecurity, in the temporal life and character of the church. Time is given a new
character in the incarnation, death and resurrection of Christ (a character that is
re-presented in baptism), a time that is no longer historical time but not yet God's
time, for that is a 'super-time that is unique to him' (Balthasar, 1998, p. 30). Christ
is the mediation between a time which is inimitably divine and the time of the
world, and this intervention or intercession between times 'is illustrated in the fact
that Christ's time recapitulates and comprehends world-time, while it also reveals
God's super-time' (ibid.).

Fundamental to Balthasar's position is the contention that it is not the future or
the 'moment' that is of absolute importance here. There is no point offering either
quantitative or qualitative assessments of the time of the end. The essential truth
of eschatology for theology is that 'the only feature that will ultimately persist
and establish itself, whether visibly or invisibly, is the "*krisis*," the decision, the
scission, that Christ has introduced into the world' (ibid., p. 46). Time is scored

by the inherent opposition and conciliation of the *protos adam* and the *eschatos adam*, in a time that is transformed but incomplete in nature and quality.

Balthasar offers a valuable illustration of the Christological starting point for any reflection on the importance and pertinence of eschatology within history. However, while the horizon he unveils complements and supplements the temporal reflections of Kierkegaard and Barth, Balthasar could be accused of squandering the urgency of the momentaneous penetration of history which grounds their reflections. But whatever the distinctions and differences that are necessary for improving and augmenting the status of theological enquiry, of building a conception of eschatology which approaches some measure of being adequate to the immeasurable, one thing is clear: for these eschatological theologians, Kierkegaard, Barth and Balthasar, the 'dialectic' of times and temporalities sits uneasily with the coherence of the theological endeavour as it is undertaken within a church which has forsaken its kairological imperative. In contrast, we might suggest (by attending to St Paul) that the reassurance of an inner coherence is only present in the very insecurity and tension of being (and being-with) that is characteristic of the interval, the stay of execution, between time and its ending. That is why Paul is the only true theologian of eschatology, the figure who appreciated the manner and status of living amid a world-time that is in some sense decomposed by, and in every sense reconfigured through, the incursion of super-time. Confronted by the resurrection and the paradoxical status of the messiah, the *christos*, Paul understood that while '*krisis*' is normalised in the event-al nature of time it is just as essentially realised in the juridico-political impact of the Christ event. It is to these two attributes of '*krisis*' that we must turn but it is essential that these two motifs are appropriately situated within the eschatological politics of the Pauline corpus. In doing so we can ensure that the temptation to exaggerate the 'decisionist' (and therefore voluntarist) tendency in crisis theology is resisted and that the performative element of a kairological disposition is given its due weight.

Legitimation and Illegitimation

One of the greatest challenges to any reconsideration of Paul's eschatology is the simple fact that the church has tended to forget its revolutionary significance. Paul's dangerous prose seems to fit only those periods of modern western history where chaos and crisis are prevalent. And yet, the identifying characteristic of the eschatological communities for which Paul writes is that of a 'normative instability' (Müller, 2001, p. 62). Here the instability is not restricted to the rejection of Jewish law. It is an instability instantiated in relation to all law – Jewish and Roman. That is why Paul's letter to the community in Rome can be understood as nothing less than 'a *political* declaration of war on the Caesar' (Taubes, 2004, p. 16). The letter to Rome establishes a relationship between this new community and the law which is marked throughout by opposition. In the letter, Paul begins with a 'declaration' of the status and consequence of Jesus. Such a declaration questions and forcibly neutralises the 'apotheosis of *nomos*' (ibid., p. 23) that is evident in the Imperial and Jewish contexts. According to Jacob Taubes, Paul's conception of law propels the Christian community into a directly antagonistic confrontation with this decidedly juridical environment and its claim to authority because he responds to the question of the law without proper recourse to the law itself. At the heart of his message is a fundamental insistence on a juridico-political transformation that is initiated by the resurrection: 'It isn't *nomos* but rather the one who was nailed to the cross by *nomos* who is the imperator!' (ibid., p. 24). It would be a misunderstanding to think that Paul, who presents an attack on the law and its very order, was creating a new type of political theology, even if such a political theology would inevitably fail to correspond to the ancient bond of gods and *civitas*. Paul's intervention, while undoubtedly a theological intrusion within a closely circumscribed political context, does not represent at any point a theological justification of any specific political system or programme. Into the void of mundane political time and purpose Paul delivers what might be designated a *negative* political theology (see Taubes, 2004, p. 122), a theology that should never be considered as the foundation of a new and alternative political regime. Nor for that matter is Paul attempting to supplant the imperial political form through revolutionary violence. Paul's letter opens up a more radical possibility: a theological delegitimation of all political power as a profoundly *political* attitude.[8]

It is this attitude that Jacob Taubes has rescued from Paul's letters, a disposition which refuses the tendency to condense Paul's theology into a pious deposit of theological niceties or exegetical innovations. The originality of Taubes's position lies in is his construction of a political performativity that is scripted by Pauline messianism and which eschews the security of political form, citizenship and the law. Life is realised not on the basis of mundane authority but on the ineluctable fact of dislocation that arises from the resurrection. The consequences of this Pauline challenge to the law and order of political authority is also a persistent theme of Martin Heidegger's lecture on Paul's first letter to the Thessalonians, a theme that is relevant to our understanding of the radical character demanded in the light of the coming of the Messiah. In this lecture Heidegger contrasts the standpoint of the worldly individual with the comportment that follows from Christian factical life experience.

> Those who find rest and security in this world are those who cling to this world, since it provides them with peace and security. ... Sudden death [*Verderben*] befalls them. ... They are surprised by it, they do not expect it (Heidegger, 1995, p. 103).

---

[8]   For an excellent discussion of the nature of a Pauline 'negative political theology' as it is exposed by Jacob Taubes, see Terpstra & de Wit, 2000.

In one important sense, Heidegger offers a precise diagnosis of the significance and challenge of the resurrection. The world is now confronted with a new and unprecedented economy of life and death. Thought-provoking as it may be, however, this reading of the Pauline *corpus* is myopic. If we take Taubes's political reading of Paul seriously then Heidegger has domesticated Pauline messianism by reducing it to an ontological-existential force. Take the term 'peace and security' which, as *pax et securitas*, was the principal slogan of Roman imperial propaganda and appears in Paul's consideration of the times and the seasons (*chronoi kai kairoi*) in 1 Thessalonians (5:3): 'Whenever they say "peace and security (*eirēnē kai asphaleia*)" then sudden destruction comes upon them as birth pains come upon the pregnant woman and by no means may they escape.' Paul here introduces the 'martial' element of eschatology that the church has forsaken. The day of the Lord, the temporal interjection of *kairos* upon *chronos*, will shatter the impotent posturing of any imperial pretensions to power and its justification. It is this negation of rule and norm, the vigorous refusal of political authority, which gives Paul's analysis of time its transformative and abnormal quality. Although now largely alien to a Christianity that has forsaken its shocking force, the exceptional nature of eschatology is succinctly and precisely excavated in Franz Kafka's reflection upon the juridical and temporal identity of the end: 'It is only our conception of time that makes us call the Last Judgement by this name. It is in fact a kind of martial law' (Kafka, 1954, p. 42). It is only in this light, through the disclosure that the end of time is a form or type of martial law, that the juridico-political status of eschatology is clarified. And martial law means, in the words of the Duke of Wellington, 'no law at all' (quoted in Hussain, 1999, p. 98). Inasmuch as the Christian denizen has been freed from the law by the eschatological event of the resurrection, there cannot be any compromise with, or concession to, the principles of judgment espoused by the law and executed by its adherents.

The eschatological thrust of the Pauline letters provides a type of 'shooting script' for the performance of a life that is lived in the face of this martial law, in between the law and its termination. In particular, the letter to the Romans identifies the followers of Jesus as living in the time of the exception as the law is now fulfilled and Christ takes its place (see Sanders, 1985, p. 83). The Jewish Law which identifies the chosen people, and a Roman law which legislates for the proper place and standing of those who fall under its command – citizens, women, children, slaves and barbarians – are surmounted in the event that is the resurrection. For Alain Badiou, it is Romans 6:14 which reveals the logic of this negative political theology: 'you are *no* longer under the law, *but* under grace' (Badiou, 1997, p. 67). The logic of the Pauline exception, for the Pauline Church in the midst of the suspension of the law, is then simply 'no ... but'. The rejection of the imperial establishment and its legitimacy is accompanied by the institution and validation of a new people of God formed in the light of grace. The originality of this *non*-economy of grace is that it opposes 'law insofar as it is what comes *without being due*' (ibid., p. 81). There is no longer a political arrangement or legal framework that can find the measure of grace or stand in a relation of adequacy to its demands. The resurrection undoes the limits of distinctiveness and security. This dissolution of closed particularities and identities, settled homes and secure borders, presents a Christian politics of refusal – Paul's eschatology proclaims that 'this is not it!'[9] Paul provides us with a form of being that, in relation to the economic and nomological taxonomies of politics, is actually unidentifiable because the subject of the messianic age is contingent upon the disjunction between the world (as it is) and its redemption through grace. As a consequence, the terms which he employs when designating the nature of the people of God are specific and unambiguous. Paul never utilises the common terms which indicate and authorise a community as such – *laos, demos* or *ethnos* – because the Christian community is not constituted through such substantive provisions with their attendant task, their laws, or those determinations and their requirements that constitute an enclosed finality. The Christian community is identified – or to be more precise here, unidentified – through the essentially illimitable pronouns 'we' and 'us'. In the political context of Rome or of capital, of the *nomos* of the empire or the war on terror, this unidentifiability is both dangerous and inherently precarious. It reconstitutes a political space in a deterritorialised world, but one that cannot be exploited by power or priced by capital.

The Time Between

The impress of eschatology modifies the very nature of time as time. Its critical impression upon history and upon those who pass this time (or kill time) in expectation is not primarily futural but intermediate between time and its ending. Indeed, the temporal identity of the end must always remain in question for the simple reason that 'of that day and hour no one knows' (Matt. 24:36). Even when that day does arrive its advent will never be something calculable or foreseeable because it 'will come like a thief in the night' (1 Thess. 5:2). Eschatology does, nevertheless, convey a distinctive form of temporal experience that cannot be discerned from an historical point of view or dissected for the sake of anatomical assessment. This elusive feature of the eschatological effect is clarified in various passages in the New Testament. A good example is provided by Mark 13:20 where, following the narration of a range of natural and individual tribulations that are to come, Jesus suggests that on behalf of those chosen the Lord has shortened the days. In the parallel text of Matthew 24:22, we see a similar claim. The vocabulary used for this radical abbreviation or condensation of time conveys a drama – flamboyance even – that is lost in translation: *ekolobōsen*, the formulation in Mark, along with *ekolobōthēsan* and *kolobōthēsontai* in Matthew, is indicative of a process that results in the stunting, mutilation and swallowing of history as progression and *telos*. This is the experience of time of those situated between, on the one hand, the time of 'fulfilled promise with fulfilment promised' and, on

---

[9]   I borrow this term from Paolo Palladino.

the other, the time of complete fulfilment. Time, along with those subject to this time, is imprinted with an urgency and ultimacy that reconstitutes the very nature of time. The consequences, course and texture of such a radically condensed time demand a disposition to temporal experience that is singular and strange.

As a counterpart to the swallowing of time, we can distinguish in Paul's understanding of the structure of that epoch which follows the resurrection a conception and inception of a temporality that is in no way dissimilar. In 1 Corinthians 7:29, a text to which we shall return, Paul announces that the time is short, *ho kairos synestalmenos estin*. The time here, *kairos*, is not merely shortened or forestalled. It is, to be more precise, contracted, pressured (*sustellō*) in a course of action that bears down upon the temporal interim which subsists between out-and-out *chronos* and an all-embracing *kairos*. Being between and being pressed, shortened time – or time 'having been shortened', *synestalmenos* – is ready to burst to the extent that its status and identity is never quite, but is always more than, the moment. It is a laborious time in which temporality bares and bears the pregnant meaning of an event and an experience that repeatedly questions history and its truth. Ready to burst, swollen to the point of rupture, the superimposition of *kairos* upon *chronos* composes a strange and transvalued history that is a site or temporal location of struggle. As Taubes understands it, this new and re-ordered temporality is the 'place upon which the substance of time and the substance of eternity, death and life cross paths' (Taubes, 1991, p. 4). By attending to the significance of this crossing of time and eternity, we can see how it is that, *pace* Moltmann, Volf and those eschatological theologians for whom the future is everything, the character of a paroxysmal, resistant time is never straightforwardly teleological or rhythmic, oscillating and vacillating amid discord and resolution. Its generative principle is an intensity, an energy, a dynamic that opens up a stage upon which to perform, as the early Heidegger claimed, a mode of 'enactment' [*Vollzug*] (Heidegger, 1995, p. 121). But this enactment is not excited by the to and fro of dialectical fluctuation between history and its end, a performative necessity while rapt and ensnared by the incessant revolutions of time. The dialectic might well be understood as a chaotic continuum, but it is a continuum all the same. Rather, the specific performance of the 'time between' relates to its singular configuration as summons to inconformity. That is why the most pertinent example of the kairological instantiation of a fructifying prolepsis is the birth of the Christ: 'when the fullness of time [*plemōra tou chronou*] was come, God sent forth his Son, born of a woman, born under the law' (Gal. 4:4). The fullness of time, of *this* time, is laden with substance, a body in time and beyond time which encroaches, interrupts and invades the 'now' [*nun*] (Rom. 13:11). Now is a time that is a 'proper time' or 'its own time' [*kairos idiois*] (see 1 Tim. 2:6 & 6:15), a concept of time which, according to Herman Ridderbos, is interchangeable with the fullness of time or the 'moment' [*ton kairon*] (Ridderbos, 1975, p. 47 n. 12). The time that the church embodies is not that of a time to come. It is a proper time; a time proper to the fecundity and interruptive vitality of the incarnation, the resurrection and their aftermath. It is a special, unique and distinctive time, a time in which the parody of the accepted *doxa* is most fully revealed: the Messiah conforms neither to the *necessitas rerum*, the inevitability of things (hence, a virginal conception) nor to the order of received opinion and truth (hence, he is no 'ruler' in the normal juridical sense and is crucified as a criminal). It is a time, in every sense, of *paradox*.

From the perspective of the nature of the fullness of time, then, we can formulate two preliminary conclusions. First, it is clear that with the tendency in the annals of Christianity (and without) to radically historicise eschatology, as a millennial phenomenon in history itself or as the exclusive concern of posthumous or historical finality, comes the always inherent danger of repudiating the character and import of *kairos* as a time that applies to time. The choice of history and futurity over the proper time and its impending force is basically dependent upon the modern effort to recuperate freedom from the logic of redemption. It is a thoroughgoing accommodation with a view of life which holds to an exclusively immanent horizon of existence. It is, in consequence, a rejection of a specifically Christian idiom of participation and transformation. It is also a choice that incessantly ventures to shake off a melancholy which inevitably accompanies the absence of salvation. And it can never do so. The character of hope which dominates eschatological reflection is therefore fettered by the commitment to a curtailed or deficient understanding of practical involvement in the proper time. Second, the inauguration of a 'time between' as a corollary of the birth of Christ, the Messiah, intensifies a specific 'questionability' of timing, temporality and history that persistently generates the contours of a theological politics – of living life within the horizons of what Barth calls 'the true revolution' (Barth, 1933, p. 483). Challenging rather than comforting, and unlike the *habitus* of any other form of life, this phase or stage in which life is to be enacted in the eschatological community cannot be recovered for any political blueprint. And yet, it is also true that this phase or stage sets the scene for emphatic political action. That is because, in Frederick Bauerschmidt's words:

> The eschatological character of Jesus' proclamation of the Kingdom of God is not primarily found in its 'future oriented' prediction of 'the end of the world (in the sense of the end of time and space), but in its bringing to an end a particular 'world order' (Bauerschmidt, 1996, p. 508).

The new 'world order' which in time questions and undercuts the dominant flow of historical power and the immanent dynamic of worldly authority is, however, idiosyncratic to the extent that its nature is comparable to the status of the time between. Its form is distinct from revolutionary or utopian concepts of transformation because it is not, in any real sense, a blueprint of a future *topos*. From the perspective of the eschatological imperative we have the formation of a type of Christian existence that is strange and estranged in nature because it is a spaceless form of life for which, and in which, the world orders of politics, identity and power are delegitimated. Christian eschatology must be understood, from this perspective, as a resolute context within which there is nothing less than the rejection 'on principle' of '*all political and eudaemonist elements*, so decisively that the world to come is *God's* world' (Deissner, 1969, p. 254). *The Epistle to Diognetus* characterises the existential ramifications of this negation of political boundaries and designations in uncompromising terms. It is the fate of Christians to 'share all things as citizens, and suffer all things as strangers. Every foreign country is their homeland, and every homeland is a foreign country' (*Epistle to Diognetus*, 1950, p. 360).

Theological Politics

Between theocracy and sectarianism, without the security of spatial bounds or the assurance of a new political identity that overpowers or withdraws from all others, the Christian comportment after history and before the *eschaton* is necessarily improper or awry. It is a stance that cannot undertake the standard, determinate modes of human conduct. It is a disposition that questions the very certainty of political identities and roles: familial, sexual, ethnic or economic. The 'questionability' that resides at the heart of such a theological politics is already clarified in the synoptic accounts of a transformation of relations, commitments and bonds that overturns, ruins and destabilises the *status quo*. There we can see, for example in Mark 9:35 and 10:43–44 (and parallels), a characterisation of household service (*diakonia*) as a principle of action, where being last of all and servant (*diakonos*) is of paramount political importance. Here we have a valuable example of the 'political impact of the new evolving Christian community', the impact of which was to de-totalise politics (Wannenwetsch, 1996, p. 279). This church is a community in which contingent and historical forms of action and arrangement are trans-valued in the light of a different and divergent temporal logic. The socio-economic and political structures of power which include and exclude through the force of law are 'now' no longer justifiable in the wake of the fulfilment of the law, even if they 'once' held authority. Ecclesial time, engendered by the very surmounting of juridico-political divisions constituted by power, law and force is identified through the delineation of an historical conclusion, a logic of 'once-now' because that which was 'once' justified as the norm is no longer applicable 'now' (see Bornkamm, 1971, p. 200). The classic division between *oikos* and *polis*, between the domestic context of naked reproductive life (*zoē*) and the public and exclusive context of political life (*bios*), is sublated. The political as such, as a sphere of ordering, exclusion and power, is not only brought into doubt but is, according to Paul, invalidated. The 'new' life that is offered in Christ wipes out any of those obligations that are intrinsic to the measure and evaluation of the 'old' life (see Gal. 5:19ff & 1 Cor. 6:11).

But we must be careful to understand the significance of this transformative process in and for the present. This de-totalisation of politics, so thoroughly examined by Bernd Wannenwetsch, is also the reality in our contemporary age. Following Hannah Arendt (1958, pp. 28–37), Wannenwetsch exposes the manner in which the 'public' realm of political action has been transformed by the paradigmatic dominance of economics in the political realm. Public affairs are treated in this economic arrangement 'as if they were a huge household or business' (Wannenwetsch, 1996, p. 279). It would lead us to triviality, and more crucially to confusion, if we were to understand (as Wannenwetsch does) that this development is somehow countered or questioned by a liturgy in which there is 'full participation of all of the representatives of the debased *oikos*' (ibid.). In contrast, we must conclude that capitalist-parliamentariansim has followed an identical course to this liturgy in that the concerns of the private sphere (*oikos, zoē*) have become central concerns of modern biopolitics (as we saw in Chapter Six) and are becoming more fully and more completely the focus of the managerial procedures of public politics (*polis, bios*). The de-totalisation of politics is a fundamental principle of modern biopolitics.[10] Thus we must not think that the de-totalising of politics which Christianity effected in its first centuries is, alone and in itself, the means to an interruption of 'the course of the world' in our times (ibid.). For while there is no doubt that the inclusivity of the church is different in kind to the politics of liberal governance, the motif of inclusivity is at the heart of a politics that is predicated on the very thing that holds all in common – rich and poor, male and female, Christian and atheist. And that 'thing' is life itself, the point and principle of the 'communism' of biopolitical democracy.

There is, however, a character that opens up a form of being-with that is both inclusive in nature and non-appropriable by biopolitical regimes. The *doulos*, the slave, becomes in the new time which is inaugurated by the resurrection the Christian political exemplar of living life in the 'time between'. It is essential to remember that in any authentic attempt to understand the significance of this title and role we ought to refuse the temptation to sentimentalise this figure of service and exclusion. In the Pauline text, as Giorgio Agamben reminds us, the term *doulos* refers 'to a profane juridical condition and, at the same time, the transformation that this condition undergoes in its relation to the messianic event' (Agamben, 2000b, pp. 27–28). He or she who is slave is devoid of *bios*, of political existence, he or she is the figure who has no legal identity as such, and he or she is the abnormal norm who discloses 'the neutralization that the division of the law and all juridical and social conditions undergo as a consequence of the messianic event' (ibid., p. 28). The slave figure is not simply the one who assists, aids and attends to the other, and is certainly not the one who is called upon to embody some excess of civility and courteousness. Paul's teaching here echoes the characterisation of *diakonos* in the synoptics; we are confronted with a mode of service and a style of existence that cuts right to the heart of the norm through an eschatological procedure in which the normative is fundamentally transvalued in the messianic event. The status and identity of those who constitute the *ecclesia* is

---

10   Indeed, for this reason Carl Schmitt suggested (in 1923) that the Roman Catholic Church was the only truly political institution remaining in Europe. See Schmitt, 1996c.

freed from the demands of the *polis* – any *polis* (theocratic, autocratic, democratic or monarchic) – because the order of the world is suspended with the coming of the Christ.

Accompanying this essential questioning of political life is the fact that the early Christians were no longer tied to the *oikos* as such. The *doulos* or, as Paul suggests elsewhere, the *hyper doulon*, 'super-slave' or 'beyond the slave' (Philem 1:16; see Agamben, 2000b, p. 28), cannot be confined to the household alone but is a political figure who stands outside the demarcation of that which is standard and conventional within the Graeco-Roman world: *polis* or *oikos*. It is something like this peculiar 'otherness' of the early Christian identity, an identity pursued outside the boundaries drawn so definitively by the juridico-political traditions of the *status quo*, which is evident in the claim that Christianity marks the beginning of a new race (*genos*) or practice (*epitēdeuma*) (*Epistle to Diognetus*, 1950, p. 351).[11] The placing of Christian identity beyond the parameters of those designations known as 'Greek' and 'Jew' or 'slave' and 'free' serves to establish a new kind of collective, a novel people who fit neither the community relevant to a univocally political sphere nor the sub-political mass of the *oikos*. More crucially, within the present situation of the near-universal reach of biopolitics, the third race exceeds the parameters formed by the convergence of *oikos* and *polis*. The third race takes its lineage from that line which cuts through the mundane divisions of ethnicity, society or gender. The new *genos* has no place in which to settle, as political or economic natives. Its members are denizens who are strangers even if they are citizens. Insofar as the *ecclesia* breaks out of the juridical straitjacket of slavery or citizenship in the enactment of an intensified slavery, it will now constitute a body which is impossible to classify in juridical, political or religious terms, the members of which secure their freedom 'from all natural, organic attachments – from nature, art, cult, and state – and for whom emptiness and alienation [*Entfremdung*] from the world, as well as the separation [*Entzweiung*] with secularism, accordingly reach a high degree' (Taubes, 1991, p. 64).

The early church, in its constitution of new forms of being ('race' and 'practice') and forms of expression (syntaxes and grammars), fractures the meaning and refuses the discourses of any religio-political forms which bound communal identity. Relative to the fixed contours of communal identity – 'Jew' or 'Greek' – the condition of the Christian is, then, one of alienation. The messianic community lives as an alien body in the world, always diasporic and never static (see Breton, 1988, p. 100). The Christian community as such can no longer be categorised according to type or rule. Rather than providing the established and unwavering ground upon which identity and meaning is predicated, as the political demands, the political, in itself and for itself and in its juridical divisions of groups and classes, is annulled.

---

[11]   See also Clement of Alexandria, 1985, VI.5.41: 'we who worship Him in a new way, as a third race, are Christians'.

Only with this radical perspective in mind might we fully understand St Paul's description of how the Christian is to live in the between-time, the 'time that remains', and how the appropriate *habitus* might be constituted for a messianic time that is, strictly speaking, neither *chronos* nor *kairos*. The overcoming of the law, Paul suggests, demands a radically different rehearsal of what has, and is to, come and how the third race which is improper for, and unfitting in, the order of things should enact its singular role: 'I mean, brethren, the appointed time (*kairos*) has grown very short; from now on, let those who have wives live as though they had none, and those who mourn as though they were not mourning, and those who rejoice as though they were not rejoicing, and those who buy as though they had no goods, and those who deal with the world as though they had no dealings with it. For the form of this world is passing away' (1 Cor. 7:29–31). This Pauline text consistently repeats a specific motif of the negation of a given historical nature of things in order to set up the possibility of living in the time that remains, a motif which signifies the arrival of a very different temporality to historical time. That motif, repeated five times in this short text, is *hōs mē*, 'as if not'. It denotes a radical reconstitution of the nature of life, because its *telos* in the wake of the risen Christ is the new creation, and it daringly questions the state and status of the order of things, whether economic or affective but especially political. These historico-social phenomena are irrelevant in the context of a stay of execution. Yet this fact of irrelevance is not the premise of a withdrawal from the world but the principle upon which the Christian community is required to engage with the world.

What exactly is it, though, that distinguishes this new time, the stay of execution, from chronological time? Simply put, it is a time that engenders a fundamentally different imperative and a radically different arrangement of things. It is a time in which those conditions and principles through which the norm gains its validity and efficacy are made inoperative. A delegitimation is sanctioned by the interruption of a new ontology and a new politics. The *oikodespotes* and *oikonomia*, the sovereign rule and the sovereign ordering of the body of Christ are unsuitable for, and inconsistent with, the rule and ordering of the *polis*. In unfolding the negative disposition that is required in the time between, St Paul offers a clue to the status and practice of the *oikonomian tou plērōmatos tōn kairōn*, the ordering of the fullness of the times (Eph. 1:10).

A Theologico-Political Example

The crucial affinities between a Christian disposition that is engendered by a formative dislocation in time and space and the very fact of being beyond the law are embodied by a character hidden in the annals of the tradition. In a letter composed by St Jerome in the latter half of the fourth century and addressed to the priest Innocent, we are offered a vivid portrayal of a character who is fashioned in the course of a miraculous event (Jerome, 1963, pp. 21–27). The letter presents a story of such detailed violence, along with the smatterings of an anachronistic misogyny, that it is easy to pass over the central theme of Jerome's deliberation: the paradoxical relationship between the law and justice or between judgement and the perpetual deferral of its execution in the context of grace.

The missive tells of a visit by a governor to the city of Vercelli. During the visitation, 'a certain woman and a man accused by her husband of being her paramour were brought before him'. The couple are described by Jerome as utterly blameless but are imprisoned on the governor's word. During a period of sustained torture which is employed to extract the truth, the young man attempts to save himself by heaping his accusations onto the woman; she, as a result, no longer has an opportunity to deny the allegations. 'But, as a matter of fact,' Jerome suggests, 'the woman was more courageous than her sex.' Tied to the rack and subjected to horrific pain, she will not submit. Pain and death are nothing in the face of her commitment to the truth and, looking to heaven, she vows to welcome the executioner's sword if it means that she had not sinned. Her tortures are doubled but still she refuses to confess.

The pair are eventually condemned to death and the 'entire populace poured forth to see the sight. … As for the wretched young man, his head was cut off by the very first stroke of the sword.' As for the virtuous woman, she kneels on the ground in readiness for her death. But when the sword falls to her neck, propelled by every ounce of the executioner's strength, it cannot fulfil its purpose and the woman suffers no more than a nick to the skin. The execution is attempted for a second time but once again 'the sword lost all its force as it fell upon the woman, and, as though the steel feared to touch the accused, it rested harmlessly on her neck'. Since even a third attempt to kill the woman ends in outright failure – Jerome informs us that 'it too the mystery of the Trinity had rendered naught' – an alternative strategy is employed. The man assigned to kill her tries to bring the farce to a conclusion through a piercing of her body. This time, however, the sword itself 'bent back to the hilt and, as though vanquished and looking to its master, confessed that it could not give her the death blow'. The woman, whom Jerome informs us had been condemned by the judge, was absolved by the sword.

In response to the miracle the crowd 'take up arms' and liberate the woman. But in the face of the exigencies of the law even a miracle is insufficient for salvation. A meeting of the governor's council despatches a representative to confront the people with the truth of the situation and, what amounts to the same thing, the force of law. His words are uncompromising:

> Fellow citizens, is it my life you are seeking? Are you making me a substitute for her? You may be compassionate, you may be merciful, you may wish to save the condemned woman, but surely I, who am innocent, ought not to perish?

The law demands its execution, its price and its answer. Faced with this need and the injustice that would occur if the law were to be satisfied by the sacrifice of another, the people accept that while its 'defence of her had seemed the path of duty, it now seemed to be a sort of duty to permit her to be executed'. Faced with the unwavering claim of the law and the requirement that its violence be accomplished upon her body and no other, the crowd gloomily accepts that she must die. A new sword is acquired, along with a new executioner who brings the sword down upon her three times and, as a result of his third stroke, the woman falls to the ground. It appears that she has died so that 'an innocent man need not die in her stead'. The body is shrouded and a tomb is prepared but as the sun sets and nightfall arrives 'the woman's bosom quivers, her eyes seek the light and her body is restored to life'. When the woman's resuscitation is complete she offers her first words, pronounced with defiance and an undiminished trust: '*The Lord is my helper: I will not fear what man can do to me.*'[12]

But the miracle is not quite concluded. An old woman suddenly dies and her body is placed in the tomb prepared for the corpse of the innocent woman who has come back to life. Meanwhile the devil, disguised as the executioner, is not convinced that our protagonist is dead. He is shown the grave by the clergy who, in response to the devil's scepticism, object to his disbelief and rebuke him for his stupidity. While this fracas continues, the woman is spirited away and hidden from public view. She is dressed in male garb and her hair is cut short and because she exists between the law and its suspension, between life and death, between bondage and freedom she remains *incognita*. Only after a series of petitions to the emperor, the one who in himself embodies – indeed, exceeds – the law, can her case be resolved. And this is precisely how the chronicle is concluded: 'the emperor restored to freedom the woman who had been restored to life.'

This restoration to freedom which, in turn, signifies the restitution of the law and its force, marks the cessation of the woman's abandonment. Crisis is terminated. Yet the restoration also indicates the foreclosure of a messianic comportment and its dangerous corollaries, both in the sense of closing fast an exilic aperture within the very centre of this world and in the sense of hindering its intensive efficacy. That she is restored to the status of a political and legal person seems only just and right. The account seems to grant the reader a morally agreeable finale. A closer analysis of the narrative, however, alerts us to the fact that she must be restored to a *normal* identity because her very status beyond the reach of the law is a demonstration of a form of life that refuses to countenance the law or its force. While *incognita* – as neither free nor slave, as neither male nor female (she was dressed in male garb and her hair cut short) – she embodies the crisis of the law which resides at the heart of the time that remains between the resurrection and the *parousia*. This crisis has nothing to do with decision, a motif of modern theology that only has relevance because of the recurrent crises surrounding the meaning and manifestation of liberal notions of 'consent'. Rather it is a juridical crisis within which the political as such is delegitimated.

Throughout Jerome's report of this woman's terrible experience, the law is enforced with all the might of its judicatory authority over bodies that only possess an identity, and therefore bear any kind of identifiable character, because

---

[12]   The quotation echoes, of course, Psalm 118:6.

of *its* rule, its *oikonomia*. And while even in her exceptional case the law is still in force and its judgement as decreed must stand, a radically improper logic is at work. The judgment of the law endures but this judgement is inexecutable (see Scholem, 1999, p. 357). This is the paradox of justice and justification from the standpoint of the time between. Taking the standpoint of the law is a stance that is ultimately impotent. It may well be that a judgement is made, that a moment of decision is involved, that a figure who represents the law delivers its verdict but its implementation is fundamentally invalid because law can no longer be executed on the bodies of the third race.

There is an inherent and ineluctable strangeness about this (non)identity that the women enacts, a strangeness that is shared by the early Christian community *as such* (see *Epistle to Diognetus*, 1950, p. 359). But we have already witnessed the manner in which Paul exhorts the community at Corinth to live a paradoxical, strange life now that the time is short (1 Cor. 7:29–31). The early Christian community may well live under the judgement of law – in the context of legal and economic relations – so that some of the brethren are identified as married or renowned for their commercial dealings. But what constitutes the singular character of the Christian in this time is that all these injunctions and demands of the law, of economy and of history, are actually irrelevant. They are inconsequential in the face of the end. Thus we might say that the woman celebrated by Jerome belongs to a race or *genos* that is characteristically and onto-politically paradoxical. The new *genos* lives 'as if not'. And living by the principle of subjunctive renunciation marks both the refusal of the catastrophe of the *status quo* and the tragedy of the legitimacy of progress. Consequently this figure of the stranger is a more radical figure than the revolutionary because the latter still wishes to reconfigure the *nomos*, the law as the principle measure of all subsequent measures, even if that measure is corrected or modified in a new order created by a novel orientation. She, in contrast, presents us with the figure of a community without community where 'being-with' is no longer conceived of as a composition – at least in terms of the fixed boundaries that determine order and orientation – but as a disposition. It is a disposition from which any action or activity is, to borrow a phrase of Barth's, 'void of purpose' (Barth, 1933, p. 483).

Impolitical Theology

It is this incongruity or abnormality that resides at the heart of a Christian (non)identity and which is so difficult to accept, let alone embrace. The austere place (*locus severus*) that is inimitable within any normal situation can only be faithfully inhabited if it is never possessed by citizens or marked and bounded by the codification of values and statutes. But this (im)potent disposition is something of a well-kept secret within modern theology. The repudiation of the kairological imperative that we have charted necessitates a concomitant abandonment of a 'being-with' that is impolitical and ill-fitting for the acceptable demands of a privatised, moralised and interiorised faith. There have been, nevertheless, moments whereby the force and significance of the form of life proposed by the New Testament (and within the tradition) have come to light despite this process of evasion and neglect. A remarkable feature of such disclosures is the manner in which they persistently identify the principles of formation of the Christian community as antithetical to the political *per se*. Moreover, they also suggest that these principles by no means stipulate the shift towards a simplistically converse stance, or that which is apolitical. As thoroughly impolitical, these disclosures act as the representation of that which it is impossible to represent, as a mode of political sacrament, through which the violence and determinacy of representation – legal, political or cultural – is disclosed for what it is.

Perhaps no modern thinker has so consciously appreciated the significance of these outlandish and fantastical exigencies that are professed in the name of Christ than the young Hegel. Between 1793 and 1794, in his so-called 'Berne Fragments', Hegel exposed and analysed the threatening and intolerable character of many of the precepts of Christ. Indeed, so menacing are the commands of the Messiah to the proper and just workings of civil society, is it any surprise that Hegel must conclude that they are fundamentally destructive?

> Were a nation to introduce Christ's precepts today – ordering at best external compliance with them, since the spirit cannot be effectively commanded – it would very quickly come apart (Hegel, 1984, pp. 70–71).

Hegel's argument is founded upon the fact that a whole range of the teachings and principles expounded in the gospels 'are contrary to the foundational principles of legislation (the principles governing the rights of property, self-defence, etc.) in civil societies' (ibid., p. 70). The teachings upon which the practice of Christianity is to be based can only be defined, therefore, as 'useless and pernicious' (ibid.). In his estimation of the nature of the generative principles of the church, it would seem that the young Hegel is absolutely correct. However, his consideration of why this might be so is dreadfully wide of the mark. In the context of his sentimental attachment to and advocacy of a *Volksreligion*, Hegel misses the very challenge of the significance of the socio-political uselessness of Christian precepts when he suggests that 'the teachings of Jesus, his rules of conduct, were really suited only for the cultivation of singular individuals, and were oriented accordingly' (ibid., p. 71).

The political community is here contrasted with the particularised and individualised heroism of Christian antinomianism. The formation of such a disparity and divergence of purposes is essential because of the 'absurdity' that would occur if Christianity were actually rehearsed in concrete terms. From this perspective, it is wholly reasonable to reject the political import of Christianity. But it is in pursuing this very point that Hegel effectively discloses the substance and impact of Christian teaching: in relation to the foundational contours of any political community, the Church is a race or *genos* that is impolitical in nature. The impolitical quality of Christian precepts is such that they question and to all intents and purposes invalidate the auto-legitimating logic of (modern) politics. Hegel's concern is to provide and promote a ground to political community from which the organising conventions of authority, representation and juridical relations will effortlessly merge with the politico-theological principles of Absolute Spirit.

In contrast, an impolitical theology cannot take this route or its opposite.[13] If the Church is to accept its place within the 'time between' it is essential that it succumbs neither to the requirements of political constitution (as juridico-political representation or, in the context of biopolitics, depoliticisation) nor to the valorisation of the political that is achieved as a result of the recourse to a theological legitimation (which habitually occurs even within the context of secular modernity). In fact, these two alternatives are simply the two sides of the one coin.

It is on the basis of this uncertain and irrepresentable terrain, this testing zone between and betwixt time and its cessation, between and beyond the political and the apolitical, that the forms and substance of a theological politics must be thought and practised. In the nineteenth century, David Friedrich Strauss asked a challenging and still pertinent question: are we still Christians? (Strauss, 1873, pp. 13–107). His negative response enraged those who represented the pillars of bourgeois society in his day. In our day, the diagnosis and prognosis of Strauss demands that we truly consider whether theology ought to accept the contemporary pressure to be acceptable and relevant. Or, indeed, whether such an arrangement marks the death and decomposition of the tradition, along with its inherent vitality. This study has suggested that there is also an alternative response – that we might embrace the sheer irrelevance of theology as thought and practice in the knowing faith that its rehearsal proceeds from alternative principles, that we do not conform to the age. In order to fully justify such a step, however, it will be necessary to interrogate how it was possible that faith became beholden to the force of law, and how the historical development of juridico-politics brought theology to a point beyond which it survives only as a parasite.

---

[13]   Throughout this reflection on the impolitical I am drawing on the insights provided by Roberto Esposito's *Catgorie dell'impolitico* (1999).

Published Works by Paul Fletcher

Monograph

2009. *Disciplining the Divine: Toward an (Im)political Theology*. Ashgate: Aldershot.

Edited Collections

2009, forthcoming. *The Politics to Come: Power, Secularity and the Messianic*. Co-edited with A. Bradley. Continuum: London.

2009, forthcoming. *The Messianic Now: Religion, Politics and Culture*, Special Issue of *The Journal of Cultural Research*. Co-edited with A. Bradley.

2001. *Religions in the Modern World: Traditions and Transformations*. Co-edited with H. Kawanami, D. Smith and L. Woodhead. Routledge: London.

2000. *Violence, Sacrifice, Desire,* Special Issue of *Cultural Values*. Co-edited with M. Dillon.

Articles

2008. 'Real Time: The Instant of my Death'. Co-written with M. Dillon. *Journal of Cultural Research*, 12:3, 389–402.

2008. 'Prolegomena to a Theology of Death'. *Neue Zeitschrift für Systematische Theologie und Religionsphilosophie* 50, 139–157.

2004. 'The Nature of Redemption: Post-Humanity, Post-Romanticism and the Messianic'. *Ecotheology*, 9:3, 276–94.

2004. 'The Political Theology of the Empire to Come'. *Cambridge Review of International Affairs* 17:1, 49–61.

2001. 'Incognito ergo sum: Political Theology and the Metaphysics of Existence'. *New Blackfriars* 82:961, 121–132.

2000. 'Making Bowels Move: Justice Without the Limits of Reason Alone'. *Cultural Values* 4:2, 228–238.

1997. 'Writing of(f) Victims: hors texte'. *New Blackfriars* 78:916, 267–278.

Essays in Edited Volumes

2008. 'Self-Knowledge and the Problem of Experience' in *Self-Knowledge and Agency*, ed. M. Sen. Cambridge University Press: New Delhi, 186–199.
2007. 'Anti-Marriage' in *Queer Theology: Rethinking the Western Body*, ed. G. Loughlin. Blackwell: Oxford, 290–304.
2003. 'Fantasy, Imagination and the Possibility of Experience' in *Difference in Philosophy of Religion*, ed. P. Goodchild. Ashgate: Aldershot, 157–169.

Other

2001. 'Violence, Desire and the Gospels: The Theory of René Girard'. *Farmington Papers*.
2001. Contributions on 'Romanticism', 'Giorgio Agamben', 'George Bataille', 'Walter Benjamin' and 'Emmanuel Levinas' in *Encyclopedia of Religion and Language*, ed. J.F.A. Saywer and J.M.Y. Simpson. Pergamon: Oxford.

Bibliography

Adorno, T.W. (1998), *Critical Models: Interventions and Catchwords*, trans. W. Pickford, Columbia University Press: New York.

Agamben, G. (1998), *Homo Sacer: Sovereign Power and Bare Life*, trans. D. Heller-Roazen, Stanford University Press, Stanford.

—— (2000a), *Means Without Ends: Notes on Politics*, trans. V. Binetti and C. Casarino, University of Minnesota Press: Minneapolis.

—— (2000b), *Le temps qui reste: Un commentaire de l'Épître aux Romans*, trans. J. Revel, Bibliothèque Rivages: Paris.

—— (2005a), *Profanations*, trans. M. Rueff, Bibliothèque Rivages: Paris.

—— (2005b), *State of Exception*, trans. K. Attell, University of Chicago Press: Chicago.

Ahmed, E. (2004), 'John Calvin's Portrayal of Francis I as a Minister', *Neophilologus* 88, pp. 493–498.

Arendt, H. (1958), *The Human Condition*, University of Chicago Press: Chicago.

—— (1961, 1977), *Between Past and Future: Six Exercises in Political Thought*, Faber & Faber: London.

Aristotle (1976), *Nicomachean Ethics*, trans. J.A.K. Thomson and H. Tredennick, Penguin: Harmondsworth.

Assmann, J. (1992), *Politische Theologie zwischen Ägypten und Israel*, Carl Hanser: Munich.

Augustine, St (1951), *Letters, Volume 1 (1–82)*, trans. W. Parsons, The Catholic University of America: Washington, DC.

—— (1953), *Letters, Volume 2 (83–120)*, trans. W. Parsons, The Catholic University of America: Washington, DC.

—— (1961), *Confessions*, trans. R.S. Pine-Coffin, Penguin: Harmondsworth.

—— (1972), *Concerning the City of God Against the Pagans*, trans. H. Bettenson, Penguin: Harmondsworth.

—— (1991), *The Trinity*, trans. E. Hill, New City Press: New York.

Ayres, L. (2000), '"Remember That You Are Catholic" (serm. 52.2): Augustine on the Unity of the Triune God', *Journal of Early Christian Studies* 8:1, pp. 39–82.

—— (2004), *Nicaea and its Legacy: An Approach to Fourth-Century Trinitarian Theology*, Oxford University Press: Oxford.

Badewein, J. (1978), 'Euseb von Cäsarea', in A. Schindler (ed.), *Monotheismus als politisches Problem? Erik Peterson und die Kritik der politischen Theologie*, Gütersloher Verlagshaus Mohn: Gütersloh, pp. 43–49.

Badiou, A. (1997), *Saint Paul: la fondation de l'universalisme*, PUF: Paris.

Balthasar, H. Urs von (1965), 'Some Points on Eschatology', in *Word and Redemption: Essays in Theology 2*, trans. A.V. Littledale, Herder & Herder: New York, pp. 147–175.

—— (1982), 'The Unknown God', in *The Von Balthasar Reader*, ed. M. Kohl and W. Löser, trans. R.J. Daly and F. Lawrence, T. & T. Clark: Edinburgh, pp. 181–187.

—— (1985), *Theologik II: Wahrheit Gottes*, Johannes: Einsiedeln.

—— (1992), *The Theology of Karl Barth*, trans. E.T. Oakes, Ignatius Press: San Francisco.

—— (1995), *Presence and Thought: An Essay on the Religious Philosophy of Gregory of Nyssa*, trans. Mark Sebanc, Ignatius Press: San Francisco.

—— (1998), *Theo-Drama: Theological Dramatic Theory, Volume V: The Last Act*, trans. G. Harrison, Ignatius Press: San Francisco.

Barnes, M.R. (1995a), 'Augustine in Contemporary Trinitarian Theology', *Theological Studies* 56, pp. 237–250.

—— (1995b), 'De Régnon Reconsidered', *Augustinian Studies* 26:2, pp. 51–79.

—— (1999), 'Rereading Augustine's Theology of the Trinity', in S.T. Davis, D. Kendall and G. O'Collins (eds), *The Trinity*, Oxford University Press: Oxford, pp. 145–176.

—— (2001), *The Power of God: Dynamis in Gregory of Nyssa's Trinitarian Theology*, The Catholic University of America Press: Washington, DC.

—— (2002), 'Divine Unity and the Divided Self: Gregory of Myssa's Trinitarian Theology in its Psychological Context', *Modern Theology* 18:4, pp. 475–96.

Barth, K. (1928), *The Word of God and the Word of Man*, Hodder & Stoughton: London.

—— (1933), *The Epistle to the Romans*, trans. E.C. Hoskyns, Oxford University Press: Oxford.

—— (1956), *Church Dogmatics* Vol. I/2, ed. G.W. Bromiley and T.F. Torrance, T. & T. Clark: Edinburgh.

—— (1957), 'An Introductory Essay', trans. J.L. Adams, in Feuerbach (1957), pp. x–xxxii.

—— (1960a), *Church Dogmatics* Vol. III/2, ed. G.W. Bromiley and T.F. Torrance, T. & T. Clark: Edinburgh.

—— (1960b), *The Faith of the Church: A Commentary on the Apostles' Creed*, trans. G. Vahanian, Fontana: London.

—— (1972), *Protestant Theology in the Nineteenth Century*, trans. B. Cozens and J. Bowden, London: SCM.

—— (1975), *Church Dogmatics* Vol. I/1, trans. G.W. Bromiley and T.F. Torrance, T. & T. Clark: Edinburgh.

—— (1992), *Church Dogmatics*, trans. T.H.L. Parker, Edinburgh: Continuum.

Basil of Caesarea (1895), *Letters and Select Works*, trans. B. Jackson, James Parker & Co.: Oxford.

Bauckham, R. (2001) *God Will Be All in All: The Eschatology of Jürgen Moltmann*, Fortress Press: Minneapolis.

Bauerschmidt, F.C. (1996),'Walking in the Pilgrim City', *New Blackfriars* 77:909, pp. 504–518.

Béguin, S., O. Binenbaum, A. Chastel, W. McAllister Johnson, S. Pressouyre and H. Zerner (1972), *La galerie François Ier au chateau de Fontainbleau*, Flammarion: Paris.

Beiser, F.C. (2003), *The Romantic Imperative: The Concept of Early German Romanticism*, Harvard University Press: Cambridge, MA.

Bell, D.M, Jr. (2001), *Liberation Theology After the End of History*, Routledge: London.

Benjamin, W. (1973), *Illuminations*, trans. H. Zohn, Fontana: London.

—— (1974), *Gesammelte Schriften* Vol. 1, Pt. 2, ed. R. Tiedemann and H. Schweppenhäuser, Suhrkamp: Frankfurt am Main.

—— (1977a), *Gesammelte Schriften* Vol. 1, Pt. 3, ed. R. Tiedemann and H. Schweppenhäuser, Suhrkamp: Frankfurt am Main.

—— (1977b), *The Origin of the German Mourning Play*, trans. J. Osborne, Verso: London.

—— (1985), 'Kapitalismus als Religion', in *Gesammelte Schriften* Vol. 6, ed. R. Tiedemann and H. Schweppenhäuser, Suhrkamp: Frankfurt am Main, pp. 100–103.

—— (1996), *Selected Writings,* Vol. 1: *1913–1926*, ed. M. Bullock and M.W. Jennings, Harvard University Press: Cambridge, MA.

—— (1999), 'Experience and Poverty'in *Selected Writings*, Vol. 2: *1927–1934*, ed. M.W. Jennings, H. Eiland and G. Smith, Harvard University Press: Cambridge, MA, pp. 729–736.

Bethune-Baker, J.F. (1903), *An Introduction to the Early History of Christian Doctrine*, Methuen & Co.: London.

Bloch, E. (1962), *Thomas Münzer als Theologe der Revolution*, Frankfurt am Main: Suhrkamp.

—— (1986), *The Principle of Hope*, trans. N. Plaice, S. Plaice and P. Knight, 3 vols, Blackwell: Oxford.

—— (2000), *The Spirit of Utopia*, trans. A.A. Nassar, Stanford University Press: Stanford, CA.

Blondel, M. (1964), *The Letter on Apologetics and History and Dogma*, trans. A. Dru and I. Trethowan, T. & T. Clark: Edinburgh.

—— (1984), *Action (1893): Essay on the Critique of Life and a Science of Practice*, trans. Olivia Blanchette, University of Notre Dame Press: Notre Dame.

Blumenberg, H. (1983), *The Legitimacy of the Modern Age*, trans. R.M. Wallace, MIT Press: Cambridge, MA..

—— (1987), *The Genesis of the Copernican World*, trans. R.M. Wallace, MIT Press: Cambridge, MA..

Boethius, (1973), *Contra Eutychen et Nestorium*, in H.F. Stewart, E.K. Rand and S.J. Tester (trans.), *The Theolological Tractates*, 2nd edn, Harvard University Press: Cambridge, MA, pp. 72–129.

Boff, L. (1988) *Trinity and Society*, trans. P. Burns, Burns & Oates: London.

Bonhoeffer, D. (1966), 'Creation and Fall', trans. J.C. Fletcher, in *Creation and Temptation*, SCM Press: London.

Bornkamm, G. (1971), *Paul*, trans. D.M.G. Stalker, Hodder & Stoughton: London.

Braaten, J. (1995), 'From Communicative Rationality to Communicative Thinking: A Basis for Feminist Theory and Practice', in J. Meehan (ed.), *Feminists Reading Habermas: Gendering the Subject of Discourse*, Routledge: New York, pp. 136–159.

Bracken, J.A. (1973), 'The Holy Trinity as a Community of Divine Persons', *Heythrop Journal* 15, pp. 166–182 and 257–270.

Brague, R. (2003), *The Wisdom of the World: The Human Experience of the Universe in Western Thought*, trans. T.L. Fagan, University of Chicago Press: Chicago.

Breckman, W. (1992), 'Ludwig Feuerbach and the Political Theology of Restoration', *History of Political Thought* 13:3, pp. 437–462.

Breton, S. (1988), *Saint Paul*, PUF: Paris.

Brown, D.W. (1985), *The Divine Trinity*, Duckworth: London.

—— (1989), 'Trinitarian Personhood and Individuality', in R. Feenstra and C. Plantinga (eds), *Trinity, Incarnation, and Atonement*, University of Notre Dame Press: Notre Dame, pp. 48–78.

Brown, S., J. Bell and D. Carson (eds) (1996), *Marketing Apocalypse: Eschatology, Escapology and the Illusion of the End*, Routledge, London.

Brunner, E. (1949), *The Christian Doctrine of God: Dogmatics, Vol. I*, trans. O. Wyon, Lutterworth Press, London.

Buckley, M.J. (1987), *At the Origins of Modern Atheism*, Yale University Press: New Haven, NJ.

Bultmann, R. (1958), *Jesus Christ and Mythology*, T. & T. Clark: Edinburgh.

Cantalamessa, R. (1977), 'The Development of the Concept of a Personal God in Christian Spirituality', *Concilium* 103, pp. 57–66.

Carras, C. (1989), 'The Doctrine of the Trinity in Relation to Political Action and Thought', in *The Forgotten Trinity*, British Council of Churches: London.

Carroll, E.A. (1987), *Rosso Fiorentino: Drawings, Prints, and Decorative Arts*, National Gallery of Art: Washington.

Cascardi, A.J. (1992), *The Subject of Modernity*, Cambridge University Press: Cambridge.

Casey, E.S. (1999), 'The Time of the Glance: Toward Becoming Otherwise', in E. Grosz (ed.), *Becomings: Explorations in Time, Memory, and Futures*, Cornell University Press: Ithaca, NY, pp. 79–97.

Cavanaugh, W.T. (1995), 'A Fire Strong Enough to Consume the House: The Wars of Religion and the Rise of the State', *Modern Theology* 11:4, pp. 397–420

—— (1998), *Torture and Eucharist: Theology, Politics and the Body of Christ*, Blackwell: Oxford.

Caygill, H. (1998), *Walter Benjamin: The Colour of Experience*, Routledge: London.

Certeau, M. de (1966), 'Culture and Spiritual Experience', *Concilium* 19, pp. 3–16.

—— (1992), *The Mystic Fable: Volume One, The Sixteenth and Seventeenth Centuries*, trans. M.B. Smith, Chicago University Press: Chicago.

Clement of Alexandria, (1985), *Stromateis*, in *Clemens Alexandrinus* Volume 2, ed. O. Stählin, Akademie-Verlag: Berlin.

Coakley, S. (1999), '"Persons" in the "Social" Doctrine of the Trinity: A Critique of Current Analytic Discussion', in S.T. Davis, D. Kendall and G. O'Collins (eds), *The Trinity*, Oxford University Press: Oxford, pp. 123–144.

Condorcet, Marquis de (1966), *Esquisse d'un tableau historique des progress de l'esprit humain*, Editions sociales: Paris.

Congar, Y.M. (1981), 'Classical Political Monotheism and the Trinity', *Concilium* 143, pp. 31–36.

Connolly, W.E. (1998), *Why I am Not a Secularist*, University of Minnesota Press: Minneapolis.

Cunningham, A. (1970), 'Cultural Change and the Nature of the Church', in N. Lash and J. Rhymer (eds), *The Christian Priesthood*, Darton, Longman & Todd: London, pp. 251–269.

Cunningham, D.S. (1998), *These Three Are One: The Practice of Trinitarian Theology*, Blackwell: Oxford.

Dawkins, R. (1995), *River Out of Eden: A Darwinian View of Life*, Phoenix: London.

Deissner, K. (1969), 'The Eschatology of Primitive Christianity', in J. Pelikan (ed.), *Twentieth Century Theology in the Making*, Volume 1: *Themes of Biblical Theology*, Fontana: London, pp. 249–260.

Deleuze, G. (1986), *Spinoza et le problème de l'expression*, Éditions de Minuit: Paris.

Descombes, V. (1980), *Modern French Philosophy*, trans. L. Scott-Fox and J.L. Harding, Cambridge University Press: Cambridge.

Donagan, A. (1996), 'Spinoza's Theology', in *The Cambridge Companion to Spinoza*, ed. D. Garrett, Cambridge University Press: Cambridge, pp. 343–382.

Duquoc, C. (1985), 'Monotheism and Unitary Ideology', *Concilium* 177, pp. 59–66.

Dupré, L. (1993), *Passage to Modernity: An Essay in the Hermeneutics of Nature and Culture*, Yale University Press: New Haven.

Epistle to Diognetus, The (1950), *The Apostolic Fathers* Volume II, trans. K. Lake, Harvard University Press: Cambridge, MA, pp. 350–379.

Esposito, R. (1999), *Categorie dell'impolitico*, 2nd edn, Il Mulino: Bologna.

Eusebius of Caesarea (1902), *De laudibus Constantini*, ed. I. Heikel, in *Eusebius Werke* Vol I, Leipzig.

—— (1975), *Vita Constantina*, ed. F. Winkelmann, Berlin.

Evans, C. (1999), 'Jesus' Self-Designation 'The Son of Man' and the Recognition of His Divinity', in S.T. Davis, D. Kendall and G. O'Collins (eds), *The Trinity*, Oxford University Press: Oxford, pp. 29–47.

Ferrari, L. (1996), 'Augustine's Cosmography', *Augustinian Studies* 27: 2, pp. 131–180.

Feuerbach, L. (1957), *The Essence of Christianity*, trans. G. Eliot, Harper Torchbooks: New York.

—— (1964), *Sämtliche Werke* Vol. X, Bad Cannstatt: Stuttgart.

—— (1972), *The Fiery Brook: Selected Writings*, trans. Zawar Hanfi, Anchor: Garden City, NJ.

Fichte, J.G. (1978), *Attempt at a Critique of All Revelation*, trans. G. Green, Cambridge University Press: Cambridge.

Fletcher, P. (2003), 'Fantasy, Imagination and the Possibility of Experience', in P. Goodchild (ed.), *Difference in Philosophy of Religion*, Ashgate: Aldershot, pp. 157–169.

—— (2004a), 'The Political Theology of the Empire to Come', *Cambridge Review of International Affairs* 17:1, pp. 49–61.

—— (2004b), 'The Nature of Redemption: Post-Humanity, Post-Romanticism and the Messianic', *Ecotheology* 9:3, pp. 276–294.

Forte, B. (1989), *The Trinity as History: Saga of the Christian God*, trans. P. Rotondi, Alba House: New York.

Foucault, M. (2003), *'Society Must Be Defended': Lectures at the Collège de France, 1975–1976*, trans. D. Macey, Picador: New York.

Franklin, D. (1994), *Rosso in Italy: The Italian Career of Rosso Fiorentino*, Yale University Press: New Haven.

Funkenstein, A. (1986), *Theology and the Scientific Imagination from the Middle Ages to the Seventeenth Century*, Princeton University Press: Princeton, NJ.

Giddens, A. (1998), *The Third Way: The Renewal of Social Democracy*, Polity Press: Cambridge.

Gregory of Nazianzus (2002), *On God and Christ: The Five Theological Orations and Two Letters to Cledonius* (1894), trans. F. Williams and L. Wickham, St Vladimir's Seminary Press: Crestwood, NY.

Gregory of Nyssa, (1893), *Dogmatic Treatises, Etc.*, trans. W. Moore and H.A. Wilson, Parker & Co.: London.

Grenz, S.J. (2001), *The Social God and the Relational Self: A Trinitarian Theology of the Imago Dei*, Westminster John Knox Press: Louisville.

Gresham, J.L. (1993), 'The Social Model of the Trinity and its Critics', *Scottish Journal of Theology* 46, pp. 325–343.

Grey, M. (1990), 'The Core of Our Desire: Re-imaging the Trinity', *Theology* 93, pp. 363–373.

Grillmeier, A. (1975), *Christ in Christian Tradition*, 2nd edn, John Knox Press: Atlanta.

Guéhenno, J.-M. (1995), *The End of the Nation-State*, trans. V. Elliot, University of Minnesota Press: Minneapolis.

Gunton, C.E. (1989), 'The Triune God and the Freedom of the Creature', in S.W. Sykes (ed.), *Karl Barth: Centenary Essays*, Cambridge University Press: Cambridge, pp. 46–68.

—— (1991), *The Promise of Trinitarian Theology*, T. & T. Clark: Edinburgh.

—— (1993), *The One, the Three and the Many*, Cambridge University Press: Cambridge.

Gusdorf, G. (1972), *Dieu, la nature, l'homme au siècle des lumières*, Payot: Paris.

Habermas, J. (1987), *The Philosophical Discourse of Modernity: Twelve Lectures*, trans. F. Lawrence, MIT Press: Cambridge, MA.

—— (1992), *Postmetaphysical Thinking*, trans. W.M. Hohengarten, MIT Press: Cambridge, MA.

Hamacher, W. (2002), 'Guilt History: Benjamin's Sketch "Capitalism as Religion"', *Diacritics* 32:3–4, pp. 81–106.

Hanby, M. (2003), *Augustine and Modernity*, Routledge: London.

Hanson, R.P.C (1988), *The Search for the Christian Doctrine of God: The Arian Controversy, 318–381 AD*, T. & T. Clark: Edinburgh.

Hardy, D.W. (1989), 'Created and Redeemed Sociality,' in C.E. Gunton and D.W. Hardy (eds), *On Being the Church: Essays on the Christian Community*, T. & T. Clark: Edinburgh, pp. 21–46.

Harrison, P. (1998), *The Bible, Protestantism, and the Rise of Natural Science*, Cambridge University Press: Cambridge.

Harrison, V. (1991), 'Perichoresis in the Greek Fathers', *St Vladimir's Theological Quarterly* 35:1, pp. 53–65.

Hegel, G.W.F. (1977), *Phenomenology of Spirit*, trans. A.V. Miller, Oxford University Press: Oxford.

—— (1984), 'Berne Fragments', in *Three Essays, 1793–1795*, ed. and trans. P. Fuss and J. Dobbins, University of Notre Dame Press: Notre Dame, pp. 59–103.

—— (1999), 'The Relationship of Religion to the State', in *Political Writings*, ed. L. Dickey and H.B. Nisbet, Cambridge University Press: Cambridge, pp. 225–234.

Heidegger, M (1987), *Nietzsche*, Volume III: *The Will to Power as Knowledge and as Metaphysics*, ed. David Farrell Krell, trans. Joan Stamburgh et al., Harper & Row: New York.

—— (1995), *Gesamtausgabe II*. Band 60, *Phänomenologie des religiösen Lebens*, Klostermann: Frankfurt am Main.

Hein, H. (1983), 'Liberating Philosophy: An End to the Dichotomy of Spirit and Matter', in C.G. Gould (ed.), *Beyond Domination*, Rowman & Littlefield: Totowa, NJ, pp. 123–141.

Hellwig, M.K. (1991), 'Eschatology', in F. Schüssler Fiorenza and J.P. Galvin (eds), *Systematic Theology: Roman Catholic Perspectives*, Vol. 2, Fortress Press: Minneapolis, pp. 347–372.

Hennesssy, K. (2007), 'An Answer to de Régnon's Accusers: Why We Should Not Speak of "His" Paradigm', *Harvard Theological Review* 100, pp. 179–197.

Hill, E. (1985), *The Mystery of the Trinity*, Geoffrey Chapman: London.

—— (1991), 'Introduction', in St Augustine, *The Trinity*, trans. E. Hill, New City Press: New York.

Hill, W.J. (1982), *The Three-Personed God: The Trinity as the Mystery of Salvation*, The Catholic University of America Press: Washington, DC.

Hobbes, T. (1983), *De Cive: The English Version*, ed. H. Warrender, Clarendon Press: Oxford.

—— (1996), *Leviathan*, ed. R. Tuck, Cambridge University Press: Cambridge.

Hopko, T. (1992), 'Apophatic Theology and the Naming of God in Eastern Orthodox Tradition', in A.J. Kimel Jr (ed.), *Speaking the Christian God*, Eerdmans: Grand Rapids, MI, pp. 144–161.

Howell, K.J. (2002), *God's Two Books: Copernican Cosmology and Biblical Interpretation in Early Modern Science*, University of Notre Dame Press: Notre Dame, IN.

Hussain, N. (1999), 'Towards a Jurisprudence of Emergency: Colonialism and the Rule of Law', *Law and Critique* 10:2, pp. 93–115.

Jenson, R.W. (1995), 'What is the Point of Trinitarian Theology?', in C. Schwöbel (ed.), *Trinitarian Theology Today*, T. & T. Clark: Edinburgh, pp. 31–43.

—— (1997), *Systematic Theology*, Volume 1: *The Triune God*, Oxford University Press: Oxford.

Jerome, St (1963), *The Letters of St Jerome*, Volume 1, trans. C.C. Mierow, Ancient Christian Writers 33, Longman, Green & Co.: London.

Jüngel, E. (1976), *The Doctrine of the Trinity: God's Being is in Becoming*, trans. H. Harris, Scottish Academic Press: Edinburgh.

Käsemann, E. (1969), 'Thoughts on the Present Controversy About Scriptural Interpretation', in *New Testament Questions of Today*, trans. W.J. Montagne, SCM Press: London.

Kafka, F. (1954), 'Reflections on Sin, Suffering, Hope, and the True Way', in *Wedding Preparations in the Country and Other Posthumous Prose Writings*, trans. E. Kaiser and E. Wilkins, Secker & Warburg: London, pp. 38–53.

Kant, I. (1929), *Critique of Pure Reason*, trans. N. Kemp Smith, Macmillan: Basingstoke.

—— (1956), *Critique of Practical Reason*, trans. L. White Beck, Bobbs-Merrill: Minneapolis.

—— (1960), *Religion within the Limits of Reason Alone*, trans. T.M. Green and H.H. Hudson, Harper & Row: New York.

—— (1979), *The Conflict of the Faculties*, trans. M.J. Gregor, University of Nebraska Press: Lincoln, NE.

—— (1993), *Opus postumum*, trans. E. Förster and M. Rosen, Cambridge University Press: Cambridge.

—— (1995), 'The End of All Things', in *Religion Within the Boundaries of Mere Reason and Other Writings*, ed. A. Wood and G. di Giovanni, Cambridge University Press: Cambridge, pp. 193–205.

Kantorowicz, E. (1931), *Frederick the Second: 1194–1250*, trans. R.O. Lorimer, Constable & Co.: London.

Karatani, K. (1995), *Architecture as Metaphor: Language, Number, Money*, ed. M. Speaks, trans. S. Kohso, MIT Press: Cambridge, MA.

Kasper, W. (1983), *The God of Jesus Christ*, trans. M.J. O'Donnell, SCM Press: London.

Kerr, F. (1999), 'Transubstantiation After Wittgenstein', *Modern Theology* 15:2, pp. 115–130.

—— (2002), *After Aquinas: Versions of Thomism*, Blackwell: Oxford.

Kevern, J.R. (1997), 'The Trinity and Social Justice', *Anglican Theological Review* 79:1, pp. 45–54.

Kierkegaard, S. (1941), *Concluding Unscientific Postscript*, trans. W. Lowrie, Princeton University Press: Princeton, NJ.

—— (1971), *Either-Or* 2, trans. D.F. and L.M. Swenson and W. Lowrie, 2 vols, Princeton University Press: Princeton, NJ.

—— (1980), *The Concept of Anxiety*, trans. and ed. R. Thomte and A.B. Anderson, Princeton University Press: Princeton, NJ.

Kilby, K. (2000), 'Perichoreis and Projection: Problems with Social Doctrines of the Trinity', *New Blackfriars* 81:956, pp. 432–445.

Kojève, A. (1947), *Introduction à la Lecture de Hegel*, ed. R. Queneau, Gallimard: Paris.

—— (1980), *Introduction to the Reading of Hegel*, ed. Allan Bloom, trans. J.H. Nichols, Cornell University Press: Ithaca.

Koselleck, R. (1985), *Futures Past: On the Semantics of Historical Time*, trans. K. Tribe, MIT Press: Cambridge, MA.

Koyré, A. (1957), *From the Closed World to the Infinite Universe*, Johns Hopkins University Press: Baltimore.

LaCugna, C.M. (1986), 'Philosophers and Theologians on the Trinity', *Modern Theology* 2:3, pp. 169–181.

—— (1991), *God for Us: The Trinity and Christian Life*, Harper SanFrancisco: San Francisco.

LaCugna, C.M. and K. McDonnell (1988), 'Returning from "The Far Country": Theses for a Contemporary Trinitarian Theology', *Scottish Journal of Theology* 41, pp. 191–215.

Lancaster, S.H. (1996), 'Three-Personed Substance: The Relational Essence of the Triune God in Augutine's *De Trinitate*', *The Thomist* 60:1, pp. 123–139.

Le Goff, J. (1988), *Your Money or Your Life: Economy and Religion in the Middle Ages*, trans. P. Ranum, Zone Books: New York.

Lessing, G.E. (1956), *Lessing's Theological Writings*, trans. H. Chadwick, Adam & Charles Black: London.

Levinas, E. (1989), 'Martin Buber and the Theory of Knowledge', in *The Levinas Reader*, ed. Seán Hand, Blackwell: Oxford.

Lienhard, J.T. (1999), 'Ousia and Hypostasis: The Cappadocian Settlement and the Theology of "One Hypostasis"', in S.T. Davis, D. Kendall and G. O'Collins (eds), *The Trinity*, Oxford University Press: Oxford, pp. 99–121.

Loades, A. (1985), *Kant and Job's Comforters*, Avero Publications: Newcastle upon Tyne.

Lochman, J.M. (1975), 'The Trinity and Human Life', *Theology* 78, pp. 173–183.

Loemker, L.E. (1969), *Gottfried Wilhelm Leibniz: Philosophical Papers and Letters*, 2nd edn, Kluwer: Dordrecht.

Löwith, K. (1949), *Meaning in History: The Theological Implications of the Philosophy of History*, Chicago University Press: Chicago.

Loughlin, G. (2000), 'Time', in *The Oxford Companion to Christian Thought*, ed. A Hastings et al., Oxford University Press: Oxford, pp. 707–709.

Lubac, H. de (1949), *Corpus Mysticum: L'Eucharistie et l'Église au moyen âge*, 2nd edn, Aubier: Paris.

Luther, M. (1972), *The Bondage of the Will, 1525*, trans. P.S. Watson, in *Luther's Works*, Volume 33: *Career of the Reformer, III*, ed. P.S. Watson, Fortress Press: Philadelphia.

Manuel, F.E. and F.P. Manuel (1979), *Utopian Thought in the Western World*, Basil Blackwell: Oxford.

Margerie, B. de (1975), *La Trinité chrétienne dans l'histoire*, Éditions Beauchesne: Paris.

McCluskey, S.C. (1998), *Astronomies and Cultures in Early Medieval Europe*, Cambridge University Press: Cambridge.

McFadyen, A. (1992), *The Call to Personhood: A Christian Theory of the Individual in Social Relationships*, Cambridge University Press: Cambridge.

McGinn, B. (1985), *The Calabrian Abbot: Joachim of Fiore in the History of Western Thought*, Macmillan: London.

Melanchthon, P. (1969), *Loci Communus Theologici*, in *Melanchthon and Bucer*, The Library of Christian Classics 19, ed. W. Pauck, SCM Press: London.

Meredith, A. (1995), *The Cappadocians*, Geoffrey Chapman: London.

Metz, J.B. (1970), 'Political Theology', in K. Rahner et al. (eds), *Sacramentum Mundi*, Volume V, Burns & Oates: London, pp. 34–38.

Michel, P.-H. (1962), 'La querelle du géocentricisme', *Studi Secenteschi* 2:1, pp. 95–118.

Migliore, D.L. (1980), 'The Trinity and Human Liberty', *Theology Today* 36:4, pp. 488–497.

Milbank, J. (1986), 'The Second Difference: For a Trinitarianism Without Reserve', *Modern Theology* 2:3, pp. 213–234.

Moltmann, J. (1967), *The Theology of Hope*, trans. J.W. Leitch, SCM Press: London.

—— (1970), 'Theology as Eschatology', in F. Herzog (ed.), *The Future of Hope: Theology as Eschatology*, Herder & Herder: New York.

—— (1974), *The Crucified God*, trans. M. Kohl, SCM Press: London

—— (1975), *The Experiment Hope*, trans. M.D. Meeks, SCM Press: London.

—— (1979), *The Future of Creation*, trans. M. Kohl, SCM Press: London.

—— (1981), *The Trinity and the Kingdom of God*, trans. M. Kohl, SCM Press: London.

—— (1983), 'The Reconciling Powers of the Trinity in the Life of the Church and the World', in *The Reconciling Power of the Trinity*, Conference of European Churches: Geneva.

—— (1984), 'The Unity of the Triune God: Remarks on the Comprehensibility of the Doctrine of the Trinity and its Foundation in the History of Salvation', *St Vladimir's Theological Quarterly* 28:3, pp. 157–171.

—— (1985), 'The Inviting Unity of the Triune God', *Concilium* 177, pp. 50–58.

—— (1991), *History and the Triune God*, trans. M. Kohl, SCM Press: London.

—— (1996), *The Coming of God*, trans. M. Kohl, SCM Press: London.

Montesquieu (1989), *The Spirit of the Laws*, trans. and ed. A.M. Cohler, B.C. Miller and H.S. Stone, Cambridge University Press: Cambridge.

Müller, D. (2001), 'Le Christ, relève de la Loi (Romains 10, 4): La possibilité d'une éthique messianique à la suite de Giorgio Agamben', *Studies in Religion/ Sciences Religieuses* 30:1, pp. 51–63.

Nancy, J-L. (1997), 'The Insufficiency of "Values" and the Necessity of " Sense"', *Cultural Values* 1:1, pp. 127–131.

Nicholls, D. (1989), *Deity and Domination: Images of God and the State in the Nineteenth and Twentieth Centuries*, Routledge: London.

—— (1993), 'Trinity and Conflict', *Theology* 96, 19-27.

Nichtweiß, B. (1992), *Erik Peterson: Neue Sicht auf Leben und Werke*, Herder: Freiburg im Breisgau.

Nietzsche, F. (1967), *The Will to Power*, trans. W. Kaufmann and R.J. Hollingdale, Vintage Books: New York.

—— (1968), *The Twilight of the Idols and The Antichrist*, trans. R.J. Hollingdale, Penguin: Harmondsworth.

—— (1974), *The Gay Science*, trans. W. Kaufmann, Random House: New York.

—— (1994), *On the Genealogy of Morality,* ed. K. Ansell-Pearson, trans. C. Diethe, Cambridge University Press: Cambridge.

—— (1983), 'On the Uses and Disadvantages of History for Life', in *Untimely Meditations*, trans. R.J. Hollingdale, Cambridge University Press: Cambridge, pp. 57–123.

Norton, R.E. (1995), *The Beautiful Soul: Aesthetic Morality in the Eighteenth Century*, Cornell University Press, Ithaca.

O'Collins, G. (1975), *Has Dogma a Future?*, Darton, Longman & Todd: London.

O'Donnell. J. (1988), 'The Trinity as Divine Community: A Critical Reflection upon Recent Theological Developments', *Gregorianum* 69:1, pp. 5–34.

Osthasios, G.M. (1979), *Theology of a Classless Society*, Lutterworth Press: London.

Overbeck, F. (2001), 'On the Christian Character of Our Present Day Theology (Chapter One)', trans. M. Henry, *Irish Theological Quarterly* 66, pp. 51–66.

Pannenberg, W. (1990), *Metaphysics and the Idea of God*, trans. P. Clayton, Eerdmans: Grand Rapids, MI.

—— (1991), 'The Christian Vision of God: The New Discussion on the Trinitarian Doctrine', *Asbury Theological Journal* 46, pp. 27–36.

Parker, T.D. (1980), 'The Political Meaning of the Doctrine of the Trinity: Some Theses', *The Journal of Religion* 60:2, pp. 165–184.

Patočka, J. (1996), *Heretical Essays in the Philosophy of History*, trans. E. Kohák, Open Court: Chicago.

Pelikan, J. (1984), *The Christian Tradition: A History of the Development of Doctrine, Volume 4: Reformation of Church and Dogma (1300–1700)*, University of Chicago Press: Chicago.

Peterson, E. (1935), *Der Monotheismus als politisches Problem: Ein Beitrag zur Geschichte des politischen Theologie im Inperium Romanum*, Leipzig: Hegner.

—— (1983), 'Kaiser Augustus im Urteil des antiken Christentums', in J. Taubes (ed.), *Der Fürst dieser Welt: Carl Schmitt und die Folgen*, Wilhelm Fink: Munich, pp. 174–180.

—— (1994), 'Der Monotheismus als politisches Problem' (1951), in *Ausgewählte Schriften*, Volume 1: *Theologische Traktate*, Echter: Würzburg, pp. 23–81.

—— (2004), 'Politik und Theologie: Der liberale Nationalstaat des 19. Jahrhunderts und die Theologie', *Ausgewählte Schriften*, Volume 4: *tOffenbarung de Johannes und politisch-theologische Texte*, Echter: Würzburg, pp. 238–246.

Pickstock, C. (1998), *After Writing: On the Liturgical Consummation of Philosophy*, Blackwell: Oxford.

Plantinga, C. (1986), 'Gregory of Nyssa and the Social Analogy of the Trinity', *The Thomist* 50 (1986), pp. 325–352.

Plato (1977), *Timaeus and Critias*, trans. D. Lee, Penguin: New York.

Powell, S.M. (2001), *The Trinity in German Thought*, Cambridge University Press: Cambridge.

Ptolemy, (1957), *Claudii Ptolemaei Opera quae extant omnia*, Volume I: *Syntaxis mathematica*, Bibliotheca Teubneriana: Leipzig.

Rahner, K (1970), *The Trinity*, trans. J. Donceel, Burns & Oates: Tunbridge Wells.

Reardon, B.M.G. (1981), *Religious Thought in the Reformation*, Longman: Harlow.

—— (1988), *Kant as Philosophical Theologian*, Macmillan: Basingstoke.

Ridderbos, H. (1975), *Paul: An Outline of His Theology*, trans. J.R. de Witt, Eerdmans: Grand Rapids, MI.

Rikhof, H. (2002), 'Aquinas' Authority in the Contemporary Theology of the Trinity', in P. van Geest, H. Goris and C. Leget (eds), *Aquinas as Authority*, Peeters: Leuven, pp. 213–234.

Ritschl, A. (1902), *The Christian Doctrine of Justification and Reconciliation: The Positive Development of the Doctrine*, ed. H.R. Mackintosh and A.B. Macaulay, T. & T. Clark: Edinburgh.

Roberts, R. (1990), *Hope and Its Hieroglyph: A Critical Decipherment of Ernst Bloch's Principle of Hope*, Scholars Press: Atlanta.

Rose, G. (1992), *The Broken Middle: Out of Our Ancient Society*, Blackwell: Oxford.

—— (1995), *Love's Work*, Chatto & Windus: London.

—— (1996), *Mourning Becomes the Law: Philosophy and Representation*, Cambridge University Press: Cambridge.

Rudman, S. (1997), *Concepts of Person and Christian Ethics*, Cambridge University Press: Cambridge.

Ruether, R.R. (1985), *Womanguides*, Beacon Press: Boston, MA.

Ruggieri, G. (1985), 'God and Power: A Political Function of Monotheism?', *Concilium* 177, pp. 16–27.

Rummel, E. (2000), *The Confessionalization of Humanism in Reformation Germany*, Oxford University Press: Oxford.

Rupp, E.G. (1978), 'Christian Doctrine from 1350 to the Eve of the Reformation', in H. Cunliffe-Jones (ed.), *A History of Christian Doctrine*, T. & T. Clark: Edinburgh, pp. 287–304.

Sanders, E.P. (1985), *Paul, the Law, and the Jewish People*, SCM Press: London.

Santner, E. (2001), *On the Psychotheology of Everyday Life: Reflections on Freud and Rosenzweig* University of Chicago Press: Chicago.

Schindler, A. (1978), 'Einführung', in A. Schindler (ed.), *Monotheismus als politisches Problem? Erik Peterson und die Kritik der politischen Theologie*, Gütersloher Verlagshaus Mohn: Gütersloh, pp. 3–15.

Schlegel, F. (1991), *Philosophical Fragments*, trans. P. Firchow, University of Minnesota Press: Minneapolis.

Schleiermacher, F. (1928), *The Christian Faith*, trans. H.R. Mackintosh and J.S. Stewart, T. & T. Clark: Edinburgh.

Schmidt, H. (1876), *The Doctrinal Theology of the Evangelical Lutheran Church*, trans. C.A. Hay and H.E. Jacobs, Lutheran Publication Society: Philadelphia.

Schmitt, C. (1970), *Politische Theologie II. Die Legende von der Erledigung jeder Politischen Theologie*, Duncker & Humbolt: Berlin.

—— (1985), *Political Theology: Four Chapters on the Concept of Sovereignty*, trans. G. Schwab, MIT Press: Cambridge, MA.

—— (1996a), *The Leviathan in the State Theory of Thomas Hobbes: Meaning and Failure of a Political Symbol*, trans. G. Schwab and E. Hilfstein, Greenwood Press: London.

—— (1996b), *The Concept of the Political*, trans. G. Schwab, The University of Chicago Press: Chicago.

—— (1996c), *Roman Catholicism and Political Form*, trans. G.L. Ulmen, Greenwood Press: London.

Scholem, G. (1999), 'On Jonah and the Concept of Justice', trans. E.J. Schwab. *Critical Inquiry* 25, pp. 353–361.

Schweitzer, A. (1954), *The Quest of the Historical Jesus*, 3rd edn, trans. W. Montgomery, Adam & Charles Black: London.

Schwöbel, C. (1995), 'Introduction: The Renaissance of Trinitarian Theology: Reasons, Problems and Tasks', in C. Schwöbel (ed.), *Trinitarian Theology Today*, T. & T. Clark: Edinburgh, pp. 1–30.

Segundo, J.L. (1974), *A Theology for Artisans of a New Humanity*, Volume 3: *Our Idea of God*, Orbis: New York.

Soelle, D. (1974), *Political Theology*, Fortress Press: Philadelphia.

Soskice, J.M. (1994), 'Trinity and "the Feminine Other"', *New Blackfriars* 75, pp. 2–17.

Southern, R.W. (1995), *Scholastic Humanism and the Unification of Europe*, Volume 1: *Foundations*, Blackwell: Oxford.

Spaemann, R. (1984), 'Remarks on the Ontology of "Right" and "Left"', *Graduate Faculty Philosophy Journal* 10:1, pp. 89–97.

Spener, P.J. (1983), 'From the *Pia Desideria*, 1675', in *Pietists: Selected Writings*, ed. P.C. Erb, Paulist Press: New York, pp. 31–49.

Spinoza, B. de (1989), *Tractatus Theologico-Politicus*, trans. S. Shirley, E.J. Brill: Leiden.

—— (1995), *The Letters*, trans S. Shirley, Hackett: Indianapolis.

Steiner, G. (1971), *In Bluebeard's Castle*, Faber & Faber: London.

Steiner, U. (1998), 'Kapitalismus als Religion: Anmerkungen zu einem Fragment Walter Benjamins', *Deutsche Vierteljahresschrift für Literaturwissenschaft und Geistgeschichte* 72:1, pp. 147–171.

Stoeffler, F.E. (1965), *The Rise of Evangelical Pietism*, E.J. Brill: Leiden.

—— (1973), *German Pietism in the Eighteenth Century*, E.J. Brill: Leiden.

Strauss, D.F. (1873), *The Old Faith and the New: A Confession*, 2nd edn, trans. M. Blind, Asher & Co.: London.

Strauss, L. (1997), *Spinoza's Critique of Religion*, trans. E.M. Sinclair, University of Chicago Press: Chicago.

Tappert, T.G. (ed.) (1959), *The Book of Concord: The Confessions of the Evangelical Lutheran Church*, Fortress Press: Philadelphia.

Taubes, J. (1954a), 'Dialectic and Analogy', *The Journal of Religion* 34:2, pp. 111–119.

—— (1954b), 'Theodicy and Theology: A Philosophical Analysis of Karl Barth's Dialectical Theology', *The Journal of Religion* 34:4, pp. 231–243.

—— (1961), 'The Copernican Turn of Theology', in Hook, S. (ed.), *Religious Truth and Experience: A Symposium*, Oliver & Boyd: Edinburgh, pp. 70–75.

—— (1963), 'Nachman Krochmal and Modern Historicism', *Judaism* 12:2, pp. 150–164.

—— (1967), 'On the Nature of the Theological Method: Some Reflections on the Methodological Principles of Tillich's Theology', in T.J.J. Altizer (ed.), *Towards a New Christianity: Readings in the Death of God Theology*, Harcourt, Brace & World: New York, pp. 221–237.

—— (1980), 'Leviathan als sterblicher Gott: Zur Aktualität von Thomas Hobbes', *Evangelische Kommentare* 13, pp. 571–574.

—— (1987), *Ad Carl Schmitt: Gegenstrebige Fügung*, Merve Verlag: Berlin.

—— (1991), *Abendländische Eschatologie*, Matthes & Seitz: Munich.

—— (1996), *Vom Kult zur Kultur: Bausteine zu einer Kritik der historischen Vernunft*, ed. A. and J. Assmann, W.-D. Hartwich and W. Menninghaus, Wihelm Fink: Munich.

—— (2004), *The Political Theology of Paul*, trans. D. Hollander, Stanford University Press: Stanford, CA.

Terpstra, M. and T. de Wit (2000), '"No Spiritual Investment in the World As It Is": Jacob Taubes's Negative Political Theology', in I.N. Bulhof and L. ten Kate (eds), *Flight of the Gods: Philosophical Perspectives on Negative Theology*, Fordham University Press: New York, pp. 319–353.

Thiselton, A.C. (1995), *Interpreting God and the Postmodern Self: On Meaning, Manipulation and Promise*, T. & T. Clark: Edinburgh.

Thompson, J. (1991), 'Modern Trinitarian Perspectives', *Scottish Journal of Theology* 44, pp. 349–365.

Thompson, J. and D. Held (eds) (1982), *Habermas: Critical Debates*, Macmillan: London.

Tieck, L. (1965), *Werke in vier Bänden*, Bd. III, *Novellen*, ed. M. Thalmann, Winkler Verlag: Munich.

Timiadis, E. (1985), 'The Holy Trinity in Human Life', *One in Christ* 21:1, pp. 1–18.

Toulmin, S. and J. Goodfield (1961), *The Fabric of the Heavens*, Harper: New York.

Troeltsch, E. (1991), *The Christian Faith*, trans. G.E. Paul ed. G. von le Fort, Fortress Press: Minneapolis.

Tuck, R. (1979), *Natural Rights Theories: Their Origin and Development*, Cambridge University Press: Cambridge.

Turcescu, L. (2002), '"Person" Versus "Individual", and Other Modern Misreadings of Gregory of Nyssa', *Modern Theology* 18:4, pp. 527–539.

Vanhoozer, K. (1997), 'Human Being, Individual and Social', in *The Cambridge Companion to Christian Doctrine*, ed. C. Gunton, Cambridge University Press: Cambridge, pp. 158–188.

Virilio, P. (2000), *A Landscape of Events*, trans. J. Rose, MIT Press: Cambridge, MA.

Volf, M. (1998), '"The Trinity is our Social Program": The Doctrine of the Trinity and the Shape of Social Engagement', *Modern Theology* 14:3, pp. 403–423.

—— (1999), 'After Moltmann: Reflections on the Future of Eschatology', in R. Baukham (ed.), *God Will Be All In All: The Eschatology of Jürgen Moltmann*, T. & T. Clark: Edinburgh, pp. 233–257.

—— (2000a), 'The Final Reconciliation: Reflections on a Social Dimension of the Eschatological Transition', *Modern Theology* 16:1, pp. 91–113.

—— (2000b), 'Forgiveness, Reconciliation, and Justice: A Theological Contribution to a More Peaceful Social Environment', *Millennium: Journal of International Studies* 29:3, pp. 861–877.

—— (2003), '*Liberation Theology After the End of History*: An Exchange', *Modern Theology* 19:2, pp. 261–269.

Voltaire (2000), *Treatise on Tolerance and Other Writings*, ed. S. Harvey, Cambridge University Press: Cambridge.

Wallace, R.M. (1981), 'Progress, Secularization and Modernity: The Löwith-Blumenberg Debate', *New German Critique*, 22, pp. 63–79.

Wannenwetsch, B. (1996), 'The Political Worship of the Church: A Critical and Empowering Practice', *Modern Theology* 12:3, pp. 269–299.

Weber, S. (2005), *Targets of Opportunity: On the Militarization of Thinking*, Fordham University Press: New York.

Webster, J. (2000), 'Eschatology, Anthropology and Postmodernity', *International Journal of Systematic Theology* 2:1, pp. 13–28.

Weil, S. (1962), 'Human Personality', in *Selected Essays, 1934–1943*, trans. R. Rees, Oxford University Press: London, pp. 9–34.

Welch, C. (1953), *The Trinity in Contemporary Theology*, SCM Press: London.

Williams, R. (1979), 'Barth and the Triune God', in S.W. Sykes (ed.), *Karl Barth: Studies of His Theological Method*, Clarendon Press: Oxford, pp. 147–193.

—— (2000), *On Christian Theology*, Blackwell: Oxford.

Willis, W.W. (1987), *Theism, Atheism and the Doctrine of the Trinity*, Scholars Press: Atlanta.

Wilson-Kastner, P. (1983), *Faith, Feminism and the Christ*, Fortress Press: Philadelphia.

Woodruffe, H. (1997), 'Eschatology, Promise, Hope: The Utopian Vision of Consumer Research', *European Journal of Marketing* 31:9/10, pp. 667–676.

Zinzendorf, N.L. Count von (1983), 'From Nine Public Lectures, 1746', in *Pietists: Selected Writings*, ed. P.C. Erb, Paulist Press: New York, pp. 305–324.

Zizioulas, J.D. (1975), 'Human Capacity and Human Incapacity: A Theological Exploration of Personhood', *Scottish Journal of Theology* 28, pp. 401–448.

—— (1985), *Being as Communion: Studies in Personhood and the Church*, DLT: London.

—— (1995), 'The Doctrine of the Holy Trinity: The Significance of the Cappadocian Contribution', in C. Schwöbel (ed.), *Trinitarian Theology Today*, T. & T. Clark: Edinburgh, pp. 44–60.

Index

Lightning Source UK Ltd.
Milton Keynes UK
UKHW022005300419
341900UK00006B/32/P

9 780754 667223